The Only Way Is Up

Also by Polly Toynbee and David Walker:

*The Lost Decade: 2010–2020, and
What Lies Ahead for Britain*

*Dismembered: How the Conservative
Attack on the State Harms Us All*

*Cameron's Coup: How the Tories took
Britain to the Brink*

Dogma and Disarray: Cameron at Half-Time

The Verdict: Did Labour Change Britain?

*Unjust Rewards: Exposing Greed and Inequality
in Britain Today*

Better or Worse?: Has Labour Delivered?

*Did Things Get Better? An Audit of Labour's
Successes and Failures*

The Only Way Is Up

How to Take Britain from Austerity to Prosperity

Polly Toynbee and David Walker

Atlantic Books
London

First published in Great Britain in 2024 by Atlantic Books

A CIP catalogue record for this book is available from the British Library.

Trade paperback ISBN 978 1 80546 266 8
E-book ISBN 978 1 80546 267 5

Printed and bound by CPI (UK) Ltd, Croydon CR0 4YY

10 9 8 7 6 5 4 3 2 1

Atlantic Books
An imprint of Atlantic Books Ltd
Ormond House
26–27 Boswell Street
London WC1N 3JZ

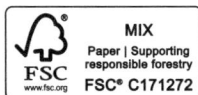

MIX
Paper | Supporting
responsible forestry
FSC
www.fsc.org
FSC® C171272

Contents

Introduction: Their Legacy   1

1   Children: A Case of Neglect   23

2   The Economy: Going Nowhere   46

3   Climate: High Water Everywhere   73

4   Housing: A Property-Owning Plutocracy   95

5   Health: Waiting and Waiting   116

6   Misgovernment   141

7   Security: Criminal Neglect   170

8   Equalities: Unjust Rewards   195

Conclusion: Up, Up and Away   225

Endnotes   248

Index   273

INTRODUCTION

Their Legacy

THE QUEUES LASTED three long days, curling round the corner and out of sight down Ashley Road from before dawn till the clinic slammed its doors at 5 p.m. Swelling crowds of all ages came back day after day to try to register with the newly opened surgery in St Pauls: Bristol was one of the dentistry deserts, nine out of ten practices across England having shut their doors to new NHS patients.

Norman Stephenson, aged 66, was desperate; he had been forced to superglue his broken dentures. An 80-year-old shivering in the February cold was brought a chair and a blanket by one of the campaigners who had fought long and hard to get the NHS to open a practice. Standing for hours, some people had taken time off, losing precious pay from zero-hours jobs. Others had brought children with them: without check-ups, they would later become emergency cases. Among those turned away when the patient quota had been filled was Bristol's poet laureate, Miles Chambers, his teeth falling out.

Welcome to what was Tory-governed England. The rest of the UK was not very much different, except maybe in retaining some sense of hope and possibility that came from not being ruled by Tory Westminster. Scotland and Wales still depended on decisions made there but had leeway, ambitions, contrasting values; England could at least attend and learn something. That Bristol queue represented the multitude waiting for NHS treatment: 7.7 million on official lists that included parents hoping for a diagnosis of their child's worrying behaviour, pensioners fearful a precious podiatry appointment wouldn't turn up, all those hanging on phones at the witching hour of 8 a.m. to see a GP. In this England, NHS care could no longer be taken for granted, no longer reliably serving need. For health, read the public sector: threadbare, precarious, understaffed and stretched beyond reasonable limits. That was what had become of the realm under the Westminster governments elected in 2010, 2015, 2017 and 2019.

Dicing with diarrhoea

The 2024 picture did not make for pre-watershed viewing. People were lonelier, saw friends and family less often. It's hard to untangle COVID, austerity and Tory policies, but the condition of public services explained a lot. Referrals of children with mental health problems skyrocketed. Saudi money had captured Heathrow Airport and Newcastle United FC, with scant interest in getting to net zero in either. Sewage poured into rivers so that to row or swim was to dice with diarrhoea. Gardens were bereft of bees and butterflies; more than half the gulls, gannets and other seabirds that used to breed off the coast had gone. Victims and perpetrators of crime waited months, often years, for hearings put off because roofs leaked, computer systems crashed and magistrates' courts were sold off. A plaintive voice on the GWR train intercom: sorry, no coffee, we've a defective urn on the line. Money and the cost of living vied with health as people's top concerns. Once growth and improvement had been the norm; now you were lucky to earn today what you earned yesterday, the year before or the decade before. The

Office for Budget Responsibility (OBR), set up by Tory ministers, said it would take till 2028 for employees to earn what they had been making in 2008.

You can sample an era through its buzzwords. Such as 'precarity', 'living on the margins'. Fully a quarter of adults had no safety net, getting by with less than £100 in savings. What happened if they had an accident, lost a job or a child fell sick? Citizens Advice estimated five million people were stuck: however hard they tried to make repayments, however good their debt advice, there was no way their income would ever cover their outgoings. These were not the shirkers sneered at by Liz Truss: they worked, often at more than one job. The strivers lauded by Theresa May were having to strive even harder.

Those are two of the era's five Tory prime ministers, but this isn't another story about politics: books and podcasts have poured out as the borderline between politics and entertainment has slipped and slid. Johnson's shtick worked for a while and the death of a clown made for good copy. People were briefly pleased to escape doom and gloom, but the buffoon on a zip wire did things that affected everyone's lives and livelihoods, outcomes often ignored in the raucous Westminster charivari. We've tried in successive books to capture what happened outside the big top – the effect of new laws, regulations, ministerial whims and the orders they give civil servants. We look too at what ministers and MPs didn't do, when they left in place dysfunctional structures of power, bad taxes and unjust spending, increasing unfairness and inefficiency. Exploring what went wrong, we can at least point up what could now go right. It's like Captain Flint's map of Treasure Island. We now know where the gold is buried, but it's up to you, citizens and voters, to get the better of the pirates.

A reserve price of a pound

Economic and political pessimism was pervasive. But the Scottish thinker Adam Smith appeals to optimists, who quote his saying to the effect that bad as things might be, there remains a 'great deal of ruin in a nation'. It's good counsel not to wallow in adversity, so here's a tale from the sage's hometown of Kirkcaldy in Fife, a fine old burgh with spectacular views across the Firth of Forth. We were monitoring retail while researching for our book *The Lost Decade* and noted the fate of Kirkcaldy's Postings shopping centre. Anchor tenant Tesco had departed in 2015. Within a couple of years, 13 of its 21 units were empty. The Columbia Threadneedle pension fund put it up for auction with a reserve price of just £1. In fact the three-acre site went for a still modest £310,000, to a developer who demolished the shops ostensibly to build housing.

That left an eyesore, Kirkcaldy's centre deadened, a word describing too many former high streets across the UK. Delay stretched on. Hoarding assets on your balance sheet was allowed to be more profitable than development, regardless of the effect on a townscape or residents' sense of loss. There are bright sparks in the gloom: despite council penury, Kirkcaldy's Adam Smith Theatre complex in a fine late-Victorian building was given a makeover and in spring 2024 was able to mount at least one new live musical production. It's true that towns and theatres in Scotland depended, to some extent, on decisions taken by the Edinburgh government, which had been controlled by the nationalists. This book focuses on England, where most people live, offering side glances at Wales and Scotland, leaving the special case of Northern Ireland on one side.

You will say, keep a sense of proportion. There's always more to life than politics and policy. Adam Smith's moral

sentiments had not entirely shrivelled up. During these individualist years, people found joy and solace coming together,
supporting the Lionesses, doing Parkrun, joining book groups
(increasingly popular among younger readers), buying more
vinyl (and even audio cassettes) and – at least in the capital –
reviving pie and mash shops (eels were critically endangered,
and besides, who'd eat anything that had swum in English
waters?). One of the central social facts of the era was work.
Jobs remained plentiful even in Yosser's Liverpool, and the
minimum wage climbed. Crime declined, the reasons for its
long-run descent across Europe uncertain but surely welcome.
Thousands more Chinese and other overseas tourists arrived,
the silver lining to sterling's weakness. Money might be
tighter, but thousands still thronged Jet2.com and Ryanair
desks for flights to the slopes and the Lanzarote sun. Beavers
were successfully reintroduced in Devon and Argyll. In other
words, millions got on with their lives, many oblivious to
politics, just coping, despite insecurity at work, rent increases
and the impossibility of buying your own home if you were
young. But pressure on GPs and prevalent mental ill-health
were consequences of financial and emotional stress, amid a
pervading country-wide sense of underachievement, wasted
lives, blighted chances. How much more content, fulfilled
and stretched people could be, young and old. Things could
have been and might still be so much better.

Bizarre, erratic, freakish

At Westminster we have to rerun the bizarre, erratic and
sometimes eye-poppingly freakish behaviour of the party so
long in power there and across swathes of English local government. Law-breaking, quick-fire dismissals of leaders and
warped choices made on tax, spend and public services don't
make a happy story. It's hard not to rub your eyes in disbelief

at the infantile phenomenon of Liz Truss, but also wrong to paint her as somehow deviant when she was indeed the life and soul of the party during these years.

Politicians and those who report on them deceive themselves if they think ministers and civil servants are ever fully in charge. Economy and society are complex and social science is primitive. Behaviour and attitude may be influenced by but aren't steered in any linear way by decisions made at Westminster (or Cardiff or Holyrood). Sensibility shifts in subterranean spaces where ministers' speeches and rabid radio outbursts may be unheard – they are not what the people with AirPods in their ears are listening to. Consciousness changes at its own pace. The judgements people make about the fairness of things follow their own trajectory. So, for example, Labour's 2010 Equality Act remained a fixed point for courts, public services and private companies despite the *Daily Mail*, whose ranting sounded increasingly out of touch with the bulk of the public. Just about everyone was now 'woke', meaning general consciousness had absorbed the rights and wrongs of race, gender, sexuality and disability. And, in an era of rule by mega-rich men and Old Etonians, also of class.

At the National Portrait Gallery in London, newly redone, the wall captions reflected this altered awareness. Sir Francis Drake in his ruff and doublet may or may not have played bowls on Plymouth Hoe as the Duke of Medina Sidonia and his armada approached: it's indisputable and uncontroversial that he and the Spanish traded slaves. Online attention-seekers and reactionary GB News presenters made no headway against spreading awareness of racial injustice in the UK's imperial past. As history was amended in the light of contemporary perceptions, that was a sign of progress.

There weren't many. Data journalist John Burn-Murdoch pored over the graphs and concluded the UK was now to be classed as a poor society that happened to have some very rich people. Our European neighbours were simply better off. Being middle income in the UK was now to be poorer than someone of equivalent status in France or Germany. Teachers or managers in Tours or Tübingen might or might not be happier than their peers in Trowbridge or Tayside, but look at their clothes and lifestyle and there was no denying they were just more affluent. Debates about benefits and dependency were lively across the Channel too, but a British family on Universal Credit struggled on an income nearly one third less than families at the bottom of the scale in France and Germany.

Airy self-confidence

Decay and dilapidation became themes. Our neighbours endured the same financial crash, they too were locked down during COVID and suffered the Ukraine war's energy spike, yet the UK fared worse. It had to be Brexit and the quality of Westminster government that made the difference, with ministers' and MPs' ideological tics and half-articulated theories about the benignity of markets and the malign state doing the damage. Bad ideas were one thing; the era was also marked by breathtaking incompetence. And scandal, both personal and systemic: take your pick from Windrush, Grenfell, the late detection of reinforced autoclaved aerated concrete in public buildings. Here's the acronym, RAAC, because it's going to crop up again, an all too obvious symbol of the UK's failure to rebuild and renew.

The Post Office revelations were another symbol. The indefensible prosecutions antedated the period, though the post-2010 governments shared culpability. Other scandals had Tory fingerprints all over them. David Cameron attempted to dismantle the NHS in 2012, and years later it was still grappling to stitch itself back together again. The privatization of the probation service by arch-incompetent Chris Grayling had to be reversed in chaos within three years. He moved on and up, and as transport secretary tried to award a £14 million ferry contract to a pizza delivery firm with no ships. Help to Buy – an impressive example of economic illiteracy, someone said – was hindrance to buy, inflating house prices. COVID contracts were let to companies connected to an underwear-maker fitted up with a Tory peerage. Airily self-confident, Cameron exited whistling a happy tune after one of the most spectacular failures in modern times, losing the Brexit vote: his autobiography is much mea and very little culpa. Then, a miracle, resurrection: a desperate Tory successor plants him in yet another Tory seat in an ermine-stuffed House of Lords. His predecessor as foreign secretary had chosen to continue sunning himself on a Greek beach rather than return to supervise the chaotic exit from Kabul. However, 74 cats and 94 dogs were airlifted out, leaving loyal Afghans who had worked at great risk for the UK government waving on the tarmac.

Austerity

The sorry tale starts with austerity, a deliberate Tory decision in the wake of the financial crash not to ask the better-off to pay more in taxes but instead to cut back welfare and public services. The national accounts did not need to be balanced, as claimed in the puerile analogy played out by George Osborne: the Treasury is not a household account. He won congratulatory headlines, but for the country this was epic failure, as economic growth was stymied, with enduring consequences for household incomes. For all his claims to prudence, Osborne increased national indebtedness to the tune of £555 billion. The cuts were no way to gird an economy in urgent need of investment at a time when the cost of borrowing had never been so cheap. Stripping away social and physical fabric planted the seeds of the Brexit vote and left the UK vulnerable when the pandemic hit.

The vaunted civil service Rolls-Royce took a battering and now resembled a jalopy, its drivers dizzied by the speed at which their departmental doors revolved: in just 14 years, 7 chancellors of the exchequer, 10 education secretaries, 10 environment secretaries and 16 housing ministers. The standing of permanent secretaries wasn't raised by alcohol-fuelled singing and dancing at Number 10. Officials might have forcefully said no, minister, but few did. 'Well, I would have advised them against it', an ex-panjandrum told us privately. And that was about it, despite those devastating reports on misspending from the National Audit Office (NAO). The era exposed the fatal weakness of the 'good chaps' theory of government, which said it didn't matter that things were not formalized or publicly accountable because gentlemen were in charge. These gents had been to Eton, Winchester and remarkably often to Oxford, but quads and cloisters did not turn them into trustworthy holders of power; all too many were charlatans and incompetents.

At least they were under some surveillance. Watchdogs mostly remained rigorous and honest. Ministers later regretted inventing the Office for Budget Responsibility, Truss refusing to let it cast an eye over her 'true conservative' catastrophe. Its chair, Robert Chote, was the former head of another of these valiants for truth, the Institute for Fiscal Studies (IFS), which like the research charity the Resolution Foundation was conscience, inquirer and generous provider of data and analysis; books such as this could not be written without them. The Office for National Statistics (ONS), on reduced cash, ran mostly reliable numbers for households and habits and the state of the nation. The NAO became more caustic as the years went by, the chickens of austerity coming home to roost amid greater inefficiency and ineffectiveness. The Commons Public Accounts Committee packed a punch under Margaret Hodge and her successor Meg Hillier, compiling a devastating database of waste and misgovernment. However, MPs and ministers could ignore it and did, consigning inconvenient evidence to the shelf.

Fag-end Thatcherism

Tory ministers speed-dated around the cabinet table. What they had in common was fag-end Thatcherism. Her battered copy of Friedrich Hayek's *Road to Serfdom*, her grocer's daughter's aversion to regulation and taxation and her romance with Ronald Reagan might never have amounted to a doctrine, but it was a coherent enough world view, with its blind faith in markets and rejection of collectivism. They all signed up to the pledge, 'no such thing as society, there are only individuals and families'. This was ideology, in the sense that belief overrode evidence.

Thirty-plus years after Thatcher's fall, the evidence was in, and it was clear. The experiment has run its course. It divided; we fell. Her talismanic privatizations created monopolies putting shareholder dividend before investment in vital national assets. Regulators proved no match. Think Thames Water, the company teetering towards bankruptcy and state supervision of a kind already imposed on failed railway franchisees, leaving the network a chaos of moving parts. Breaking up energy supply made net zero even harder to attain. Another shibboleth was exposed: cutting taxes for business did not bring promised productivity gains or growth. Thatcher's flagship Right to Buy depleted the stock of affordable social housing, part of the cause of the housing crisis. All this we cover in the following chapters.

The governing party had never been philosophically coherent, for all the fogies' invocations of Edmund Burke. Anti-individualism in matters of cannabis or gender identity contradicted pro-individualism over markets. A necessary Tory quality these days was selective amnesia, picking parts of their shape-shifting history when it suited; and what a mixed history, from the aristocratic paternalism of Harold Macmillan and Alec Douglas-Home, via Grantham to Ashfield and Lee Anderson, appointed deputy chair of the party by Rishi Sunak for his plebeian racism, then sacked by Rishi Sunak for his plebeian racism. Here was a Conservative Party that attacked the very institutions that conserved British identity: the BBC, the NHS and recently the National Trust and the Royal National Lifeboat Institution.

A daily hate

They came to power with Cameron acting the moderate, but privately they vowed to foment 'chaos' and 'creative destruction' to show people the state didn't work. If that sounds conspiratorial, read Oliver Letwin, supposedly a moderate, let alone the barmy army of *Britannia Unchained* and Truss, the self-destructor. The party's long hegemony rested on ruthlessness, staying in power at all costs. And putting your own people in, as they proved time and again with ostensibly meritocratic public appointments (chair of the BBC, chief executive of the British Museum, board of NHS England).

They weren't united. Especially after Brexit, they turned fissiparous, with new strains of Trump-inflected extremism, each with its pet think tank and coterie of journalist supporters. But there they stayed. Sustained by a deeply unjust voting system and a stuffed House of Lords, the Tories remained the party of the haves, of tax-fearing small business and white suburbanites, favoured by corporate boardrooms and successful upwardly aspiring ethnic minorities. Historically they relied on social contradiction. Mothers once voted for a party that consistently opposed their rights and benefits. They would never have won down the decades without backing from at least a third of workers, despite their attacks on trade unions and employment protection. Theirs was the party of the old, though they used to oppose raising pensions and recently degraded older people's health and social care.

The Tories are the *Daily Mail*'s party, the *Daily Telegraph* their parish newsletter: these papers inflated Johnson's bank account for dashed-off columns. The *Daily Mail*'s founder, Lord Northcliffe, said his mission was to give readers 'a daily hate', the objects of which have serially been Jewish people, Liberal and Labour politicians or anyone of progressive mien in public life, the poor, welfare recipients, the BBC, greens, advocates of LGBTQ rights, migrants, sportspeople, media folk or actors with liberal opinions, the European Union, universities and academics. Add to it Murdoch's media and the new broadcast channels such as GB News, copying its hate formula to target, harangue and victimize. Social media, contrary to earlier hopes, started to amplify the right, stoking up culture wars over transgender issues, 'cancel culture', and diversity and inclusion initiatives in the armed forces and the NHS. Cutting aid from 0.7 to 0.5 per cent of GDP, diverting it to fund migrant accommodation at home and abolishing the international development department were sops to the daily haters, resulting in another loss of UK credibility and soft power abroad.

Writing in the *Daily Express*, a cruder and more extreme version of the *Daily Mail*, the implausible defence secretary Grant Shapps claimed 'woke culture has seeped into public life poisoning common-sense discourse'. Here was Tory opportunism on display. They had all voted for Cameron's very woke legalization of same-sex marriage. 'Woke' makes for a case study of failing to swim against the cultural tide. Despite the big bellows of their media, they failed to ignite many sparks over the iniquities of no-platforming in universities, to take one example. Liberal social attitudes were here to stay. Trying to wrench back Big Ben's hands over abortion, LGBTQ rights, racial and disability equality was bad politics. The culture war was well and truly lost long ago.

Merry-go-round

The Brexit referendum was supposed to put out the fires. Cameron thought a referendum would finally cauterize the wound, so he took a gigantic risk with the UK's future for the sake of internal party management. And lost on both counts. The Europhobes' anarchic demands simply accelerated after their 2016 victory. All those comings and goings at Number 10 did not signify pluralism. Cameron was slick, camouflaging juvenile Thatcherism behind the PR operation he had mounted in opposition, hugging huskies and devising a new green party logo. Even then he didn't win outright, forced into coalition with the Liberal Democrats. Four successors stood on the steps of Number 10, each podium personally designed, each arrival proclaiming itself some kind of novelty. May, tongue-tied and gauche, benefited from astute slogan-writers, but she left her JAMs ('just about managing') worse off. If her own beliefs were essentially tea-party-on-the-lawn-with-the-vicar Toryism, over the Brexit negotiations she still put party unity ahead of any wider national interest, even over the interests of Brexit-alarmed business.

For a while Johnson mesmerized, one of several right-wing journalists who clambered into the seats of power. Columnists tend to believe their work is done once they have found a telling word or phrase. He coined 'levelling up' but proved incapable of – was probably uninterested in – giving it meaning or substance. Dishonesty will out, and eventually it did, his Commons mendacity beyond cover-up. Back to the 1850s with Truss, as viewed through the prism of American think tanks funded by reactionary moguls: the markets she worshipped had her for breakfast. Sunak struggled to give his promised makeover any content whatsoever. Strangely, Truss might turn out to be the most significant of them. By taking Thatcherism to its extreme, she dealt the doctrine a finishing death-blow.

But this zombie has risen from the grave before, so don't abandon garlic, stakes or whatever weapons are needed to dispatch it. COVID looked at first as if it might be pivotal. For a while its lethal brutality forced the Tories to abandon gut precepts. A stale joke at right-wing conferences used to be Reagan's epigram, 'I've always felt the nine most terrifying words in the English language are: "I'm from the Government, and I'm here to help."' Then a Tory government – a Tory government! – had to forbid people to leave home while it pumped in billions to people and businesses. Reality trumped ideology when public health brooked no fiscal faint-heartedness. Remember beaming Sunak, a plate precariously balanced in each hand, advertising Eat Out to Help Out, the subsidy for restaurant food. Here was this no-such-thing-as-a-free-luncher handing out free lunches, which also unfortunately revived transmission of the virus. Companies large and small were propped up by the job retention scheme. Individual employees were sustained in paid furlough. People who had never touched a benefit in their lives were kept afloat on state credits. But once released from COVID masks, the Tories reverted to form, and within their ranks the *Spectator* and *Telegraph* crowd turned their flame-throwers on those who had ordered the lockdowns and payouts, in a new round of infighting.

Come together?

Inequality grew, not accidentally. Many on the right regarded it as a healthy and inevitable feature of competition: the poor more or less deserved their fate; only markets should decide soaring chief executive pay. UK billionaires burgeoned and the top tenth triumphed. And yet the facts about growing inequality that leapt from the graphs and expert analysis had curiously little social resonance. The rich keep themselves to themselves, hence those gates; the poor ditto, in peripheral estates and high-rises. The physical distance between Grenfell Tower and Holland Park is a few hundred metres, the wealth gap enormous but curtained, out of sight.

Can a country where maldistribution of resources is so large ever come together, even in the face of threats to collective security from AI and cyberattack, let alone hostile states? Climate change predicates more equality of sacrifice. The wicked issues ahead, such as migration, demand collective strength to guard the barriers and passport gates, check the visas and vehicles and inspect places of work. Undocumented people will continue to cross frontiers across the world, including the English Channel. Migratory flows pose hard questions for progressives, but dogmatic marketeers have the deeper dilemma. Pulling up the drawbridge entails paying higher wages and higher prices. There is no easy solution, but among preconditions is close cooperation with European neighbours we have offended, as well as a strong, well-resourced UK state.

Back to those children queuing in St Pauls. Tooth decay so extreme that it needed surgery had become the single most common reason for those aged five to seventeen being admitted to A&E. Long gone were the days when dental check-ups, like school medicals and eye tests, were part of the ordinary furniture of childhood. Soaring autism diagnoses, with many parents waiting months and sometimes years for appointments, followed the disappearance of educational psychologists and support staff from schools. This can be remedied. Boomers could begin to make amends.

Back to the future

That's the legacy of these years. What now? If not yet a new world, then a new world view is struggling to be born. Its midwives are climate disaster, the bank crash, the COVID shock, the lived experience of austerity, and international tensions of an intensity unknown for many years. In gestation is a renewed belief in the necessity of a good and strong state. Will Hutton says we need to go back to the future and rework the Edwardian coming-together of progressive liberalism and employees, workers by hand and brain. We need drones not *drones*. Whatever the electoral recipe, some kind of social-market democracy grows out of the earth scorched by austerity.

Aspects may even be guaranteed. Take housing. Dust to dust, says the scripture: bricks and mortar crumble. New-build will have to replace the old dwellings in which so many live – one in six in England built before the First World War. In an alarming recent leap upwards, 5.7 million properties in England were now at risk of being flooded. The Victorian heritage has stood us in astonishingly good stead, but every accumulating year of underinvestment in repair and renewal brings more collapsed timbers, sewers and pipes, more cracks in the concrete, more disconnected cables. Labour failed to fix the roof while the sun shone, sneered Osborne. During the Tory era the sun shone mercilessly, raising temperatures and storms and further damaging the tiles, but these householders failed to invest despite conspicuously low interest rates. Osborne loved photo ops at construction sites in a high-vis jacket and helmet. Choose your idiom: all mouth and no trousers, fur coat and no knickers.

Generational tensions will out. Those born in the 1980s were wondering why their pay peaked in the 2000s and why fewer of them owned their own homes compared to their parents. As for those in their twenties and thirties, they simply had less; more were still living with parents because they couldn't afford to rent or buy. Rents kept rising, having children looked unaffordable, the length of time they would have to save until they could afford a deposit kept growing. The political implications seem plain. Formerly, said an expert commentator, 'young Britons had realistic expectations of upward mobility and home ownership, and their political interests naturally allied with the party of homeowners and low taxes', i.e. the Tories. Not today.

A peak period for wealthy retirement

Demographics are destiny. A society where couples can't afford children will die out. In 2022, England and Wales recorded the lowest number of live births since 2002, when the population was smaller: it was now below replacement rate. Births rose in the Labour years, suggesting policy can make a difference. Now the average number of children born to a woman was 1.49, on a falling trend since 2010 and the lowest rate since good data was first collected in the 1930s. Ageing is inexorable. By 2024, nearly one in five people were over retirement age, their numbers up nearly three million during the last decade. Over-85s will double in number in the next quarter-century. Even if they will then make up only one in twenty-five, the intensity of their need for health and social care in the later stages of life will press hard.

If the policy consequences of ageing point one way, what about the politics? In 2019, the over-70s were more than twice as likely to vote Tory as those aged 30. But the 2010s may turn out to have been the peak period for wealthy retirement. Future retirees will have less generous pensions, with their increased housing wealth less spectacular. Each year the age at which a majority of older cohorts tend to vote right has been advancing, with no sign the young are turning Tory as they age in the way of previous generations.

Those likely to be most reliant on home helps, district nurses, bus passes, smooth pavements and open community centres should be voting for decent provision, and paying the taxes needed to support them. They should also take a sane view of who the home helps and district nurses will be. If they are not migrants, the domestic workforce will have to grow in pay and number. Those contemplating their later life as pensioners and dependants may rue their support for the anti-statists when their need grows, when they feel the effects of those cuts in training for nurses and doctors or in career progression for teachers and public servants. Polling suggests more women of childbearing age wish they had one more child but are deterred by the cost of their upbringing and childcare when wages are stagnant. Making life better for mothers and would-be mothers is a necessity. Children were the principal victims of austerity and anti-collectivism. The UK, or at least England, had turned its back on its own future.

Growth culture

There's no way up without reviving growth, in incomes, in opportunities, but also in basic technical capacities. Market dogmatics having failed, the new formula marries public interest and corporate ambition through planning. To secure long-term private investment requires the state to lead, steer and where necessary de-risk and reassure. To those who say, that's back to the future, we've been there, we say, no, we haven't. Glimmerings in the 1960s weren't followed through. The circumstances the UK finds itself in now and into the 2030s require government to spur enterprise in biosciences, digital technologies, energy and communications as well as the arts, education, the law and organizational services, on which the UK balance of trade has come to depend. The UK is the second largest exporter of services in the world; the very phrase 'industrial strategy' was narrowing and anachronistic. How to harness, stimulate and promote: government alone can fuel business ecosystems, keeping an eye on training and physical infrastructure and, as necessary, protecting against undercutting and dumping by foreign predators. Only a strong central government can mitigate overconcentration of GDP growth in London and the south-east, which accounts for two thirds of the UK's trade surplus in services, to better exploit the talents of less-favoured areas.

A concomitant of all this is a shift in UK corporate culture. The quid pro quo for government assuring the future is that boardrooms accept social responsibility, meaning reasonable levels of taxation on company and individual gains and an attitudinal shift among directors against widespread tax evasion. Misalignments between the interests of shareholders and directors have to be rectified; also between fundholders with a long-term interest against private equity manipulators out for a short-term hit. The City and financial sector were badly shaken by Brexit. The London Stock Exchange has been losing business to New York, Paris and Frankfurt. Here too is scope for better matching private enterprise and the pursuit of profit with a wider interest, mediated by the state as planner, regulator, tax authority and trade negotiator.

If trends in ageing are inexorable and the consequences of failing to invest are already visible all around us, what happens if the sharp increases in inequality in the UK keep widening? Tory politicians have surfed the indifference or ignorance of many, but social bonds are not infinitely elastic. In an earlier book we used the metaphor of a camel train crossing the desert, the sheikhs at its head having long passed out of sight, no longer part of the train at all. What then if the middle and lower ranks refuse to go any further? Or branch out in a completely different direction? In the case of the UK, a long history and relative absence of disturbance should not be taken for granted.

Turning point?

In the following chapters, we weigh the legacy of the last 14 years. The story of what the Tories did and didn't do is a baseline, a tally for judging what comes next. At the end of each chapter we offer some pointers. Generous volunteering at local food banks shows this has not entirely become the kind of society *they* wanted. But society has to connect with the state, and that can only happen through the ballot box and metamorphosis at Westminster, together with the other parliament and assemblies and local authorities. We wrote this hoping an account of failure would first anger and provoke but second whet the appetite for change, knowing what we can do about those mistakes made.

This book is dedicated to today's children. They will reach adulthood on a globe heating even faster than predicted, which in 2023 hit 1.5 degrees above pre-industrial temperatures, with all its consequences for sea levels, climate and crop failure. Will they get decarbonization back on track for net zero? They are going to need vocational and professional training to install solar panels and heat pumps, as well as the skills to tame AI, develop a domestic drone industry and find a hundred and one other solutions. So they need to hear why further education has been run down and technical qualifications torn up. They will ask their parents: what were you doing, voting for clowns and cakeism, and the deceit of promising European levels of public services on American levels of taxation? And why the rich got richer even as total taxes rose and public services buckled.

Emerging bleary-eyed from lockdowns, the public looked around and saw how unprepared the UK had been for the pandemic, with fewer NHS staff, beds, intensive care places and ventilators, and a lack of care homes or protection for those living in them. In the years before 2020, ministers had been lackadaisical, dismissing warnings. It wasn't just lack of protective equipment; austerity had thinned out collective capacity to endure a crisis. Schools had nothing spare as they tried to set up online lessons while still teaching key workers' children in classrooms, so many children not owning a laptop. A Southwark head teacher showed us the families gathered at her gates, hoping to catch the school's Wi-Fi so children could do homework on their mobile phones. Hardship was visible in places previously regarded as well-heeled. Food banks became the red flag marking people in need, most of them in jobs that paid too little for survival.

But it's only when your feet touch the bottom of the swamp that you can push up to the surface. We need to know what went awry, auditing what did not happen, such as investing, stimulating productivity, equipping people with the skills to survive, exploiting technologies, building, planning, greening, self-sustaining, restoring good government and a sense of orderliness and due process. We know a lot. Improvement and progress now depend on wresting all those critical reports off the shelf and mining them for what and what not to do next. Chances for improvement, economic, social and emotional, depend on collective choices. By 2024, pollsters were finding that well over half of voters wanted the government to spend more on public services, with fewer than a third choosing tax cuts instead. That felt like spring in the air. But history tells us that regimes and societies are perfectly capable of repeating error (the second time as farce, someone said). Yet it's also true that knowledge and experience cumulate. We've been down and seen what went wrong, so now ... the only way is up.

Now that we enter a new era, this book chronicles the baseline for judging the new government. This is the legacy they inherit, this audits the starting point to look back on later to see how far 'up' they have taken the country on a path to recovery, repair and renewal.

1

Children: A Case of Neglect

NOT A GREAT time to be a child. Bliss it wasn't in that dawn to be young. This generation was the least physically active generation ever, said a despairing Children's Commissioner. Exploited and intimidated online by unregulated social media companies, waiting 94 weeks for an autism assessment, never even having the chance of visiting a local library to borrow a book or disc because, as in Birmingham, two thirds had been closed, this was not a country for young people.

But consolation was at hand. Every school in England was given an oak-framed portrait of King Charles, to complement the King James Bible sent them by education secretary Michael Gove. That name rings out across the era, stamping his authoritarian seal on children's lives, as if unprecedented volumes of mental distress and later pandemic lockdowns weren't enough. His first act had been to lop children, schools and families from the title of his department, moving to abolish Every Child Matters and Sure Start, Labour programmes wrapped around the whole child.

Perhaps it was only to be expected that children were neglected. Unless their parents are affluent, they are not of much interest to markets, hence to a market-oriented government; many Tory MPs sent their own children to the private schools where they themselves had been. But Gove had missionary zeal, stemming from his partisan fear and contempt for educators as a vector for liberal and progressive politics. He shared with his cabinet colleagues an ideological rejection of the interventionist programme pursued by Labour, embracing child poverty, the Child Trust Fund and early years schemes. But Tory voters had children at state schools, which explains why educational resources, despite the Liberal Democrats' token pupil premium for poorer areas, were redistributed to schools in more affluent areas.

Laying out all the Tories' child-unfriendly actions, one after another, is shocking. Surely all governments put children and the future first? More children were living below the official poverty line, 4.2 million of them excluded from an ordinary quality of life. That was up from 3.6 million in 2010. Poor children tend to become poor and underperforming adults. In Chapter 4 we cite a Tory adviser bemoaning neglect of housing, warning that as a society we had fallen out of love with the future.

That things were not going well for children in the other UK nations serves only to remind us of a profound and banal truth. Children are posterity. Fail to cherish them, let their schools crumble, increase their class sizes, deprive them of joy and happiness as well as a solid grounding in the skills and aptitudes we need, and society will decline. Little wonder, COVID aside, that school absence was at 'crisis levels' by 2024.

Joyless

Joy was off the curriculum. Trips and outings became rarities. Municipal parks were shut, sold or left unattended; playgrounds closed and hundreds of community football pitches disappeared, along with school playing fields and swimming pools – 400 of them shut down between 2010 and 2023. Nearly 800 libraries closed their doors, those havens for children and families on winter days. Youth services disappeared; more than 4,500 youth work jobs went, with 760 council-run youth centres closed in the 10 years since 2010, said the YMCA. Labour had left a Connexions service in place, offering careers advice; it was largely abolished. The national careers service that replaced it was online only, failing confused or drifting teens who needed encouragement and support.

The 2012 Olympics generated tremendous enthusiasm for all ages, amid high hopes that success in the arena would boost involvement, stimulate children and improve their well-being. But when auditors investigated, they found participation in sport had fallen in the three subsequent years 'and the government's commitment to the sporting legacy had waned by 2016'. What a wasted opportunity.

It became more dangerous to be young. Infant mortality rose for two years in a row to 2018. The last time there was such a trend was 1939–41; it was hard to find any other cause than austerity. The fate of children drove the distinguished paediatrician Al Aynsley-Green to write a passionate denunciation when he stood down from the role of Children's Commissioner for England. He lambasted the denial of fact by the propaganda machine in the Department for Education – such as the increase in the number of four- and five-year-olds arriving in reception classes still wearing nappies. As of 2024, one in four children starting school were not toilet-trained, worsened since the pandemic's loss of nursery years.

Death and disturbance

The number of child deaths had hit record levels, including those who died because of abuse and neglect, suicide, perinatal and neonatal events and surgery. In 2023, the death rate rose by 8 per cent over the previous year. More than a third were officially declared to be avoidable. Camilla Kingdon, president of the Royal College of Paediatrics and Child Health, knew the reasons why. Most deaths were in deprived areas and 'the clear driver is rising child poverty. Figures such as these in a nation as rich as ours are unforgivable.'

Previous progress on stopping expectant mothers smoking and raising rates of breastfeeding reversed. Something bad was happening in children's lives, increasing mental distress. Even before 2010, GPs and psychiatrists were seeing more; then an explosion, a doubling of referrals of under-18s between 2017 and 2022. Numbers with probable mental health problems rose sharply from 12 per cent in 2017 to 20 per cent in 2023; waiting lists ballooned as one study found a quarter of sixth-formers had sought mental health support in the previous 12 months but many (a third) were still waiting; numbers and waits were worse in deprived areas.

One reason was COVID, which increased depression, girls suffering more than boys. Another was money: children living in households struggling with unpayable bills had higher rates of mental illness. Tory governments can't be held responsible for all the causes of this wave of distress, which included exposure to harmful social media, online bullying and intolerable peer-group pressures. The charge against them is twofold. One was austerity: more than a quarter of children with a probable mental disorder had a parent who did not have enough money to let their offspring take part in activities outside school or college. The other was a failure to react, to mobilize, to put this burgeoning distress at the top of all priorities. This government forsook them. A 2021 review of children's social care put the annual cost of not addressing the needs of all children who had ever needed a social worker at around £23 billion. Here was one of those calculations regularly dismissed by blinkered Treasury civil servants. How to calculate the costs of *not* acting, *not* intervening, *not* providing adequate services? It was possible to work it out: over a lifetime, failure to help children and young people resulted in hospital admissions, early withdrawal from the labour market, lower productivity and economic loss. The NAO concluded that the problems of children and adolescents 'may become entrenched and require intense and expensive support to reverse or mitigate any harm. For the individual, consequences could include mental health difficulties, periods not being in education, employment or training, or contact with the criminal justice system. Different outcomes often overlap, for example around three quarters of children sentenced in 2019–20 were assessed as having mental health concerns.'

Parents were desperate: schools, social workers and the NHS were failing them. Waits for diagnoses, let alone treatment, stretched into years. The causes of flaring numbers of children who might be autistic were multiple: more parents were concerned about their kids' behaviour, diagnostic criteria had broadened. But also shrunken school budgets, fewer educational psychologists and teaching assistants, and for those Tory ministers were responsible. Along with, as we see in Chapter 6, a cynical heaping of responsibilities onto councils at the same time as their grants were gutted. Autism demanded a wide strategic response; it was piecemeal.

Despite lobbying by ex-deputy prime minister Nick Clegg after he became a stooge for Facebook, the government did pass online safety legislation allowing Ofcom to detect and remove child sexual abuse material (though that would depend on the regulator's capacity and willingness, which was more doubtful once a complacent Tory peer had been parachuted in as its chair). Had the UK still been in the European Union, digital services legislation would already have been in operation.

Birth

A country hostile to children? It sounds extreme, but prospective parents seemed to think so. Births plummeted at an alarming – and economically damaging – rate, with (in England and Wales) a 12 per cent reduction in the annual tally between 2012 and 2019. Decline continued and 2022 saw the lowest number in two decades, 605,479. People had not turned against parenthood; this was no rebellion by mothers. On the contrary, women told pollsters they were sad to have fewer babies than they wanted. Child-rearing had become unaffordable to age cohorts now worse off than their parents had been at the same age. They had far higher rents and mortgages, if they could even find a place to live, with lower earnings and heavy student debts. Young families now were spending a third of their income on nursery fees, and some as much as four fifths.

If they did become pregnant, women found maternity and obstetrics had become a Cinderella in the NHS, the number of midwives down by a third. Not unconnected, the number of women dying in pregnancy and childbirth reached its highest in 20 years, though mercifully this was still a rare occurrence. Targets for reducing stillbirths and infant deaths were missed by a long way. Standards in maternity units were in the news, with scandals over needless deaths in Telford and Morecambe. At the end of 2023, the health regulator reported two thirds of maternity units as unsafe.

Overweight and unhappy

Once born, children faced higher risk. The UK slid down international assessments of child height. Almost one in four English children aged 10 and 11 were obese – a finding that exposed the long-term impact of COVID. During the first year of lockdown, obesity rates had risen by a half among 4-to-5-year-olds and by a fifth in 10-to-11-year-olds. After the pandemic, rates dropped but the proportion of children leaving primary school overweight remained at high levels, leading NHS England's national clinical director to diagnose a 'ticking health timebomb'. At least 56,000 more children would grow up at heightened risk of type 2 diabetes, cancer and other serious illnesses, at a future cost of £8 billion.

Children became significantly unhappier. The 2023 annual report on their well-being from the Children's Society found 'average happiness scores with their life as a whole, their friends, appearance, school, and schoolwork were all significantly lower', girls more than boys, with 'family the only aspect of life for which children's average happiness scores remained relatively stable'.

Children were at the sharp end of the council funding crisis. Across the country, officials tried to constrict demand for help for children whose parents sought recognition of their special needs. This was politically difficult for the government, since those parents included affluent and potential Tory support-ers. This may explain legislation making it easier in principle to access emotional health and care plans, applications for which had doubled since 2014. Applications were one thing, support was another.

As we report in Chapter 6, the ploy was to load duties onto councils, underfund them, then hope they, rather than the MPs and ministers responsible, would face the ire of parents. The 2014 changes around SEND (special educational needs and disabilities) had doubled the number of eligible children to 230,000. But they also increased the number of journeys to special schools, which cost councils dear, particularly those in Cumberland, Devon and Norfolk, paying for taxis and minibuses. The Tory councillors of Hampshire, solidly in control of the county since 1997, said that they were facing a financial meltdown, though they omitted to point out who was responsible.

Care carnage

Cases of children being neglected or subjected to cruelty were on an upward trend, according to the NSPCC; they had doubled in the five years to 2022–23. Ministers appeared indifferent. On vulnerable young people, there was limited official understanding, limited knowledge, no assessments, gaps in the evidence base, so said the NAO. The number of children taken into care shot up. The 139,000 children stuck in homeless accommodation were at high risk of harm. Social worker numbers fell, meaning remaining staff had less time for casework and were more likely to take children from parents in emergencies. The 64,400 in care in England in 2010 rose to 83,840 by the end of 2023, the highest on record.

County councils said children's services were in a state of 'carnage'. Local authority homes having closed (many under Labour), children were at the mercy of the market – privately run establishments, some small businesses, others in the grip of profit-maximizing private equity. Cash-strapped councils often dumped them far away, hundreds of miles sometimes, in homes in the cheapest, poorest places, such as Blackpool and other depressed coastal towns. Councils had very little choice and were held to ransom, according to John Pearce, president of the Association of Directors of Children's Services. Homes 'can pick and choose which referrals to accept and set the price due to overwhelming demand particularly for placements for children with complex needs'.

Such children were expensive to place. In the five years to 2022–23, the number of placements in private homes, each of which cost councils over £10,000 a week, increased tenfold. The government extolled the bigger spend on children with high needs without asking why. One reason was that they had robbed Peter (school supports and educational psychology) to pay Paul (councils' budgets for special educational needs). They were now eating up council revenues, Middlesborough spending four fifths of its entire budget on adult and child social care.

Early years

Marketization was failing to provide nurseries and arrangements to look after the children of working parents during the day, especially those with special needs, where the dwindling number of council and charity-run nurseries were vital. Close to a third of not-for-profit nurseries had closed their doors or were taken over by private companies, including private equity firms. The poorest areas where parents couldn't pay top-ups had the fewest nursery places.

Labour's legacy was 15 free hours of nursery for three- and four-year-olds, and the Tories extended it with 15 hours more, but, crucially, only for 38 weeks a year and only for working families. More two-year-olds became eligible for free care, the most disadvantaged first, but here again only if they came from working families. The prime purpose (a good one) was to help young families keep their heads above water, pay sky-rocketing rents or even buy a first home, which depended on both parents working. Reserving support just for working parents, however, excluded many: children with a single parent, those whose families had severe mental or addiction problems preventing them working. Yet it was children of parents in trouble who most needed rescuing with a good nursery start to their education.

Under pressure from parents, the Tories realized just how damaging slash-and-burn austerity had been and increased the value of the subsidy to help pay nursery fees, but still cut out the children in most urgent need with non-working parents. By 2023, ministers were trumpeting a new policy, worth £4 billion they claimed, offering free places. But for months afterwards, parents struggled to make sense of the scheme, finally started in April 2024, increasing support to all working-family two-year-olds. The promise was for all nine-month-olds, but conveniently not until after the next election. The money was not enough to entice more nursery staff. Using a recurrent analogy, Joeli Brearley of campaigners Pregnant Then Screwed said, 'yet again it feels as though planning for childcare funding has been done on the back of a fag packet'. Without ensuring places were going to be provided and by whom, the cash was likely to be wasted. In the year to 2023, there was a 5 per cent fall in the number of infant care providers in England and a 10 per cent fall in the number of childminders. Nine out of ten councils cited persistent problems with recruiting and retaining staff for childcare. That's straightforward childcare; places for children with special needs were going to be in even shorter supply.

This was not early *education*. Perhaps the most wanton and destructive move the government had made was to abandon Sure Start – a judgement validated in later reports by the IFS and even pro-Tory think tanks such as the Centre for Social Justice. Research had conclusively shown that the earliest years shape destiny. Arriving ill-equipped at primary school is too late for many. Children who qualified for free school meals were falling 12 months behind their peers by the time they headed for secondary school, on a likely path to delinquency, poor jobs and low income. Catching problems early, giving children stimulus and attention can save them. The best of the 3,500 Sure Start children's centres created during the 2000s had every kind of catch-up help, from speech and language specialists to parenting classes and meeting places for isolated families. IFS research showed that the beneficial effects of Sure Start lasted all the way up to GCSE, when Sure Start children achieved three grades higher than similarly deprived children who hadn't attended. By 2015, most Sure Starts were gone or radically reduced in scale and ambition, often to no more than a private crèche. The gap in young children's attainment widened again.

Schooling

Gove's defenders say he cared passionately about children's attainment. He made a lot of noise; if the behavioural norms he insisted on for schools had been self-applied, he would have been made to stand in the corner, failed. He recruited a noisome special adviser in the shape of Dominic Cummings (private school and Oxford), a champion hater, who directed his venom against teachers and educationists. Gove was another privately educated minister pontificating about the state sector. The financial gap in per pupil funding between private and state schools had doubled since 2010. Uninterested in preschoolers or children's social needs, he immediately scrapped Labour's innovatory register of children, which would have allowed teachers, GPs and social workers with concerns to check whether a child was deemed at risk. This won him plaudits in the right-wing press, sanctimonious about privacy in family life, though soon it was blaming teachers and social workers for not picking up the growing volume of child abuse.

Yet education was never a Tory priority, despite rhetoric from Sunak (Winchester and Oxford) that it was a silver bullet and the best economic and social policy. Overall education funding as a proportion of national income dropped substantially from its peak in 2010. By 2024, spending per primary school pupil was £4,655, 3 per cent below 2010 in real terms. Gove had arrived full of indignation at the results gap between deprived children and the rest. His sincerity was tested as he shifted funding away from schools in poorer communities to more affluent areas. This, said the Institute for Government (IfG), was 'a particular concern if we are serious about addressing the attainment gap between disadvantaged children and their peers'. Thirteen years after Gove's arrival, GCSE results revealed 'persistent inequalities in outcomes with a growing gap between London and the rest of the country. In London, 28 per cent of entries were awarded a grade seven or above, in the North East it was only 18 per cent.'

Labour had launched multiple initiatives, but in opposition they proved a poor advocate of their own programmes' successes. Among those undersold was Every Child a Reader. For infant schoolchildren in poor areas, this offered intense one-to-one teaching and adult–child talk. Not cheap, it cost £3,000 a child in the first year and £2,600 in annual follow-on. For our book *Unjust Rewards* we visited a school in Wythenshawe in Manchester and were knocked out by the programme's results. More objectively, the IFS said the scheme made a distinct difference, especially among boys, pushing up test scores, equipping them for the transition to junior school and beyond. Here was an intervention that worked but cost money. As with Sure Start, Cameron played Pontius Pilate. We didn't axe these things, he said. Instead, they removed the ring-fenced subsidy to councils that supported them while cutting overall council funding.

Gove failed in his own terms. A decade on, no social class narrowing had been detected by researchers. 'The school system has become less equitable since 2010, with higher-performing schools admitting relatively fewer disadvantaged pupils.' But the very ambition to narrow the difference had been based on empty wishes. Schooling, in and of itself, can do relatively little to reduce the inequality that stems from household income and social class. During the past 20 years, there has been virtually no reduction in the gap between children on free school meals and their more fortunate peers. To the political right, blinkered or in denial about socioeconomic inequality, schools were both a substitute and a scapegoat. If you believed, as Tories tended to, that personal merit and hard work were the keys to success (as opposed to parents' wealth and the sheer luck of your birth), focusing on how schools are run and what they teach was a useful distraction. The reality, spelled out by sociologist John Goldthorpe, was that you only reduce inequality by providing substantial financial support to those who need it, either through welfare benefits or by intervening in the labour market.

Instead, Gove stormed through the primary and secondary curriculum, decreeing that Byron, Keats, Jane Austen, Dickens and Thomas Hardy *were* English literature, and toughening requirements in maths and science. Of course there is a strong case for a core curriculum, provided schools recognize differences in pupils' preparedness and background. Every secondary student was to study Gove's EBacc, five GCSEs comprising English, maths, science, a language and either history or geography – every student, that is, except those in private schools or Gove's new 'free schools'. Nothing wrong in principle with a focus on maths; on the contrary. But where were the incentives for maths teachers, where were the interventions to stop the half of children from disadvantaged backgrounds who were top in maths at primary school not proceeding to high grades at GCSE in England?

Free schools were a fad and a favouritism that diverted a substantial sum of public money and for which no evidence was gathered, no models set out, no trials run. Self-appointed groups of parents, some with a religious commitment, were given money from the central education budget to set up schools. Councils had a duty to plan the provision of enough school places yet were given no control over where these new schools went. That was by fiat of the minister. Naturally enough, activist parents were more likely to be found in areas where schools already did well. By 2023, there were 650 free schools. In terms of results, free primaries did worse than mainstream schools, but free secondaries did better. The reason, said the Education Policy Institute, was that the best performers 'are disproportionately drawing their pupils from neighbourhood types that already achieve higher results on average'. The programme got little attention after Gove left office; no one produced a cost-benefit appraisal to check on the value for public money of this diversion of resources.

Labour had romanticized the benevolence of business tycoons devoting their wealth to improving schools. The Tories followed suit. Here is what happened in Wiltshire, when ministers approved Sir James Dyson's £6 million donation to build a centre for science and engineering at Malmesbury Church of England School, near one of his company's R&D centres. (Dyson sued the *Daily Mirror* after a columnist had assailed him for moving his global head office to Singapore after extolling the benefits of Brexit to Britain; he lost.) It was local Tory councillors who complained, pointing out that Dyson creating 200 new school places could jeopardize three local schools that already had surplus space.

This issue will get worse. By 2027–28, London will need 8,000 fewer reception and primary places compared with 2023–24, thanks to a big fall in the capital's birth rate, to families leaving the capital, some Europeans driven off by Brexit, other families moving away from the rising cost of London living. Councils would need powers to direct academy schools to reduce places, unless huge unfairness was to be introduced between them and maintained schools.

Trusting in trusts

Labour had introduced academies to replace failing schools in deprived areas, sponsored by businesses or foundations to give existing schools new buildings or to make a fresh start: there were 202 in 2010. Gove decreed all schools would be wrenched from local authorities and become academies. They would be bundled together in multi-academy trusts, MATs, mini education authorities, but not publicly accountable. The idea was that the best schools would spread their expertise to others inside these trusts, which came to encompass four fifths of England's secondary schools. Ofsted found they did not get better results. The proportion of pupils achieving the expected standard in reading, writing and maths was slightly higher in local authority schools. Trusts showed greater variation in performance: the best MATs outperformed, but the worst ones fell below the rest. It's characteristic of English schools that the highest-performing pupils do better (on international comparisons) but they are concentrated in private and grammar schools and the best MATs.

Gove's imperious order that all schools join MATs was rescinded in 2016, but schools in difficulty were still to be pushed into becoming academies. By 2023, there were over 10,000 academy schools, taking in half of all pupils. What is striking isn't just the lack of evidence and analysis before Gove's ordinance, but the indifference (hostility?) to evaluation and monitoring what it achieved. The Tory-leaning think tank the Centre for Social Justice worried about the number of children being suspended from schools and found trust secondaries more likely to rid themselves of problem pupils. That might be related to some trusts having absorbed difficult schools, but the truth was, a giant experiment in educational reorganization had pallid results.

COVID and after

COVID afflicted children. By 2023, more than 80,000 born in the years 2020 and 2021 were not reaching key measures of progress for their age group. The scars of school closure during those years will last long. Distress turned children against school life. In 2022–23, more than one in six primary and more than one in four secondary pupils were persistently absent, missing 10 per cent or more of school sessions. In surveys, a quarter of parents no longer thought it essential for children to go to school every day.

A fair test of Tory ministers must be what they did to remedy the pandemic's effects. We earlier discussed the surge of mental health problems and the inadequacy of the response, leading to bloated waiting lists. Schools got some money for catch-up tutoring, the need for which showed dramatically in the fact that by 2022, two million children were behind their peers in talking and understanding words, higher than ever previously recorded. Speech and language therapists were unable to meet the demand. Sir Kevan Collins, a distinguished former teacher, was appointed to organize the tutoring but promptly resigned. Funds were 15 times less than needed, he said, amounting to just £22 per child in primary schools. Not surprisingly, the Education Policy Institute found the government 'well behind' on its own target to get nine out of ten pupils to the expected standard in reading, writing and maths by 2030.

Schooling was disrupted across the world.

The OECD runs periodical assessments of 15-year-olds, the best data we have to measure across time and between countries, though international comparison can be treacherous. For example, it finds no clear relationship between results and the amount spent on schooling, exemplified by such countries as Singapore and South Korea. The explanation there lies in singleness of purpose, consistency and muscular state action.

The 2022 OECD rankings offered light and shade. UK schoolchildren achieved their lowest scores in mathematics and science since 2006 – the first year of comparable data. Reading results were also down, close to the previous minimum in 2009, but other countries had even greater COVID declines in attainment, which meant the UK slightly improved its overall score. So while UK maths results slumped by 13 points, the average OECD performance dropped by almost 16. French results for maths were bad, causing a national outcry.

There were marked differences between the four UK nations, with England coming top, taking it from seventeenth in the 2018 international rankings for maths to eleventh now. Oddly, given the lack of social progress in the UK in recent times, the OECD noted that socioeconomic status was weaker in predicting performance in maths than elsewhere. Against that weigh the third of all pupils failing to get crucial maths and English GCSEs and the fact that half of children on free school meals failed those subjects. Only a fifth of those who failed maths first time would ever pass, however many times they resat.

Across the globe, quality of teaching seems to matter more than class size. Actually, having a teacher matters, too. In 2022, half of UK pupils were in schools whose head reported that teaching capacity was hindered by lack of staff. In 2018, the corresponding proportion was under a third. Fewer people wanted to be teachers. Pay rates were falling and teachers went on strike over salaries 10 per cent lower in real terms than in 2010. Only half the number needed were recruited in 2023, despite the offer of bonuses. The recruitment target for physics, the worst performer, was missed by 83 per cent. So much for the future of UK science, technology and productivity. More teachers were quitting the profession caused by 'disgruntlement over workloads and a lack of flexible working as well as unhappiness over pay'. Gove's contempt – what wit to describe the profession as a 'blob' – had sent teachers the message. And then there was what the job had become. Teachers were buying hungry children food and paying for classroom materials from their own pocket, as the purchasing power of school budgets fell: the IFS said that in 2024, funds would be 4 per cent lower in real terms than in 2010.

Hard Times, the musical

Among its results, the OECD had found a quarter of UK students dissatisfied with their lives, more than in other countries. Gradgrind Gove had stripped back art, drama, music, dance and sport. From 2010, GCSE and A level arts entries fell by nearly half; many fewer children were singing in a choir or playing in an orchestra. Cultural industries were growing at twice the rate of the economy, so where was the seed corn? Love of sport keeps many attached, but physical education was also cut and playing fields sold off. Hard-pressed teachers had less time to run out-of-school clubs. Exams and progress scores drove out so much else.

Yet thankfully, in education as across other public services, dedicated and remarkable people stayed and fought. Take Vic Goddard, the head of Harlow's Passmores Academy. The Essex secondary had 60 children with special educational needs and disabilities, when the average number per school was 25. Goddard had managed to keep music going, three school shows a year. 'The world's an angrier place', he told us. More parents were up in arms; he had to endure death threats and anti-vaxxer protests. Four Ofsted inspections were looming: 'It's a lottery, depending what inspector you get. I want Ofsted to be an improver, helping me to do better.' Instead of ticking boxes for inspections, he wanted to focus on every child reaching the right reading age: 'that's what matters most for their life'.

Inspected to death

The tragic suicide of Reading head teacher Ruth Perry saw an outpouring of anger about the regime of terror, targets and inspection that had tightened the screws on schools. She killed herself after inspectors judged inadequate her previously outstanding school, Caversham Primary. Labour had encouraged a culture based on one-word judgements, in schools by Ofsted, in the NHS by the Care Quality Commission. But under Labour, resources were increasing. Now the same crude determinations were made as spending cuts bit – but the inspectors never commented on budgets. Perry touched hearts: she had been a pupil at the highly popular school, and then devoted her whole working life to it. It was the exceptional judgement of the coroner that made this sad story so remarkable. Coroners avoid giving definitive causes for suicide, but a harsh Ofsted inspection was named as the key contributor to the death of a woman previously without signs of depression. The inspection had 'lacked fairness, respect and sensitivity' and was rude and intimidating. There followed a flood of tales of unjust and bullying inspections, where one fault, often administrative, condemned an otherwise good school. No wonder a third of new head teachers quit after five years. The government promised to revise these one-word damnations. The latest Tory education secretary, Gillian Keegan, showed her sophisticated grasp of running schools by saying she would punch a rude inspector.

Learning in a school that needs rebuilding

Inspectors were conspicuously silent about leaking roofs and boarded-up classrooms. Gove had cancelled Labour's ambitious building programme, in another example of storing up trouble. Later his cabinet colleague Priti Patel protested loudly when five schools in her Essex constituency were found to be contaminated with RAAC. Maintenance budgets had been cut, directly contributing to the crisis that unfolded when some 200 other schools were found to be affected, in addition to those with asbestos. The NAO reported that 'following years of underinvestment the [school] estate's average condition is declining and 700,000 pupils are learning in a school that needs major rebuilding or refurbishment'. The government lacked information on safety; funding was less than what was needed to secure buildings. In addition, more than a third of English school buildings were past their estimated design life, making them more expensive to maintain, with poorer energy efficiency and higher running costs. In 2020, the Department for Education had asked for £5.3 billion a year for buildings; it was given £3.1 billion. An independent assessment by the Office of Government Property put the necessary spend at £7 billion a year.

Imbalance in the national skill set

Maintenance of all buildings everywhere required technical skills. During Brexit, plumbing had enjoyed a moment in the spotlight amid complaints at the number of Polish craftspeople working in the UK (usually to the intense satisfaction of their clients). Vainglorious promises were made about post-Brexit training of British plumbers, but this skill set along with most others disappeared from view once the referendum was over. The backdrop was one of confusion about vocational education and its interaction with the preparation for employment offered post-16. Vic Goddard, the Harlow head, had mentioned that his own father had been a good plumber but had never really learned reading – a loss. Now, to get on a plumbing course he would need GCSE maths and English.

Imbalance in the national skill set had been worried over for decades. Market signals went awry. Employers, in construction for example, preferred to recruit trained staff from abroad rather than invest in the workforce: they refused to take on carpenters, electricians and plumbers straight from passing FE courses unless they had real-world experience, but denied them the chance to acquire this. For Tory ministers, further education outside universities was largely about other people's children, which may explain disproportionate budget cuts after 2010. Further education teachers' real pay declined by 18 per cent while school teachers' pay fell by between 5 and 13 per cent. No wonder there was such a high staff turnover, with a quarter of FE teachers leaving after just one year.

The half of the 18–20 age group who went to university grabbed attention and generated political heat. During the first year of COVID, teachers awarded A-level marks based on coursework, tending to give higher-than-usual scores: private schools inflated their results even more than state schools. These adjustments caused more outcry than the chaos inflicted on FE after another upheaval in the curriculum and qualifications for technical and skills courses. The Tories decided to abolish the well-established and well-understood qualifications around BTECs, provided by the Business and Technology Council, across some 134 different skills (children's care, travel and tourism, hair and beauty among them) at various levels up to the equivalent of a degree. The rhetoric said 'parity of esteem', but it had been the Tories who in the 1990s had abolished the polytechnics, with their local and vocational ethos, calling them all universities with a bias towards academic qualifications.

T levels, meant to be equivalent to A levels, came in instead, combining on-the-job experience with college. They were born in confusion, students being misled and ill-informed about their content and structure. Only 10,000 enrolled in the qualification in 2022–23, with colleges unable to fill courses in several subjects. The IFS said these reforms 'are especially likely to affect the post-16 choices of poor households (eligible for free school meals), students with special educational needs, and low attainers who are not yet ready for T levels', who were now losing familiar BTEC and City and Guilds qualifications. Ofsted said they offered poor value, inappropriate work placements and had high dropout rates. The tinkering went on. At the Tory conference in October 2023, Sunak announced a new post-16 qualification to bring together the best of A levels and T levels, the 'Advanced British Standard'. Technical qualifications matter to us all, not just for economic growth. The NAO reported that the defence of the UK was imperilled by a lack of people with digital skills.

A sense of abandoning posterity has suffused this account of children, their schooling and their well-being. Put them first, wrap society around them, design every policy and every place with children and young people in mind and there's a good chance this country will have a future.

The only way is up

- Recommit to abolishing child poverty
- Bring joy back to schools, restore arts, sports, school trips
- Recreate Sure Start children's centres, plus better-trained and paid nursery staff; restore Every Child a Reader

- Train specialist clinicians for CAMHS (Child and Adolescent Mental Health Services), bring back educational psychologists and nurses for schools
- Reopen libraries, swimming pools, playing fields and community pitches
- Recreate youth services, youth centres, youth workers supporting teenagers, with face-to-face careers advice
- Raise up FE, equalize staff pay and status with schools, shore up established vocational qualifications
- Regulate social media, prevent online bullying and strengthen Ofcom
- Create a nationwide children's register of those at risk: repair family social work

2

The Economy: Going Nowhere

STAGNATION NATION. THERE'S no escape from that verdict after the Tories' 14 years. Like elsewhere, the UK suffered from the bankers' crash, COVID and the Ukraine war sending prices skywards. But why after these it trailed further behind can only be explained by austerity and misgovernment. By the end of 2023, GDP had grown 1 per cent since pre-COVID 2019, compared with the Eurozone's 3 per cent. Investors, craving consistency, wondered at the Westminster whirligig: nine business secretaries, all promising growth and none delivering. And then in a single year three prime ministers and four chancellors. One of them, Jeremy Hunt, admitted it: political instability had damaged business investment and there were 'very particular reasons why we've had that ... We had Brexit.'

Stagnation is the Resolution Foundation's word: hardship everywhere, the social contract under pressure ... and that's an independent judgement. As Hunt himself said, it was Brexit, plus 11 economic strategies and a mishmash of business support schemes; it was also, of longer standing, the poor quality and quantity of inputs into productivity growth, managers' and employees' skills and capital investment. Ideology degraded them, along with ministers' ignorance, confusion and complacency about what was happening in the economy, in boardrooms, on high streets. F**k business, said the ostensible party of business. It was more like f**k growth.

Of course there was some, but slower. Measured in constant pounds, UK GDP per head increased by £3,558 in the 12 years after 2010, which put £296 extra in the notional purse each year – just about enough to buy an iPhone 4, though you would have to find £25 in monthly charges for two years on top of that. The productivity gap with Germany, the US and France doubled to 18 per cent. With the latter, virtually all the difference was explained, economists said, by French workers having more capital to work with. By 2024, a typical UK household was 9 per cent worse off than a similar French one, while low-income families on this side of the Channel were 27 per cent poorer. Lack of productivity fed directly into sluggish growth in real wages, which had grown by one third during each decade from 1970 to 2007 but barely at all after that. Had they continued at their previous rate, the average worker would have been £10,700 a year better off. In mid 2023, wages were back to where they had been during the financial crisis. Fifteen years of … stagnation. They ended with a cost-of-living crisis, which meant seven quarters of falling GDP per head, the longest period of continuous decline in records going back to 1955. This was the slowest growth of any party's term of office since 1945.

Corporates, conservatives and capitalism

Once, the Tories had been the party of corporates, companies and capitalism. Johnson's expletive seemed a shocking repudiation but was not the whole story. For a start, business didn't reciprocate. Corporate Britain remained reluctant to put the country's longer-run interests ahead of its continuing assumption that the Tories would tamper less with directors' income and wealth. After the collapse of the Confederation of British Industry amid a sex scandal, it lacked any distinctive voice. Some tycoons had always aspired to Singapore-on-Thames. Ardent Brexiteer Sir James Dyson, who had relocated his headquarters away from the UK, protested that the Tories were ignoring entrepreneurs and complained about 'rocketing corporation tax'. (It had been restored to a reasonable 25 per cent in 2023.) In a stormy meeting with Hunt in March 2024, the chancellor finally snapped back at the vacuum cleaner magnate, 'If you think you could do a better job, why don't you just stand for parliament.' It was a misleading rejoinder. True, business had always preferred sniping from the sidelines. Had the exporters and anti-Brexiteers dared campaign hard, they might have swung the vote. But business money was seeping into politics and Tory politicians were queuing up to be bought. Dyson might have asked himself why plutocracy wasn't delivering.

Tory access to boardrooms remained open, especially in finance. Talk about a gravy train; this was the richest *au jus*. Boards – notorious examples were Thames Water and Boots – gave shareholders generous rewards, exploiting tax relief to load up with debt (interest written off against tax), then neglected to invest. Remuneration committees paid executives huge sums that bore no relationship to productivity improvement or performance. They still wanted more. Fund manager Legal & General announced it was changing its voting on boardroom pay to allow companies an increased push towards remuneration 'more closely aligned to US-style pay'. American pay for British levels of economic performance. By contrast, the Norwegians' sovereign wealth fund – which had not been copied by Thatcher when oil revenues were flowing in during the 1980s – said it would mobilize its investments to proscribe excessive payments to company bosses.

Ministers seemed either not to know or not to care about the health of UK capitalism. Pension funds and insurers based here had been dumping their shares in British companies, which had fallen from 50 to 4 per cent of portfolios during the previous 30 years. 'British' companies were increasingly owned by foreigners. Worried about the competitiveness of the UK (damaged by Brexit), the government's instinct was to buttress boardrooms by diluting the rights of shareholders. Experts warned this would harm the UK's reputation as a business centre and let in dodgy foreign outfits with even more opaque ownership. Private equity was on the rampage, buying companies on leverage, waiting for the stock market to rise then re-floating at vast profit, having added no value. Irony of ironies, City expert John Plender noted, a decade later buyout funds turned out not to have generated better returns than stocks at large, after fees were exacted.

The *Financial Times* columnist Martin Wolf diagnosed 'the strange death of corporate Britain'. Did boards even know what was happening? For years there had been talk of improving the audit of commercial companies. The spectacular collapse of Carillion and BHS in 2016 and 2018 had shown the flaws. Reformers wanted to make directors liable for internal controls on financial reporting, but this was deemed too radical. The existing regulator of audits was a catspaw of the Big Four firms — Deloitte, EY, KPMG and PwC – but the government could never quite find the time or energy to change things. The head of the chartered accountants' professional body was scathing. What the government eventually proposed had 'a half-hearted and lopsided feel to it'. The reforms were then dropped after lobbying. Here had been a test of faith in markets. Rigorous audits were the cornerstone of honesty and openness in corporate ownership. If balance sheets lied, markets were corrupted. Evidently friends in the City were more persuasive than Hayek and markets magus Milton Friedman.

A colossal muddle

Stagnation was not an accident but the result of decisions made plus willed inaction. The key period was 2010–16 and at first the Tories won public assent: pollsters found nearly half of people declaring they were personally willing to accept less from public services to pay off national debt. Cuts were necessary not because profligate banks had needed to be bailed out, said chancellor Osborne, but because Gordon Brown had built too many new schools and Sure Start children's centres.

Austerity was needed to regain the trust of the financial markets, he went on. Both at the time and since, this was a facile argument. Austerity blocked investment; the state could have borrowed far more to lift the economy, at least 95 per cent of GDP given the low level of interest rates and the maturity profile of UK state debt. During and after COVID, state borrowing did indeed rise above that level without the markets rebelling. Of course high levels of government debt require the 'kindness of strangers', willing to buy it. But many debt buyers lived in the UK and had a direct incentive to participate; others were likely to be convinced by a government's resolution in organizing the economy for growth. Not, as Truss later showed, by its floundering dogmatism.

Austerity was self-defeating because it had a strong and immediate effect on demand by shrinking social security payments and reduced growth potential by cutting infrastructure investment and local services. A fair 2010 package would have involved spending cuts – Labour had promised them, and besides, the fat years of the noughties had left parts of the public sector bloated and less effective, witness spending on management consultants and high salaries. But they should have been balanced by increased contribution from those who had done so well out of financialization and the bank boom. Stripping the knighthood from former RBS boss Sir Fred Goodwin could have flagged the start of a tax system that rewarded GDP-enhancing enterprise and penalized boardroom extravagance and the accumulation of idle property assets. That prospect remains enticing.

In the 1920s, another age of economic error, J. M. Keynes said, 'To-day we have involved ourselves in a colossal muddle, having blundered in the control of a delicate machine, the working of which we do not understand.' That pretty much applies to economic stewardship in the 2010s and perhaps also to the epoch before, given how little Labour ministers realized the depth of greed and incompetence around the board tables of the banks they had cosseted.

Too much trouble trading with the UK

Europe was the great error, compounded by wilful refusal to understand supply chains, export dependencies and the dynamizing effect of open European markets. Confronted with lorry logjams, Brexit secretary Dominic Raab made the jaw-dropping admission that he 'hadn't quite understood' how much trade relied on the Dover–Calais crossing. Never mind that his ignorance was shared by large numbers of citizens: these were ministers who had been educated at expensive private schools and the University of Oxford (an institution that carries a considerable measure of indirect responsibility for the state we are in). The OBR reported that Brexit was permanently diminishing UK productivity by 4 per cent relative to remaining in the European Union, while exports and imports to and from the EU are going to be 15 per cent lower in the long run. Such candour was one reason Truss refused to let the OBR scrutinize her disaster budget.

Here's one Brexit example among many. After the referendum we reported on the fortunes of Seetru, a middle-sized manufacturer of industrial safety valves. Overnight the Bristol company lost a tenth of its export business. 'Some customers instantly decided it was too much trouble trading with the UK and switched to EU suppliers', said managing director Andrew Varga, a Cambridge engineering PhD. Brexit knocked £4 million off turnover. 'Our EU customers were our friends, but there was a sudden chill.' Products were stuck in German customs for eight weeks. Both their imported supplies and their exports suffered from the 'hard' deal insisted on by Johnson and David Frost, his fanatical negotiator.

They did not heed warnings from the likes of Varga over the imposition of a new British kitemark on all products. This label, UK Conformity Assessed, was dreamt up purely out of nationalist pride. Conformité Européenne (CE), the gold standard among EU countries for 30 years, was anathema: after all, it was in French. Though the UKCA followed CE standards, every one of 30,000 different configurations of Seetru's products now had to be reinspected in the UK to qualify for the new kitemark. It still meant having to give the EU the provenance for raw materials and components as well as finished goods. 'It tripled our admin workload, requiring horrendous new IT systems.'

By 2023, Varga's finished products were stuck, waiting over a year for a UKCA kitemark; the government had failed to appoint inspectors. Worse still, his supplies from the EU were stuck in the same paralysis waiting for the UKCA mark. Many buyers gave up. In the end, the dam burst: the logjam was so catastrophic that the government was forced to revert to the CE. By that time UK exports of goods had fallen by 13 per cent and companies such as Seetru had spent millions upon millions on a pointless exercise.

F**k manufacturing?

In globalist theory, it didn't matter where things were made. According to Professor Patrick Minford (a 'mind' behind Brexit), manufacturing's demise was nothing to worry about. Through the magic of the market something else would take its place. In the real world, however, much depended on making things here. While only 10 per cent of GDP, manufacturing was the principal seat of productivity gains – it constituted two thirds of total research and development – and manufactured products made up nearly half of all exports.

Making certain things was coming to be a precondition of national survival, including the future of Minford's markets. Wiser countries learned the lessons of the bankers' crash, COVID and the effect of the Ukraine war. It was dangerous to rely solely on imports for essentials such as energy, PPE protection, vaccines, food. If you couldn't make drones or tanks or shells or ships, let alone surveillance cameras, switches and software, you depended on others. But what if antagonistic countries forbade exports? The West was waking from the great liberal dream. All those hubristic claims about China becoming a democratic citizen of the world drowned in naval confrontations off Taiwan; the election of Donald Trump pushed them further underwater. Cameron and Osborne had rolled out the red carpet to President Xi, announcing the golden age of Anglo-Chinese relations, and opened nuclear reactors and even surveillance cameras on the streets to Chinese companies, courting huge risks.

Take steel. It was a vital question affecting national security stretching far into the future whether some capacity should be retained at home. The answer had already been outsourced to foreigners. Jingye, the Chinese owner of British Steel, demanded £300 million to keep steelmaking at Scunthorpe. Didn't the state have an interest in reducing the carbon intensity of furnaces? The question arose acutely at Port Talbot, where Indian-owned Tata wanted both a £500m package and the right to make huge job cuts; the economy of South Wales hung in the balance.

By 2023, here was Tory peer Richard Harrington admitting capitalism had changed. 'Many of our competitors chase investments via their industrial strategies backed by substantial government support.' These included Joe Biden's America, once the avatar of market liberalism. But the Tory response had been half-hearted, unable to shake off Thatcher's veto on picking winners. Osborne – his speechwriters loved to alliterate – announced a march of the makers. It stopped well short of specific corporate or regional initiatives, leaving manufacturers to hobble along or mark time. As for May's industrial strategy, unveiled in a white paper in November 2017, it did not last long: a big notice on the government website said it was officially withdrawn in March 2023.

Jürgen Maier, former chief executive of Siemens UK, said companies were crying out for consistency, certainty and clarity. Stephen Phipson, the chief executive of manufacturers' organization Make UK, said: 'Every other major economy has a national manufacturing plan, underlining the importance of an industrial base to the success of its wider economy. The UK is an outlier and, if we are to compete on a global stage, we need one as a matter of urgency.' What the Tories could not countenance was what David Edgerton, Will Hutton and others have called a developmental state. There had been an attempt in the 1960s, extending to the Heath premiership in the early 1970s, to put public money into technologically advanced projects – nuclear reactors, aircraft, computers, trains – and to remake Whitehall, creating the Department of Economic Affairs to fight the short-termism of the Treasury. Left to its own devices business could not and would not innovate and invest. Before COVID, we visited a Sheffield spin-out company called Magnomatics, making magnetic gearboxes, its managing director having tried to talk to the then Department for Business, Energy & Industrial Strategy about grants. 'We got no response at all', chief executive David Latimer told us. 'Eventually they said they were too busy, up to their necks in Brexit. So we'll build the gearboxes abroad. China is very keen.'

Public procurement was already a mainstay of investment decisions, but they were dislocated, sporadic. There was no planning even in such sectors as shipbuilding, where the Ministry of Defence was already in the driving seat. Much had been made of the opening in 2015 of a new railway factory in Durham by Hitachi; eight years later the firm was writing down the value of the investment by £64 million. In November 2023, Alstom, another railway supplier, said 1,300 jobs at its Derbyshire plant were in jeopardy because it had no confirmed orders beyond the first quarter of 2024. Orders, that is, from the confusing mess of companies, some semi-nationalized, that made up the railways. Hoped-for orders for HS2 trains were in abeyance. Through privatization, the trains themselves had been hived off to leasing companies, which, since their profits trebled during 2023, had no need of new carriages.

Car sales rose after the financial crash, but then fell. By January 2024, the Society of Motor Manufacturers and Traders claimed to be back in the game after eight years of turmoil (i.e. Brexit). But could the UK claim a stake in the switch to electric cars without joined-up thinking in government, large-scale investment and training? Tata, the owner of Jaguar Land Rover, and arbiter of the fate of South Wales steel, announced it was building a giant battery factory in Somerset. Could local roads cope with heavy lorries; did Bridgwater and Taunton College have training capacity; would there even be UK-based carmakers to buy the batteries in 2030?

Come and buy, but not the Daily Telegraph

Modern manufacturing had to have a foreign policy, which inevitably involved the state. Motors were a global business. Vital for semiconductors and electric car batteries were gallium, germanium and graphite, and the Chinese had their heel on the supply chain. Ministers shilly-shallied over screening foreign owners and stopping takeovers, though a new National Security and Investment Act gave them powers. In 2016 they celebrated the takeover of Britain's biggest tech company, Arm, by Japan's SoftBank, facilitated by the Brexit-induced drop in sterling's value; a few years on, Arm's new owners decided to list its stock only on Wall Street, which was hardly a vote of confidence in the City. The government changed course: in 2022 they blocked the takeover of the UK's only significant maker of semiconductors by a company ultimately Chinese-owned, which they had initially waved through.

UK companies became cheap, having lost value because of Brexit and the economy's inherent weaknesses. Predators pounced, Americans buying the transport company Wincanton and papermaker DS Smith, with big brands such as Currys and Direct Line targeted. Deals where a foreign company bought a UK one rose to £8.6 billion in value in the last quarter of 2023. Typical was the fate of Morrisons. Bought by an American private equity outfit in 2021 when it had debt of £3.2 billion, within two years it had been loaded with debt worth £8.6 billion, which did not make its survival in a competitive grocery market any easier. The government put its foot down when the United Arab Emirates was about to capture media titles dear to Tory hearts in the *Daily Telegraph* and *Spectator*.

Weak and unstable

Finance benefited from the blind eye turned to what had happened, no lessons learned from the crash, no punishments delivered for what reckless finance had done to living standards in 2008. Osborne did introduce a levy on banks in 2011, but it lasted in a significant form only until 2015, when the government capitulated to blackmail by HSBC, which threatened to move its headquarters. Banks were allowed to offset their tax bill against losses on loans and the government exempted some overseas income from UK tax. If before the crash banks got away with scant scrutiny from regulators, it's by no means clear that afterwards the Bank of England or anyone else knew any better what they were doing or what their balance sheets really reported. With the passage of time since the crash, it became clear that the banks had got away with their greed and folly. Professor Nicholas Crafts argued that if Brexit is seen as an outcome of the banking crisis, then the UK economy was up to 16 per cent of GDP smaller than it would have been if bankers had not gambled and been handsomely bailed out. Imagine how many schools, railways and nurses that would have bought.

London finance might be the natural retirement home for cabinet members, but that didn't help when it came to Brexit negotiations: pleas for special agreements to protect the City fell on deaf ears. Naturally Paris and Frankfurt made the most of the opportunity. The flight of new listings to New York rattled a weakened London Stock Exchange.

The Tory era turned into an experiment in cutting business tax to produce more investment. A shibboleth of market absolutists was that government is an excrescence; slice it away and wonderful gifts fall out of the piñata. So corporation tax was cut, driving the UK rates to among the lowest in the OECD, falling from 28 per cent to 17 per cent in

2020. The growth boost didn't happen. Investment decisions depended on a host of factors, among them a stable horizon, security from predatory takeover and a corporate culture that prized growth: economically, tax mattered far less than the dogmatists said. Those tax cuts didn't make Britain look particularly 'strong and stable' to investors.

Infrastructure

Productivity depended on investment going on outside as well as inside companies. Make UK said two thirds of manufacturers believed infrastructure had deteriorated, citing roads and broadband. The latter was an ironic example. The rationale for privatizing BT in the 1980s had been lack of investment, leading to technological backwardness in telecommunications; the private sector would see the UK excel. By 2023, mobile users were suffering the worst download speeds among advanced countries, with an average 5G speed of 118.2 megabits per second, a good 13 per cent lower than the previous year and a long way below France, on 221 mbps. That wasn't all BT, of course. The belated realization that Huawei, like all big Chinese companies, followed the edicts of President Xi had led to its equipment being stripped out. BT's odd non-ownership ownership of the monopolistic installer of broadband cables Openreach did not help. Its cables had reached 12.5 million homes by the end of 2023, but the promise was 25 million by 2026 and 30 million by 2030. Confusingly, smaller cable-layers were also at work. By early 2024, these 'altnets' had reached nearly 11 million premises and 2.3 million had signed up for connections. This was typical – overlapping firms providing vital infrastructure, potentially overbuilding, dispersing limited resources.

It wasn't so different with electric vehicle chargers. Where was the plan, the join-up between councils, installers, garages, car and battery makers? Why were so many grants offered to householders to install their own (private) chargers as opposed to on-street facilities? Numbers grew, from 20,000 public charging points in 2020 to 55,000 in 2024, but more than half of them were rated slow. Charging points were provided by 14 companies, posing questions about compatibility and location: there remained EV deserts and not just in rural areas such as Lincolnshire. Southend was under-served, but one councillor opined that chargers were a 'cherry on top, and flood prevention and sewage works had priority'.

Holes in the road

Maybe he was right. Investment was in deficit everywhere. Potholes became a symbol for gaps in all public services. They were political dynamite on the doorstep, as we found out when out with canvassers in Lightwater in Surrey. That very day two cars had got stuck in a single local pothole and were waiting to be winched out. On doorstep after doorstep in a ward Tory since the dawn of time, potholes topped the litany of woes. 'Britain used to drive on the left, but now it drives on what's left', joked one householder.

The Asphalt Industry Alliance said in 2023 that the backlog of road repairs was the highest ever, with a tenth of the local road network in England in poor condition. At this rate roads would only be resurfaced once a century. In October 2023, the AA said its patrols were called to 52,541 incidents involving wheel, tyre and suspension damage, a figure 12 per cent higher than in the previous year. Storm Babet – bad weather increasing in frequency and virulence – had not helped by diverting road maintenance crews, where they existed, to fallen trees and floods. A panicked government offered a new road fund, but the first payments would not be made till Easter 2024.

The state of transport reflected the state of the nation. And of productivity, said the former Bank of England official Andy Haldane, recruited as government adviser on infrastructure. Only four out of ten people could reach their nearest city centre within half an hour compared to six out of ten in comparable European regions. It was, he reckoned, no coincidence that towns with below-average GDP per head tended to be badly connected to regional networks, such as Runcorn, Cumbernauld and Thamesmead.

At least the latter now had buses going to Abbey Wood, the terminus for a branch of the Elizabeth Line, formerly Crossrail. Building costs had overshot and completion was delayed by years, but here at last was a fast east–west link across the London conurbation. The architectural critic Edwin Heathcote praised such projects as more than a mere feat of engineering: the new central London stations, especially Paddington and Tottenham Court Road, were cathedral-like spaces. They shaped how we thought about the city and ourselves and perhaps also about how productive we could be, emotions that desiccated economic models could not begin to calculate. How quickly those caverns beneath the streets filled; barely a year after the line's opening, trains and stations were rammed. This was a rare example of Continental-style ambition, but note that the line had first been planned in 1941, rejected by Parliament in 1991 and only finally agreed in 2005. Northerners complained about the concentration of infrastructure spending in the south. London replied that the nation's capital generated the GDP that produced funds needed to improve links in the north. After many stop-starts, the Manchester to York Transpennine line did get going on its vital upgrade with £11.5 billion, but won't be completed until 2037.

No guiding mind

The state of the railways reflected the absence of the state. British railways lacked a guiding mind, said a review by Keith Williams, former head of British Airways. Or, as the transport minister Mark Harper put it, it was 'mad'. Mental capacity had not been on display during the succession of seven mediocre transport secretaries. A timetable fiasco in 2018 had forced the review. Fares rose, train delays and cancellations worsened. Reputation suffered: one company executive told the *Guardian* privately that his own son had laughed at the idea of taking the train: 'too expensive, too unreliable'.

COVID hit the railways hard, with more people working from home and fewer season tickets sold, arresting a long upswing, though they were back to 82 per cent of prior levels by the end of 2023. Johnson had grandiosely announced Great British Railways (GBR), which then got stuck in a siding for years. The new body would run and plan the network, providing rational ticketing and information nationwide, yet another half-remedy for the 1994 privatization catastrophe. A bill was promised; it was a ghost train. State subsidy rose. Semi-nationalization followed, as train companies now acted as mere providers (if you were lucky) for a fixed sum. But with the state collecting ticket revenues, the companies lost any incentive to encourage more travellers. At the end of 2023, two fifths of trains were late, many with fewer carriages. But rolling-stock companies renting out trains made a fortune from their contracts, profits trebling in a year to 2024.

Avanti West Coast, owned by the Italian state railway company Trenitalia, didn't channel Mussolini; its trains not only failed to run on time, many didn't run at all. It was cancelling 26 trains a day by March 2024. That's the same company whose executives chortled with indecent glee at how much it was making from its government contract, putting up a slide entitled 'Roll up, roll up, get your free money here!' The Thameslink franchisees were told they could lower standards. Executives stood to claim millions in bonuses because they could save money from Bedford and Cambridge to Brighton and Horsham by running dirtier trains with fewer staff and lower levels of customer service. Trains had to be a greener alternative to cars and planes, but the Department of Transport's commitment to zero-carbon rail emissions by 2050 flagged, along with the government's waning environmental enthusiasm. An end to diesel trains by 2040 looked unlikely when electrification of the proposed new line from Oxford to Cambridge was postponed. While the French restricted domestic inter-city flights, the UK government encouraged them, priced far cheaper than rail. Trying to cut spending, the government announced the closure of ticket offices, but it was a sign of public emotional attachment to trains that in the resulting outcry they had to back off. Railway unions struck intermittently from 2022 onwards, strike days becoming regarded as just another element in an unreliable service.

How perverse it was for Rishi Sunak to choose his party conference in Manchester in 2023 to insult the city by announcing the axing of the long-promised high-speed rail link. HS2 was a sorry saga of stop-start dithering, delays and changes to plan. The Leeds leg was cancelled in 2021. In 2013, the London to Birmingham stretch was costed at £19.4 billion, but by 2024 it had ballooned to £66 billion. The proposed Euston terminus became another symbol of failure, a black hole in the ground, with blocks of flats and a street of restaurants bulldozed but work then suspended, with no funding agreed to bring HS2 any further than Old Oak Common in west London. Funds must be raised privately, Sunak said, but investment was not forthcoming. The NAO despaired of the government's capacity to roll out major capital projects, and even those who originally opposed HS2 expressed a sense of doom and failure at the UK's inability or unwillingness to undertake enterprises on the scale and ambition of other countries.

The £36 billion 'saved' by truncating the service at Birmingham would be used on road and rail projects in the north and Midlands, Sunak promised. But when he announced a rough sketch of such schemes, they included previous plans such as a West Yorkshire tram/trolley bus and a Manchester airport tram that was already operating. Each time he came back to re-announce schemes, they shrank along with the sums to be spent. A promised 50 new railway stations were never heard of again.

Buses were the cheapest and most used daily transport, but not by the people who made decisions in Westminster. In the Margaret Thatcher book of antisocial aphorisms, she said anyone taking a bus over the age of 25 was a failure. (Independent fact-checking organization Full Fact said the phrase had been coined by the Duchess of Westminster.) Thatcher's 1986 deregulation of buses outside London had shrunk networks and cut passengers – journeys fell by a billion a year between 2009 and 2022, mainly attributable to COVID. Bad buses affected productivity: the Centre for Cities found that poor service cut access to jobs and hurt city economies. Birmingham and West Yorkshire were worst for that, said watchdog Transport Focus. The May government made a partial correction. Councils and mayors got new powers to franchise services on the London model, where the public sector planned the system and collected fares, paying private companies to run specified services. In Greater Manchester, mayor Andy Burnham faced an uphill financial struggle to integrate bus, train and tram across the conurbation; his oppo in West Yorkshire hoped to use her new powers to improve. But Tory ministers still would not countenance municipal bus services, even though the only two left, Reading and Nottingham, regularly won awards.

Jobs galore, but low-paid

However they travelled or worked from home, productivity depended ultimately on people, but in a paradoxical way. The UK's chronically low productivity – 20 per cent below that of France – was partly caused by employers' ability to hire plentiful cheap labour instead of investing in equipment or systems. The trade-off was that France had higher unemployment. This era's jobs count was remarkable. Unemployment fell from 8.2 per cent in 2012 and kept on falling to 3.9 per cent, returning to that level after COVID. The strongest rates of jobs growth were in Merseyside and South Yorkshire, though total employment levels there remained lower than in the south; regional economies remained fragile and dependent on the state, to the extent of 75 per cent of GDP in Northern Ireland. This extraordinary growth in jobs was seen in other countries. Vacancies reached record highs in Japan, the US and across the Euro area. AI, robots and automation had yet to take them away.

But not all jobs are good jobs. A million secure positions were lost in the public sector. The UK economy employed large numbers on low pay, in low-skill jobs, insecure with haphazard hours. Uber began operations in 2012; in 2014, Just Eat floated on the stock exchange. Two thirds of the new jobs were classed as low-paid. The size of the 'gig economy' along with agency working should not be exaggerated: the Chartered Institute of Personnel and Development (CIPD) said it was under 2 per cent. But adding in all who worked part-time at least once a week, the TUC put it at 14 per cent. Numbers on zero-hours contracts, which destabilized household income, had expanded from under 200,000 in 2010 to

1.2 million in 2023. Self-employment grew strongly during the decade to 2020, often with dubious tax arrangements, especially among managers and professionals.

Vacancies did not mean that pay rose: the economics textbooks got that one wrong. A new word was picked up by the lexicographers – 'barista'. Hospitality accounted for two thirds of the growth in lower-paid employment, and the proportion of total consumption represented by hotels, bars and restaurants was higher in the UK than anywhere else in Europe. The reason was they were cheap, because servers were badly paid. Improving things for baristas or delivery drivers would mean adding to the cost of lattes and Amazon purchases. The benefit would be large: the UK would become a better and fairer place as poorer households gained. But wealthier households that spend proportionately more in Costa and on internet deliveries would have to pay more.

Unfit

The ubiquity of low-quality, low-pay work where managers rigidly controlled hours and access to slots had consequences. Suddenly a lot of people became unfit; growing numbers of working-age people gave up work. Some 2.7 million were now claiming sickness benefits, while claims for Personal Independence Payment (PIP) rose by two thirds in the four years to 2024. The OBR predicted that spending on PIP would nearly double between 2024 and 2029. This was a uniquely UK problem, and the OBR warned that it was having a serious impact, pulling down growth projections.

Over half of claimants were in their fifties and sixties, but some were now under 25. These were not students, and they weren't dropouts, either. The number of 16-to-24-year-olds not in education or employment (NEETs) – many not claiming benefits at all – fell from 958,000 in 2011 to 794,000 in

2023, which was welcome even if it still meant one in ten of this crucial age group were wasting their potential or resorting to crime.

Predictably the right-wing press cried 'idlers', but the criteria for claiming disability benefits were as tough as ever, work capability assessment tests notoriously harsh. NHS waiting lists played their part, many people unable to work until they were diagnosed and treated. The increase in mental ill-health coincided geographically with rising poverty: those who couldn't feed and clothe their children, heat their homes or pay for transport became too stressed to cope, severely enough to make them eligible for disability benefits. That was a lose-lose effect of neglecting the poor.

Jobs didn't pay partly because migration increased the labour supply, aided by the UK's lack of regulation and inspection, and because staff were unable or unwilling to organize to fight for more. Study after study confirmed that restoring decent pay required a fairer balance of power at work. People could not move house because of high rents, so reducing their bargaining power with landlords. Lack of flexible choice in childcare limited where and when parents could work, preventing them from seeking better pay.

A Britain that can't

Johnson's expletive about business was matched by Gove's jibe at experts. Knowledge, hard-earned skills, specialist understanding – these were for the oiks deprecated by effortlessly superior Etonians. If that sounds harsh, read the OECD's survey showing skills shortages in construction and engineering as well of course as in medicine and healthcare, and the pending impact of the green transition and artificial intelligence. Its inspectors noted how the British still wanted to discriminate in favour of thinkers (presidents of the Oxford

Union naturally, in their white ties and tails) over doers, lesser beings. NAO reports ran in the same direction. The country faced a major challenge in ensuring it had a sufficiently skilled workforce, 'but it is unclear whether [government] interventions will deliver the step change in skills required'.

The tight labour market was sucking in foreigners with skills that might have been taught and acquired at home. By 2019, in England, Northern Ireland and Wales, a quarter of vacancies were caused by a lack of the required skills, qualifications or experience among applicants, with gaps especially big in construction and manufacturing. The story was one of confusion between a plethora of bodies, training organizations, colleges, local economic partnerships, the Departments for Education and for Business, employers and would-be trainees. It had long been the case that relying on employers' willingness to spend and train was futile. Indeed, firms' spending on workforce training per employee had fallen by about a tenth in real terms in the decade before COVID. A survey found that over a third of employers had provided no training at all in the previous 12 months. Meanwhile participation in state-backed further education and training fell, most damagingly in the country's disadvantaged areas. All those Brexit voters did not want their grandchildren or relatives anticipating the golden future outside the EU by acquiring skills, it seemed. In the decade to 2021, the number of adult learners in England halved.

Employers know best, ministers said, implying not just that they were going to cooperate with one another (which flew in the face of the dogma of competition) but that they were able to identify tomorrow's skills needs. UK companies spent nearly a third less per employee on training between 2011 and 2022. Employers were even reluctant to pay the levy introduced in 2017 through which larger firms (with a payroll above £3 million) paid into a central pot, rebated if they ran training schemes. They tried to divert the money to train existing and older employees. Apprenticeship starts for younger people aged 19 to 24 fell by a third. Meanwhile record numbers of pupils in England were 'severely absent', missing half their lessons.

Employers complained they didn't understand the government programmes. No wonder, when initiative followed initiative, among them a Lifetime Skills Guarantee, and schemes were duplicated between Whitehall departments. What was the point of the big and disruptive reform of vocational qualifications, the new T levels, launched in 2020 and advertised as an alternative to either A levels or apprenticeships? They failed to attract young people. The government next pushed in another direction: a Lifelong Loan Entitlement was scheduled for 2025, which would let anyone up to the age of 60 borrow to pay for up to four years of education at degree level or above, theoretically opening second chances for all. But the New Economics Foundation pointed out how few could take time out from earning and supporting families: added subsistence costs were going to be needed to make it possible to train and study. A third of British young people left any form of education behind by the age of 18 – compared to a fifth in France and Germany. GCSE or A level and its equivalents, and that was it.

Dens of wokery

Where was education money best spent to secure long-run productivity, high or low? Among OECD countries, the UK was one of the highest spenders on higher education but one of the lowest on early years. All the evidence showed that every pound spent on the youngest yielded far more future education and employment progress. But universities were a prime source of national status, a key exporter and a fount of invention that should drive growth in knowledge in key sectors, such as biosciences. Four UK universities sat in the global top ten, and twenty in the global top fifty. They were also very diverse and high-cost, and some still highly exclusive. Chinese tourists thronged King's Parade in Cambridge and some paid to send their offspring there, but why were fee levels the same as Cambridge's at the universities of Bolton, Bangor and Bournemouth?

Over the years the Tories became increasingly ambiguous in their attitudes towards academe. They had suckered the Liberal Democrats into extending loans to pay for undergraduate courses, which helped do electorally for their coalition partners for a decade. The number of 18-year-olds was rising, so university expansion was necessary – Tory voters included ambitious parents. What had been achieved under Labour was retained, so around half of 18-to-22-year-olds went on spending three years of their early adulthood accumulating debt, acquiring a stamp of employability and, maybe, having a good time (though alcoholic debauchery seemed to be on the wane, not least because some students 'have 50p a week to live on after rent'). As for that other old staple of studentdom, sex, one in ten expected to have it during welcome or freshers' week, and if surveys are to be believed, in 2021 the same proportion were succeeding.

It wasn't student morals that alarmed the government but their politics. The Tories and their press outriders took to vigorous attacks on universities as dens of neo-Marxism, political correctness, green campaigning, wokery and other ideological failings. Their fears were well founded. Psephologists found that a new divide had opened; those with degrees voted leftwards. The right-voting degreeless old would die out, to be replaced by progressive-minded graduates. With sneers about Mickey Mouse degrees, Tory right-wingers were deeply suspicious. They pushed the imposition of employability tests through a new, interventionist Office for Students: universities to be graded on how much their graduates earned a year.

The general answer was not enough. Tuition fees of £9,000-plus were greeted in 2012 as a bonanza by the universities; cranes swung above expanding campuses; universities took over (and regenerated) city centres in such places as Preston and Huddersfield. But only a fraction of student loans was going to be repaid and the long-term costs rose to astronomical sums, £400 billion or so. After interest rates were pushed up by the Truss madness, loan conditions were tightened, pointing to a large increase in likely repayments by women and moderate earners including teachers and nurses.

Given their high costs, universities now needed foreigners to keep them afloat – and to stay in the mainstream of international exchange. By refusing to keep students out of the migration count, the government made a rod for its own back, which the *Daily Mail* wielded with relish. Net migration into the UK was 670,000 in the year to June 2023, nearly half of whom were students and most of whom would leave, said Oxford University's Migration Observatory. One study said overseas students brought the UK a net economic benefit of £37.4 billion. In 2023, over a quarter of the world's countries, 58 of them, were headed by someone educated in the UK, second only to the US. But such soft power was acquired in a competitive market. Refused the right to work after graduation or banned from bringing in family members, students had other countries to study in. In 2024, Universities UK found a drop of a third in overseas student applications, damaging not only higher education and international goodwill but the economy of university towns.

Producing and applying knowledge

This love–hate relationship with the universities reflected the Tories' chronic inability to accept that the state should plan and organize the production of knowledge and smooth its take-up and application by firms and public sector organizations. Knowledge was being generated: the UK was the fourth-highest R&D spender in the G7, at nearly 3 per cent of GDP, about two thirds of it from the private sector. The challenge was specialization, anticipation of future opportunities and, an old British failure, application – turning academic research into products, services and innovation in start-ups, then sustaining them in British ownership as they thrived. AstraZeneca, Cambridge-based, flexed its muscles as the UK's biggest R&D spender by putting a new $400m factory in Ireland, because of its lower corporation tax rate. Might it have stayed, despite tax differentials, if the Tories had not abandoned the would-be arc of science-oriented development between Oxford and Cambridge?

'We don't do any prioritization of the science base', complained Sir John Bell, the Oxford University Regius professor of medicine. Scientists did great things, in space research and astronomy, in genomics and life sciences, but they cried out for strategy and scaling up to mobilize the formidable data resources of the NHS, especially for clinical trials. Policymakers were disorganized and ministers opposed to making what a Johnson-era report called 'bets on encouraging development of potentially important technologies in the face of uncertainty'. Bets that only a far-seeing, generous and courageous government could make. An Advanced Research and Invention Agency was created as a sort of halfway house, but the heroine of COVID, Kate Bingham, the vaccine tsar, warned scathingly that 'Britain is losing its chance to become a science superpower.' 'Bollocks' was her actual word. Life sciences were 'the object of suspicion and incomprehension' within government.

Science had been a victim of Brexit, though it did get a new secretary of state, a former World Wrestling Entertainment executive. Students were excluded from the EU Erasmus scheme and UK science from the Horizon programme. A would-be replacement for Erasmus, the Turing Scheme, devised by the Johnson government, was found by universities to be too complex and cheapskate. The UK was eventually permitted to return to Horizon as of January 2024, but within a month the EU research commissioner was fretting over obstacles for scientists wanting to come to the UK. The Royal Society denounced visa charges as a punitive tax on scientific exchange: the upfront costs for a five-year permit rose to nearly £6,000. So much for the mobility of talent.

The only way is up

- Borrow to invest
- Mobilize pension funds for investment
- Reopen trade negotiations with the EU
- Tighter control of takeovers
- Complete HS2 to Manchester and Leeds
- Let councils run local transport
- Set and fund priorities for science
- Grow green: EV chargers, renewables
- Connect hard-to-reach places
- Fit the 'unfit' for work
- More funding for skills

3

Climate: High Water Everywhere

JUST OFF HARRISON Way in St Ives in Cambridgeshire, downriver from the Oliver Cromwell pub, opposite Jones Boatyard, the Environment Agency maintains a giant water meter. At 4.30 a.m. on New Year's Day 2024, the height of the River Great Ouse was recorded at 5.85 metres above sea level – 'normal' was between 5.14 and 5.36 metres. Storm Henk had struck. The water was rising and public warnings had been issued. The next day the early-evening reading was 6.08 metres. The subeditors were busy preparing the headlines: *Sunak asleep at the wheel as swathes of England devastated by floods*. They wheeled out that trusty image of the Gloucestershire town of Tewkesbury, its island abbey marooned in every flood. For England, the Environment Agency had 39 flood warnings and 200 flood alerts in place. Natural Resources Wales had one flood warning and eleven flood alerts, and the Scottish Environment Protection Agency five alerts.

Back on the Great Ouse, the highest previous level recorded at St Ives had been 6.52 metres on Christmas Day 2020. That year houses and businesses were inundated. In 2024 that level was exceeded, with the river peaking at 6.53 metres at teatime on 6 January, by which point St Neots along with many other riverside towns and villages had seen extensive flooding of houses, fields and roads; sewage floated across playing fields and the Oliver Cromwell lost thousands of pounds' worth of stock.

St Ives, along with much of the East of England, had traditionally been a Tory heartland. That makes it unlikely that sodden residents would have picked up the *Guardian* story that in recent years flood defences had been damaged to the point of uselessness, leaving 203,000 properties at risk. Greenpeace found that in the East Midlands the proportion of flood defences in the worst category of disrepair had doubled in the previous five years. It's unlikely that the 15,800 residents in dwellings at risk of the Great Ouse overflowing in Cambridgeshire and Bedfordshire took comfort from the official line: a record sum of £5.2 billion was being spent between 2021 and 2027 was the claim, to reduce flood risks by 11 per cent and increase safety for four million people. That hyperbolic 'record sum' was standard in just about every government press release, whatever the topic. Interviewed on LBC or harangued on *Question Time*, ministers would say 'we've got a policy' and 'we have spent more'. The riposte – this book is peppered with examples – is that commitments turn out to have been inadequate and unimplemented, either or both. At best they came late, after austerity had washed away the foundations.

What *was* true, according to the NAO, was that the number of properties due to receive better protection by 2027 had been cut by 40 per cent, with a quarter of new flood-defence projects abandoned. The likelihood of Storm Henk being repeated was growing – already followed during January by Isha and Jocelyn. Where, MPs asked that same month, was any overall measure of resilience, so we could know whether we were making progress? Officially there was a 'vision' to the year 2100, but the Environment Agency lacked specific targets beyond 2026.

Vote blue, go cyan

Outside the lunatic fringes, few disputed the nature or scale of climate warming, rising sea levels, more intense rainfall and more deadly heatwaves. It had all started out so well, with Cameron's symbolic detoxification of his party's image with a fuzzy green oak tree logo. 'Vote blue, go green', he said, as he tried (unsuccessfully) to fix a windmill on his Notting Hill roof. He even backed Labour's 2008 Climate Change Act. In power, with a Liberal Democrat climate change secretary, things went well. Emissions continued to reduce, with more clean energy and wind and solar (at first). The UK promoted the Paris Agreement, which set the target of net zero by 2050, emissions to be halved by 2030. But then in 2013, 'cut the green crap', Cameron ordered. His sudden cancellation of subsidies caused a booming solar installation industry to collapse overnight. Loft insulations virtually ceased, along with cavity wall fillings. In 2012, 46 per cent of English housing had cavity or solid wall insulation and 78 per cent double glazing; 10 years later, the respective figures showed minuscule growth, at 52 per cent and 87 per cent.

Within three years, the Tories had privatized their own Green Investment Bank, weakened energy-efficiency schemes and then, the *coup de grâce*, appointed as environment secretary the climate denier Owen Paterson. Fracking, he said, was 'a boon'; wind turbines 'useless'. He was drummed out of Parliament later for undeclared lobbying. The revolving door at the climate department says a lot: next came Andrea Leadsom, Liz Truss, Theresa Villiers, Therese Coffey and Steve Barclay – not forgetting Ranil Jayawardena, serial voter against renewables and climate measures, who lasted 49 days. This roster of shame matters because they shared an ideological identity, not just as ardent Brexiteers but as dogmatic state-shrinkers. They did not believe that government should be active and build dams, embankments and especially windmills.

To appease well-heeled countryside voters, Cameron banned onshore wind just as it became the cheapest and most profitable of renewables: if a single local objected, a turbine would be refused planning permission. 'We're going all out for shale' was his 2014 promise, amid plans to dig up precious wildlife sites inside national parks. The government had hoped fracking could be confined to the north, then regarded as predominantly red, but it turned out some of the best shale sat underneath Tory voters. They dismantled the rigs. All this was in the run-up to the global Paris climate negotiations in which the UK was claiming to lead the nations. It entered the talks as the only G7 country increasing tax breaks for fossil fuels.

Seeing the wood for the forests

Policy zigzagged. Dominic Cummings called Johnson a trolley, as in veering from side to side, but the metaphor was especially apt here. Cameron wanted a big Thatcher-style privatization of the Forestry Commission, selling off the nation's trees, but was forced to back down by a phalanx of National Trust members and Tory voters. However, the commission was severely cut back in funds and staff.

Some 13 per cent of the UK is woodland, 10 per cent of England, much lower than in France with 32 per cent and Germany, historically and culturally a nation of tree lovers, on 33 per cent. The Tories inherited commitments to plant, with a large increase in tree cover needed both for the sake of wood supplies and to help mitigate climate change. By March 2025, the UK was to have planted 30,000 hectares of woodland, amounting to some 100 million or more trees. In 2024, the rate of planting was less than half that required to meet the target.

Was the target even realistic? No, said the auditors: rates of planting had never reached the government's annual targets during any of the past 50 years. Between 2021 and 2026, Forestry England (a division of the Forestry Commission) was only planting 303 hectares against its own target of 2,000 hectares. Thanks to the cuts, the Forestry Commission had only been able to process a limited amount of land during the planting season: it did not have the money or the staff. Besides, it was heavily dependent on private landowners. We are not 'communist', said minister Mark Spencer; Tories did not tell people what to do with their estates. But what if they planted the wrong species, asked Parliament's cross-party Environmental Audit Committee, recommending a mix of native broadleaf trees offering animal and plant habitats and conifers for timber. Such a balance was unlikely to be struck because the Forestry Commission had no way of knowing whether the woodlands were being properly managed. The fate of trees in the west and north now lay with separate bodies: Natural Resources Wales and, from 2019, Scottish Forestry, and Forestry and Land Scotland (Coilltearachd agus Fearann Alba).

The Conservative climate

In one of her last acts as prime minister, May enshrined the 2050 net-zero target in law, and issued a multi-year plan for the environment. Her successors ignored both. As a *Daily Telegraph* columnist, Johnson had declared that unprecedentedly hot weather had 'nothing to do with global warming'. The journey to Number 10 took him via the Damascus road, and after an encounter with Sir Patrick Vallance, chief scientific adviser, he now believed, he said. While he was awake, at least. At the COP26 meeting in Glasgow, he nodded off. The 2019 manifesto had hailed £9 billion investment in energy efficiency. No programme for home insulation ensued. The ban on sending waste plastic overseas never happened, the UK remaining one of the biggest dumpers. The annual report of the independent Climate Change Committee acknowledged progress on offshore wind and electric cars, but reported scant progress otherwise. The committee was left without a chair for months after the 2022 departure of Lord Deben.

It was 'not appropriate' to stop supporting a third runway at Heathrow on climate grounds (expanding passenger numbers to service the foreign-owned airport's huge £16 billion debt – an annual charge of £1.5 billion – took priority), but it was appropriate to approve the Jackdaw oil field, and the first deep coal mine for 30 years, near Whitehaven in Cumbria. Without it, so said the official justification, the UK would not be able to produce its own steel, which would otherwise have to be imported. That was 12 months before Tata, the sole remaining UK steelmaker, announced the end of coal-fired steelmaking; future electric arc furnaces would use imported steel.

As for Sunak, he appointed to a key parliamentary committee on the climate crisis Lord David Frost, a trustee of the Global Warming Policy Foundation, which staunchly opposed net-zero policies. The nominatively determined Frost said rising temperatures were welcome because fewer old people would die from cold (presumably if they had not drowned, their houses had not blown away and they had not starved when the UK could no longer import food from drought-stricken Spain). Sunak opportunistically tried to use green policy as a culture-war dividing line against Labour, his ministers aligning with opponents of companies adopting environmental, social and governance standards.

Spurred on by a surprise by-election win in Uxbridge, where the London mayor's introduction of an ultra-low emissions zone was causing indignation, Sunak pivoted further.

His party started inveighing against low-traffic neighbour-hoods, though it turned out, according to the government's own surveys, they were popular with residents (of whom, admittedly, two thirds did not know they lived inside one). He delayed a ban on the sale of new petrol and diesel cars to 2035 and slowed the phase-out of new gas boilers.

There were some sincerely committed Tories; some even resigned. Alok Sharma, president of COP26, threatened but didn't. Chris Skidmore (another example of nominative determinism) was a climate convert, sliding from ultra-non-intervention to signing the net-zero pledge into law as minister for energy and clean growth, then, after protesting at Sunak's proposal to rescind the ban on fracking, leaving Parliament when the PM restarted North Sea drilling plans, calling it 'the greatest mistake'.

Nameplates changed in quick succession. The Department of Energy and Climate Change merged with the Business, Innovation and Skills department, reorganized into Business, Energy and Industrial Strategy (BEIS), which was meant to agree a roadmap to the decarbonization of energy by 2035. On that, the NAO reported drily, 'it still had more work to do', having no clear plan, while all these policy changes were deterring investors.

Pity the Environment Agency staff in their high-vis jackets and four-by-fours, out in all weathers, heroes of public service, protecting the public in unseen ways, such as monitoring how industry, universities and the NHS handle nuclear materials. In our system of government, ministers have huge powers, to hire, fire and sideline agency chiefs. They can inspire their teams – or demoralize staff by spreading cynicism and futility about their work. Imagine you are a long-serving custodian of river basins and you see another mediocre minister appointed who believes public servants are feather-bedded timewasters.

Carbon emissions

Despite 'world-leading' rhetoric, the low-carbon and renewable energy sector failed to grow after 2014. Analysis by Carbon Brief found that maintaining the green policies the Tories had come to power with would have reduced energy costs by as much as £8.3 billion a year.

Consumption of fossil fuels was falling but still substantial, with 39 per cent of UK electricity coming from gas-fired plants and 1 per cent from burning coal. Why offer a subsidy of £22 billion to energy companies – the money to be raised from household energy bills – to subsidize the burning of wood to generate electricity at the Drax power station? The Comptroller and Auditor General (C&AG) demanded a review, fearing that government reliance on industry data and occasional assurance reports could not give it enough reliable information on what was happening to emissions.

We knew what needed to happen because the various agencies charged with monitoring environmental performance gave testimony. Emissions fell from the 1990 baseline but were not decreasing at the pace required to meet carbon commitments. Here also was the Office for Environmental Protection saying that the UK was 'largely off track' in meeting its environmental ambitions, including control of harmful chemicals, and clean rivers and drinking water. Acknowledging some improvement in air pollutants, it assessed legally binding targets and found the government was likely to achieve four out of forty, noting failure on waste disposal, sustainable fisheries, environmental chemicals and improving nature.

Progress depended on government working like a machine, its circuits joined up and strong leadership from the top. The first was never likely. The record since Thatcher shows that if you despise government, kick and diminish it, you are not going to make it work better. Little thought was given to how climate-change policy needed to be all-embracing, including the wider economy, employment and housing. For example, a quarter of those working in emissions-intensive jobs were drivers of lorries. There would have to be big changes in the 'how' of delivery – electric traction, stricter controls around last-mile delivery, better articulation between road and rail. That transition meant active, imaginative government at every turn, said the Resolution Foundation – and a transport department closely aligned with prime minister, environment secretary and the rest.

The roll-out of electric charging points proved another example of disconnection – between councils, carmakers and garage owners. A 2023 survey found that not a single English council had fully delivered its own plan for charging, and a third of them had no plan at all. No wonder over two thirds of electric vehicle (EV) owners reported their unhappiness with public chargers – with cost, access, faults, incompatibility. An expert Lords committee linked the government's 'premature' cut in consumer grants for EVs with a slowdown in purchases, which started to fall as a proportion of the market for the first time.

Blades and blows

The UK could be a great wind power; the country is estimated to have the world's sixth largest capacity. People, said Cameron, meaning the English, were 'fed up' with onshore turbines; most were in Scotland. Subsidies were removed and planning rescinded. Offshore wind was different, up to a point. The UK now had more installed capacity than any other country, lighting and heating 7.5 million homes, a tenth of UK energy supply. The official ambition was to power every home by 2030, giving the UK five years to reach 19 million dwellings. To meet such a goal, the state would need to oversee the introduction of nearly three times as much off-shore wind capacity during the 2020s as it had in the last two decades. Infrastructure takes years of preparation. Offshore possibilities, among them floating turbines, would require new quays: only government could mobilize the building of the pontoons and dock gates. It had not been happening.

While emissions from power generation had decreased 73 per cent since 1990, nearly half of electricity was still being produced from natural gas, which would need to be phased out or its carbon captured. In 2021, greenhouse gas emissions from electricity generation still made up 13 per cent of total emissions. We needed 'clear measures of overall progress, milestones reported annually to parliament', said the NAO, which failed to find any delivery plan.

Besides, generating green energy was one thing, transmitting it from turbine to household another. Ministers largely ignored the massive constrictions in electricity distribution networks. One of the most unthinking Thatcher privatizations had been National Grid, the cables and switches linking energy production and retail distribution now in private ownership and under huge strain. Energy was generated in dispersed sites, some by solar panels – another revolution stalled – owned by businesses and households themselves. Energy giant SSE, which at least retained a UK stock listing, had sold a batch of its Scottish transmission lines to the Ontario Teachers' Pension Plan together with Scottish Power (Spanish-owned, despite the name). Other players included UK Power Networks, owned by foreigners including Warren Buffett and Hong Kong billionaire Sir Li Ka-shing. What were the chances they would take a long-term view and stump up the estimated £200 billion needed for new networking by 2050? Making the connections required pylons, trenches, building sites and trucks. Not in my backyard, said Tory MPs including the former home secretary Priti Patel, a serial protester about her government's own policies. Rishi Sunak did want a better grid connection to his constituency residence in Richmond, North Yorkshire, to heat his outdoor swimming pool.

A review was commissioned from engineer Nick Winser, who recommended disturbance payments for Patel's constituents – she believed in markets and prices after all – along with more planning and investment in skills for energy technologies. Even with all that, building transmission lines would take a dozen or more years, jeopardizing the zero-emissions target. Was the regulator, Ofgem, independent enough, was it savvy about the complex financial engineering? It would have to police the companies' bids to increase household bills to make the millions they said were necessary for investment – but which recent history showed they'd prefer to divert into shareholder dividends.

Net zero offered economic opportunity; it could have driven improvement in vocational training, pushed jobs to run-down areas. But no plan, no leadership. Blades for turbines were made in the UK, in limited numbers. We visited the Vestas plant along the River Medina on the Isle of Wight and saw how the Danish company had stirred the local economy. Good news when the Siemens Gamesa plant in Hull (German) announced in 2023 that it was adding 200 to its 1,000-strong workforce, boosting UK and global blade-making capacity. But when the managing director, Clark MacFarlane, praised the government for 'strong and consistent support for offshore wind', businessman hyperbole had taken over. His view wasn't shared by the Swedish company Vattenfall, which in July 2023 stopped work on its Norfolk Boreas offshore project that promised 1.4 GW of new capacity, because it was no longer viable under the government's price cap – with knock-on consequences for, among others, Vestas.

Nuclear turkey

Some of those problematic pylons running through Patel's Witham constituency carried power from the Suffolk coast and Sizewell's ageing reactors; nuclear still produced 15 per cent of UK electricity. Within months, Johnson braggadocio about putting 'new nuclear' at the heart of energy strategy gave way to reality. The (French) nationalized energy concern EDF got official approval to extend the life of four ancient plants well beyond the date they were supposed to have been shut down for good. As for Sizewell, a reactor that had been scheduled to close in 2025 now would have to survive another two decades. At least that saved some money, since redundant reactors fell to the Nuclear Decommissioning Authority, which was to take on long-term (hundreds of years' worth) liabilities, absolving the generator of the aggregate costs of producing electricity.

The era was marked by big talk (24 GW of nuclear capacity were to be built by 2050 compared with 6 GW; new reactors would sprout in Wales and Gloucestershire) and prevarication. The new reactor being built at Hinkley Point was delayed and delayed. The epoch had been marked by Brexit's fatuous 'take back control', yet surrender to foreign powers more accurately described it. In Somerset, the Chinese state-owned company CGN was hailed as a saviour; irony alert given the Tories' hostility to nationalization. Together with EDF, fully nationalized by the French government in 2023, it would construct and run the reactor with a guarantee that future UK household electricity bills would rise and return them a profit. Construction costs spiralled and then the Chinese state was discovered to be, well, the Chinese state, the same state 'aggressively' cyberattacking MPs and peers. So keeping the lights on depended on the fate of Taiwan.

EDF's chief had boasted in 2007 that within a decade people would be cooking their Christmas turkeys with

Hinkley Point electricity: make your own cracker joke. His successor warned darkly that the government would have to help them cope with cost overruns. Or? EDF has high-value cards to play since nuclear generation produces 'base load', power to keep the lights on whatever the weather. Despite being far from finished, Hinkley Point was to be the template for a new reactor to be built at Sizewell, for which consumers would have to start paying before the JCBs swung into action.

Meanwhile, Sellafield had been hacked by cybercriminals shown by the *Guardian* to be 'closely linked' to Russia and China, who were after nuclear protocols and defence-related materials. Sellafield was the symbol of the dark side of nuclear energy's sustainability. Reactors did not produce carbon (though the construction of mega reactor sites did), but their lethal residue lasts for centuries. Sellafield had become the sole repository for nuclear waste, a rather grand word to describe a site littered with pools of contaminated water, rusting drums and leaking sheds. Problems were of long standing; from 2010 they got worse.

Pump it up

Net zero might be attainable if consumption fell and we stopped energy escaping from badly insulated homes. The Building Back Britain Commission – run by the housebuilders – reported that well over half the housing stock in an average council area wouldn't score C on the A–G Energy Performance Certificate scale: getting it up to C would cost around £200 billion. Only one in seven of all homes had been built after 1990, meaning any focus on new homes would not have much effect on global warming. Mandating that they have built-in meters, for instance, wouldn't make much difference.

Most householders were owner-occupiers and most had now paid off their mortgages. They were less inclined to do up dwellings that, because they were now getting on in years, would sooner or later become someone else's problem. Why should sturdy property owners pay any attention to ministers over installing heat pumps or insulation? They could not or would not read across from the ticking dials on their smart meters to spending on refitting windows or buying hydrogen boilers. In 2017, the government asked finance companies to develop products that would lower the cost of lending for energy efficiency; but it turned out the demand for borrowing wasn't there. And what if it simply wasn't cost-effective? In properties valued at less than £162,000 in 2023, energy-efficiency improvements were going to be financially unviable because the cost of the work would exceed any potential gain in price – and there were millions of homes in this situation.

Households' ability to pay upfront for new boilers, heat pumps and insulation depended on their income: the Resolution Foundation did the sums. With the disposable income of poorer homeowners averaging £9,100 and the cost of insulating leaky homes over £8,000 per household, 'it is plain that the necessary investment isn't going to happen without major government intervention'.

Domestic heating was responsible for 14 per cent of UK emissions, but arguments on the best technology were fierce. The National Infrastructure Commission recommended dropping hydrogen and choosing heat pumps. The government prevaricated, leaving would-be hydrogen producers in limbo. By 2023, about 250,000 heat pumps had been installed. The 72,000 fitted in 2022 were a long way off the official target of 600,000 installations per year by 2028. A straw in the wind was the decision by Macquarie Group to sell its stake in Cadent, the UK's biggest gas network, on the grounds that the future transition was too uncertain; Macquarie had previously wrought its profits magic by entering then exiting Thames Water (see below).

The past decade and a half have not been good for consumers – not just price inflation, but surreptitious loading of costs (water and energy most obviously) for the sake of profitability. Many could not afford it. Clare Moriarty, head of Citizens Advice, counted consumer energy debt at just under £3 billion – but this was debt owing for three months or more, so the real total was much higher. Some five million people lived in households behind on their bills. 'Making tangible progress', she said, 'will be so much easier if the households struggling the most but which stand to benefit the most from lower bills are supported through the green energy transition.'

In the decade to 2020 gas prices had been stable while electricity costs increased in real terms by about a third. After the invasion of Ukraine and the spike in energy prices, gas up nearly sixfold from February to December 2021, the government had to act. It extended protection through an energy price guarantee. Connoisseurs of political irony relished the sight of the arch-marketeer Liz Truss intervening to this extent. But it was knee-jerk and missed an opportunity. Price regulation might have been tied to energy-saving and measures to stem consumption.

Householders knew more about what they were consuming. More dwellings had smart meters, but the NAO said roll-out targets were not being met and progress was slowing. In 2012, the government had required energy companies to install smart meters by the end of 2019. Three times the deadline was extended and reset again to the end of 2025. Now, 57 per cent of all meters in Great Britain are smart, although around 9 per cent of them – around 3 million – were not working as intended when the auditors checked. One reason for delay was shortage of installers. No one had sought to anticipate the need and incentivize training.

It doesn't help if your energy company goes bust, as 28 of them did in the year from June 2021. The costs of these private companies failing were distributed across all energy bills, around £94 per customer. The biggest collapse was Bulb Energy, so big the government had to swallow its principles and put it into 'special administration' (don't call it nationalization), which cost an additional £2 billion over the next two years. Companies had been allowed by a complacent regulator (Ofgem) to ensnare customers without sufficient cover, so said the NAO.

Breathe in

The environment is mostly air, the thin layers of decreasingly breathable gases enveloping the planet. As well as greenhouse gases, it is made up of toxins. Emissions of most pollutants had been falling and awareness of their damage was growing. The poor air quality that degrades children's lungs was increasingly being associated with rising rates of dementia and stroke, according to UK Biobank, the biomedical database. It took the Tories till 2019 to produce a clean air strategy, its language grandiose, its targets ambitious but a long way off. The government proved reluctant to push farmers to use less fertilizer, which emits ammonia, levels of which had not fallen since 2007.

In urban areas, a primary polluter was the car, especially the big sports utility vehicles that were so lightly taxed in the UK relative to other European countries (vehicle excise duty on a BMW X5 was £1,565 here compared with £51,400 [€60,000] in France). Here the tactic was to leave responsibility to councils, despite decreasing budgets. Declaring that it was they who had to programme cuts to vehicle use for the sake of cleaner air served a neat political purpose: it exculpated ministers at the same time as MPs and their pals in the right-wing press attacked the councils – usually Labour and especially London mayor Sadiq Khan – for doing precisely that. The Tory candidate in 2024's mayoral election campaigned to scrap the ultra-low emission zone altogether, though pollution levels are a fifth lower than they would have been without it.

The public body responsible for motorways and major roads admitted there were no viable measures of air quality across much of the road network; those known to be in breach of existing targets were likely still to be in breach come 2030. Obfuscation ruled. 'Government does not clearly and consistently communicate air quality issues or its proposed solutions to the public', said the NAO. 'It publishes many sets of air quality reports, but most are inaccessible. People cannot easily find out about problems in their local area, whether pollution levels breach legal limits.'

A similar story could be told about other types of pollution, for example household waste. Long-term ambitions were set in 2018, but five years on, Defra (the Department for Environment, Food & Rural Affairs) did not know what was happening. We do know that in 2020 the UK missed the official target for recycling waste that had been set a decade previously. Announced reforms on packaging and waste collection were inexplicably delayed. However, English councils were to be given extra money to pay for weekly collection of food waste, according to an announcement squeezed in before campaigning began for local elections in 2024. The District Councils Network calculated that its members were being short-changed to the tune of hundreds of thousands of pounds in paying for new bins and vehicles.

Victimizing badgers

While the UK remained inside the European Union, greening proceeded apace. In 2011, Defra published a biodiversity strategy that set out how the government would meet

European commitments. By 2024, it had yet to publish an update. Where, for instance, was the delayed blueprint for how land was allocated in the UK?

One animal did not fit the landscape and Tory ministers fixated on it: the poor, near-blind badger. In the haplessness stakes, environment minister Paterson ranked up there alongside Grayling and Gavin Williamson. Having launched a mass cull in 2013, he claimed the badgers had 'moved the goal posts'. Scientists and veterinarians disputed the claim that badgers infected cattle with TB, as farmers asserted, but mixed evidence did not prevent the policy intensifying. Sunak wanted badgers killed to create a 'wedge' with Labour to bolster Tory support in the shires.

Sponges and sumps

Beavers were different. Wildlife trusts managed their reintroduction into watery habitats and celebrated the value of their dams in streams. But on the wider front, the Climate Change Committee predicted stormy weather: its 2023 report to Parliament 'found little evidence that government is driving adaptation at the pace and scale needed to fully prepare for climate risks facing the UK'. In the wake of heatwaves in four of the five years to 2023, with the summer of 2018 the joint hottest on record, the National Infrastructure Commission reported that roads, rail, power and data centres were simply not designed to withstand such extreme temperatures. The UK had a Resilience Framework, meant to encompass climate, cyber and defence risks. But broadly the story in recent times has been one of loose ends, lack of targets, faltering progress. The enemy of practical response to climate change was political dogma.

For example, flooding isn't inevitable. Groundwater can be channelled and diverted while planning rules prevented construction on flood plains. But such action depended not just on money and a fair split of responsibility between property owners and taxpayers, but on coordination between councils, builders and agencies. Coordination? There were 25 different unconnected bodies supposed to regulate the environment, as well as Defra, Natural England and local councils. And they, as we will see in Chapter 6, were severely depleted.

For years, practical plans had described 'sponge' cities, where watercourses are recreated, forming natural sumps and green areas where the water level rises and falls as necessary without flooding. New rules along these lines had been due by 2011, but according to Alastair Chisholm, the director of the Chartered Institution of Water and Environmental Management, they were dropped by Tory local government secretary Eric Pickles. 'Since then, we have had 13 years of delays. This has been kicked down the road and what is going on now is the result', he said of increasingly regular floods.

Insufficient treatment

Water did not run clear. Thatcherism had delivered unfishable chalk streams, stinking rivers and beaches unfit for safe bathing. Who was going to choose a seaside holiday, asked councillors from coastal districts, when bathers saw sewage bobbing in the briny and there wasn't enough testing of water quality to ensure authorities had time to hoist a red flag?

The Undertones' lead singer Feargal Sharkey had transformed himself into a persuasive campaigner, forcing Tory MPs to appear on regional news bulletins to bemoan offensive smells in local rivers and the loss of angling. Not a single waterway was reported to be in good overall health, and more than half failed to pass standard tests derived from the EU standards that used to apply. As of 2020, only 16 per cent of inland water bodies in England were deemed to be in good ecological status; the latest EU water directive had specified a target of 75 per cent by 2027. Taking back control meant failing to control the quality of water, free to be the dirty man of Europe. Treatment plants were opening their taps and letting sewage run into the watercourses with greater frequency. *The Times* mounted a Clean It Up campaign, conveniently forgetting Rupert Murdoch's support for water privatization, minimal regulation and Brexit.

Pollution was primarily a failure of regulators, who were either not allowed or chose not to monitor the water companies, and time and again failed to penalize them. The companies had cut their capital investment by up to a fifth over the past three decades, which explained why the average water trunk main in London is over a century old and one sixth of the oldest cast-iron pipes have been in the ground for 150 years. Their borrowing grew and grew, to a total of £60 billion as of March 2023, as household bills increased. Households contributed nearly all of companies' revenue. If all that borrowing wasn't spent on pipes – leakage rates grew – where did it go? It paid dividends to owners who came and went with dizzying speed, a roundabout of Australian banks, private equity funds, foreign states, pension funds. The ownership of South East Water, with 2.3 million customers, to take one example, was a labyrinth involving a Luxembourg (tax haven) holding company, NatWest Pensions, Utilities of Australia, and Desjardins, a Canadian financial services outfit, only one small part of the maze actually regulated. Was it surprising that inspectors of drinking water quality worried whether water leaving the company's plant had received 'sufficient preliminary treatment'?

For Thames, Southern and South East Water, servicing 9.4 million households and businesses, the cost of debt amounted to more than a quarter of water bills. By contrast, Scottish Water spent just a tenth of its revenues on financing debt they used to invest in water and sewerage, which the deluge of wet wipes and debris on Scottish beaches clearly necessitated. Some pipes were laid. The Thames Tideway is a 25-kilometre tunnel that was touted originally as vital to stop sewage flooding into the river. But even before it was planned, technological changes had made it redundant, thanks to green drainage and methods of sewage storage. However, a consortium of investors had spied an opportunity. Not content with the return officially allowed on the billions' worth of assets being created, they lobbied for and received a government backstop against cost overruns. Before a spade had been wielded, Thames customers were being charged, passing them the risk of excess costs.

Despite all that finance, by 2023 Thames Water was teetering on the verge of bankruptcy, underneath a pile of debt worth £18 billion. Called before a Camden council scrutiny committee in January 2024, managers denied the company was solvent. In testimony they claimed it made a loss of £11 million, which of course meant that investment would have to be paid from higher bills or government grants; the accounts showed a profit of £400 million. Balance sheets are not simple, which is why accountancy is generally a lucrative business, but shouldn't it be clear whether Thames Water, as custodian of a critical public service, was in a position to invest? Michael Benke, engagement manager, said: 'I think the point was we didn't have a profit of £400 million worth of cash … our annual turnover is about £2.1 billion, so we don't take a profit of £400 million, do you know what I mean?' No, it was as clear as the murky water flowing under Waterloo Bridge. The company had no shame. It geared up a lobbying effort to water down regulation and let it raise charges by nearly half by 2030.

Under political pressure, Ofwat started enforcement cases. But it suited the government to muddy the relationship between the water regulator and the Environment Agency, allowing companies such as South West Water to fail to prepare for drought in Devon and Cornwall and in 2022 nearly run out of water. The company, said the Environment Agency, had not been honest, had been complacent and shown a 'lack of understanding of their own supply system'. The water companies even lacked proper audit procedures, allowing South East Water, for example, to spend more on dividends and interest payments than on pipes in the two years to March 2022. 'Tell Sid', the 1980s privatization ads had said; tell him to hold his nose.

The only way is up

- Decarbonize electricity by 2030
- Insulate homes
- Speed up alternatives to gas boilers
- Get control of water and sewerage
- Restructure National Grid
- Fast-track onshore wind and solar
- A national plan for water and flooding
- Stop oil drilling and coal mining

4

Housing: A Property-Owning Plutocracy

THE GRENFELL TOWER conflagration in June 2017 that killed 72 people might have been, should have been catalytic, its flames shedding cruel light on differences in living conditions between owners and renters. It should have sparked a great turnaround for the shrinking stock let by councils and non-profits. The Royal Borough of Kensington and Chelsea, Tory since birth, had turned its back on its poorer postcodes, consigning management of Grenfell to an arm's-length organization, its physical state neglected, its tenancies a lottery. The stump still stands, Steve McQueen's silent film among powerful reminders. But after the pain and recriminations and a long inquiry, nothing much changed.

Social renters such as Grenfell's were the most overcrowded. Compared with owners and private tenants, they were unhappy, more anxious and less satisfied with their lives – which wasn't surprising, since to qualify for their homes they had to be among the poorest and most likely to be disabled or sick. Their dwellings were twice as likely to be damp as those owned by their residents.

An inheritocracy

The proportion of damp homes did fall overall, reflecting the fact that new homes were built, though many fewer than successive Tory ministers promised. We were paying more to be housed, with the share of family income dedicated to it having doubled since 1980. Among poorer families, accommodation now cost a third of their available money. The government spent billions on initiatives, but mostly directed at home ownership, motivated by electoral calculation. Policy was deeply conflicted. Here was a pro-market, anti-state party with anti-planning instincts in every fibre. Its voters didn't want planners' protection from the kindly market that kept raising the value of their homes, but yes they did if developers targeted that field where they took pooch to poo in the morning. Developers, a cosy cartel (said the Competition and Markets Authority), hoarded land, with rates of new-build sluggish. Schemes to boost home ownership perversely if predictably pushed up prices, putting homes beyond the reach of more and more. Expanding owner-occupation had been the Tory dream for decades: it declined, falling from its 2001 peak of 70 per cent to 65 per cent. Homelessness rose. The economy lost investment in productive enterprise, money tempted away from start-ups into inert bricks and mortar that made such rich returns.

Grenfell crystallized extreme inequality, the assetless poor stacked in an unsafe structure looking down on the least affordable housing in the UK. Thatcherism had concentrated the habit of seeing housing as a store of wealth and object of speculation. Domestic dwellings and their tax treatment were the dark heart of national economic failure, a one-way bet for those who could afford it, out of reach for growing numbers, a prime cause of physical and social immobility and hence of productivity stasis. Failure to build to match population growth guaranteed soaring prices for lucky owners, fencing the rest out. Price rises were celebrated in news stories, despite the economic and social harm they did. Boomers who bought 30 years ago had gained spectacularly, thanks to wave after wave of property inflation. Growing intergenerational unfairness was turning the country into an inheritocracy, where what parents owned determined the next generation's life chances far more than their own efforts ever would, solidifying class and geographic distance. At some level of political consciousness the Tories knew it and welcomed it: the winners were their people. Their indifference to this central fact of UK housing was both remarkable and banal. Their inaction is another pointer to what now needs to be done.

Renting on a treadmill

This was the age of the landlord, as a great shift in tenures unfolded. In 1991, under 10 per cent rented privately. That once least-favoured tenure had now doubled. Low interest rates post-crash made buy-to-let mortgages, already popular, a bargain; and landlords got tax relief on borrowing charges. When savings accounts yielded near zero interest, becoming a landlord was a no-brainer, so one in ten people, 5.5 million, now own more than one property. Renting out became a cottage industry, where half of landlords had just one dwelling let out: some hadn't the money or inclination to keep them up to a decent standard. Only in 2015 did the government chip away the scandalous tax subsidy given them.

Amid housing shortage, rents ratcheted up, making it near impossible for tenants to save for a deposit on their own future home. Other countries, such as Germany, had buoyant (and highly regulated) private rental sectors. Here, private renting felt like a treadmill, trapping not just the young but a growing number of pensioners. Families with children, 1.3

million of them, accounted for a third of all privately renting households, at risk of eviction and in fear of having to move far from school, friends and relatives.

Fear of eviction meant tenants dared not complain about bad conditions, damp, lack of repairs or leaps in the rent. Nearly a quarter of private rentals fell below the decency standard. Legislation in 2015 was supposed to prevent landlords evicting people in retaliation for complaints, but Citizens Advice found it weak and ineffective. Before Christmas 2023, we spent time in the Manchester evictions court, the wretched vulnerability of private tenants on display. This was the law on speed, the court processing 10 evictions an hour. Kirsty Almond had been a Shelter solicitor for 15 years, and she had never seen anything like it. She did her best for Jane, in her fifties, on crutches with a degenerative spine disease, surviving on hard-to-get disability benefit. Although her housing benefit had been frozen for four years, by scrimping and half starving she had managed not to fall into arrears. In her many years in the flat she had carried out repairs herself for fear of annoying the landlord. It made no difference: he was evicting her anyway. The law called it a 'no-fault' eviction, which meant the landlord, with minimal notice, could pursue an eviction without giving any reason. Now Jane's notice was up. She had no chance of a council home, so ahead lay an emergency B&B miles from her daughter and friends. No chance of another private tenure since rents had soared 10 per cent that year. By pleading exceptional hardship on account of Jane's health, the solicitor persuaded the judge to give the only mitigation available, a six-week stay before the bailiff's knock.

Another of Kirsty's multitude of cases that day was a family with four children, due to be evicted from a two-bedroom flat: in arrears, they couldn't pay the extra £200 the landlord was demanding. Here was a household in what Citizens Advice called 'negative income'. Try as they might, their earnings fell below their basic bills. There was nothing the court could do, so their children would join the 140,000 homeless children in temporary accommodation that Christmas.

Exposed here was fallout from a policy of insufficient building (councils effectively banned from adding stock) and depletion of social renting, thanks to Right to Buy, the most socially injurious of all Thatcher privatizations. A major shift in life experiences and expectations was ongoing, but typically without plan or strategy. It even seemed to take Tory ministers by surprise insofar as they thought about it at all. Cut investment, fail to build social housing ... but pay housing benefit that went straight into landlords' pockets. Cut revenue spending, freeze housing benefit ... but that rendered many more homeless and councils had a legal obligation to house those who were old, sick or had children. Local authorities were spending a fortune on often appalling temporary housing and B&Bs.

The landlords' party

The Tories could only be described as the landlords' party. Transparency International UK reckoned four out of ten MPs and peers had declared a property interest, and most of them were Tory. In 2018, the May government made a faltering attempt to stand up for tenants, promising to abolish landlords' right to end tenancies at whim. Six years later, the same promise was reiterated but the legislation to implement it was first delayed, then dropped, then squeezed out by the election announcement. For the moment, landlords had won.

One consequence was the rising significance of rent both in budgets and in the national economy. (Another reason for flatlining productivity and growth, except for the boom in books describing the UK's rentier economy.) Even with housing benefit, private renters were now spending more than a third of their income on rent. Here was a new social truth: poorer people paid relatively more for the basics of life. The gap between renters and owner-occupiers was growing, since owner-occupiers with mortgages paid out only a fifth of their income. Of course not all private renters were poor. But they increasingly belonged to a separate class, one from which they were less and less likely to escape.

The town of Andover in Hampshire was, like much of the south-east of England, relatively well off. It was noteworthy in building vigorously, with new housing available. At a price. A two-year-old detached three-bed house in Calico Street now cost £425,000. A mortgage would probably cost £2,250 a month. Who could afford that? Only a household earning upwards of £80,000, nearly three times the median income in 2024. Renting would be much cheaper, the same house yours for just £1,500 a month. But to afford that, you would have needed an income at twice the median. And the owners were acquiring a capital asset expanding in value. You might not consider Savills, the estate agency, an oracle of inequality, but in 2024 they did the maths. For people relying on benefits, only one in twelve private rentals were affordable. The squeeze was tightening. That year, rents were rising at the fastest rate recorded, up 9 per cent on the previous year.

Social housing under renewed attack

The 'slow death of social housing' began when Osborne's first austerity measures cut Labour's final social housing programme by two thirds, said *Inside Housing*. What funds remained were reallocated to non-profit (and some private) landlords, provided they charged what he called affordable rents. These turned out to be 80 per cent of market rents, which made them unaffordable to poorer tenants. New 'social' building in England fell away drastically: from 40,000 units completed in 2010 to just 9,500 in 2022. The NAO doesn't usually do jokes, but it reported that the Department of Levelling Up, Housing and Communities' 2016 programme would achieve nearly all its target for starting the construction of new social homes ... but many would not actually be built until 2032. And it hadn't set itself targets on size and quality or environmental sustainability.

The stock fell away at a more rapid rate once Cameron channelled his inner Thatcher and increased the financial incentives to council tenants to buy. Over the decade, 285,000 more homes were privatized. By 2023, the sale and demolition of social rented homes was three times the number of new-builds, leading to a net loss of 165,000 homes. The government expanded Labour's 'arm's-length management organizations', a wrinkle on the idea of public ownership but private control of operations. It was one such ALMO that had taken over Grenfell Tower. Genuine community enterprise ossified.

We had followed the fortunes of the Clapham Park estate in Lambeth from 2000, a monument to the era's high hopes. This was a New Deal for Communities project in a run-down estate. Clapham Park got a 10-year grant of £56 million to encourage residents to take charge and make their own improvements. The estate responded. Residents set about shutting down crack dens and prostitution; they battled the borough council for money; votes were organized around a master plan; volunteers acquired business skills, reading spreadsheets and planning budgets; some rebuilding took place. One of the project's heroines, Donna Charmaine Henry, said it had boosted confidence and skills. The 2010 government was indifferent. Tenant enthusiasm tailed off. On such estates there had always been a high churn, with four in ten of those residents when the scheme began having moved within the decade. We noted that those moving in were often in the direst need, disabled, poor, not English-speaking, less able to tend the flame of the original aspiration without continued support. Regeneration and community participation demand unrelenting effort. The master plan was abandoned. Property transferred to a big housing association, whose business model was to demolish, rebuild and sell – borrowing on the strength of prospective capital gains. Clapham Park Homes became a subsidiary of the Metropolitan Housing Trust, which promised it would keep half the stock for rent. Land was sold to private developers, who renamed it the Clapham Quarter, its luxurious flats price tbc, but judging by adjacent streets, a two-bed would be north of £650,000, implying mortgage payments of £2,500 a month, utterly out of range for those doing the jobs of Clapham Park's original inhabitants. There you have the social history of the age: from park to quarter, social rent to high-end purchase.

On re-election in 2015, Cameron set about eating further into the social stock by giving tenants of non-profit housing groups the right to buy, but fortunately many of these associations were charities and others had funded construction out of their own revenues, which made the proposal legally dubious. His successors, not least after Grenfell, felt they had to gesture towards more social housing. Under May some funding was restored and councils were allowed to borrow more. But money was needed for repairs, to the tune of billions for cladding and other safety measures. In 2023, these works together consumed nearly £14 billion. May had spoken of 10,000 new council homes a year; in the decade to 2024, councils in England built 1,400 a year.

Cutting back on heating and food

The National Housing Federation calculated that 145,000 new affordable homes were needed each year, but only a third of those were being built. Waiting lists grew to 1.2 million; record numbers (279,400) were stuck in temporary accommodation and homelessness grew. The housing ombudsman – a former Tory deputy mayor of London – called on the government to 'reimagine the future of social housing' for the sake of residents, marginalized, stigmatized and badly served. Little wonder 2024 surveys found despairing tenants, facing rent rises of 8 per cent, cutting back on heating and food. The government had whittled away support such that on its own housing allowance rates, costs were affordable for only one in twenty-five properties in England, a figure that dropped to one in fifty in London.

The loss of stock continued. The only Stirling Prize for architecture ever given to social housing was awarded to Goldsmith Street in Norwich for its sustainable eco-elegant new council homes that opened in 2019. But by 2024, seven households had already applied for right-to-buy at a large discount, denying those homes to future tenants and doubtless securing a nice little earner for themselves when they sold up. Where was the incentive for councils to build? Over the years, nearly half of former council homes had ended up owned by landlords, who let them out at rents far higher than councils had ever charged.

Social space

The UK population was rapidly rising; people needed somewhere to stay. But total dwelling space already far exceeded the number of people. As well as more housebuilding, government should have sought better to share available accommodation. Grotesquely unjust council tax benefited the rich, a prime Westminster house paying just 0.6 per cent of its value, while homes in Hartlepool paid twenty times more. Failure to tax space led to the maldistribution of people and available accommodation. Among homes people owned, the number of officially underoccupied dwellings increased by 1.3 million in the years between 2011 and 2022. Fair housing would and should be part of the drive to net zero: owner-occupiers tend both to have more space and to emit more carbon. Yet the only people to be subjected to enforced redistribution of space were poor families, with their 'extra' bedrooms penalized by benefits reduction. Taxes might have stopped housing becoming speculation. London and other cities sprouted monster towers at millions per flat, but come night-time few lights were on.

Tories had never liked sociology. Thatcher had even abolished the research body funding social science. Perhaps this explains persistent myopia around social trends and changing demographics. Nary a glance at the burgeoning number of pensioners and where they were going to live. Just 750,000 dwellings were now classed as retirement housing, barely 3 per cent of the stock, though 19 per cent of Britons were beyond retirement age. It's not just that nearly half the elderly live in homes without grab-rails in bathrooms and kitchens; a million over-75s live alone and the frailest need sheltered housing and fewer stairs. Space-rich elders wouldn't sell and developers would not build for the old. Using tax and supports to encourage the old out of too-large homes into purpose-built dwellings nearby would provide more family housing. Only the state can guide the huge adaptation that lies ahead.

Markets fail to build

The market won't do it. Land, people's expectations, culture – none are captured by the textbooks and theories. What Torsten Bell of the Resolution Foundation called a natural experiment occurred during the COVID pandemic, when in 2020 would-be workers-from-home rushed to buy larger residences. Demand rose, prices rose; where was the resulting supply? Instead, private rents in the English countryside rose by nearly a third in 2023 alone.

Half a million new dwellings are needed each year, stretching into the 2030s. The highest annual total was 248,000 in 2019. COVID was no excuse. Across the Channel in France, which had about the same size of population as the UK, housebuilding reached well over 300,000 new dwellings every year over the period. By chance that same number, 300,000, had become the Tory target as Johnson tried to channel the Tory prime minister who had managed to boost construction to 350,000 – Harold Macmillan. Johnson had plucked the figure out of the air, with little regard to migration, one of the big drivers of population growth. The government issued visas to hundreds of thousands of people to come here to work but never tried to ensure housing would keep up. This remains a Victorian country, where constant rebuilding is needed to replace dilapidation. According to the latest English Housing Survey, around 904,000 homes in England were damp, and 653,000 were so cold they posed a health risk. Damp was five times more common in private rentals than in owner-occupied homes, and the scale of the problem was probably under-reported by tenants who feared eviction. When in November 2022 a coroner ruled the death of a two-year-old was caused by prolonged exposure to mould, there was a momentary fuss. The Royal College of Paediatrics and Child Health weighed in, calling the state of housing 'a crucial issue for child health'. Doctors could prescribe drugs, but not real cures such as warm homes and adequate incomes.

Banking on the land

Why weren't more houses built? Homeowners were a Tory interest and they often resisted building on their doorsteps.

But appeasing NIMBYs conflicted with the developers who were among the party's greatest benefactors, contributing £60 million since 2010, the chief executive of Barratt, David Thomas, among them. The relationship was long and intimate and explains why so little pressure was applied to make them build. Thanks to massive windfall gains from balance sheet revaluations, this was an industry where doing nothing could be more profitable than excavating basements and laying bricks. Building required permissions, which is why the two squabbled. MPs were ever mindful of constituencies where votes depended on protecting property from market-driven change, such as new dwellings at the end of the lane. The system favoured existing over potential residents, another example of how this era turned against the future. Perhaps opinion was shifting, with a Tory think tank extolling a poll saying freedom to build was rated by two thirds against freedom to prevent building. However, the antis largely had it.

In a country where money banks were so lucrative, land banking was equally profitable. It helps explain housebuilders' old-fashioned culture and lack of productivity, which mattered when housebuilding formed 7 per cent of GDP and employed two million people. Housebuilding, said Martin Wolf, was one area where the vaunted flexibility of the UK economy was utterly absent, and indeed, the Competition and Markets Authority feared, was marked by cartels and price fixing. Among the better years was 2022–23, when total construction reached 187,000. Were these dwellings built where people were most productive, contributing most to growth, and were they sustainable, socially as well as environmentally, or just little boxes erected wherever developers had land, regardless of community needs? Children lost out as the 'no ball games' culture dominated new estates and the National Planning Framework mentioned lorries more than children. Newts and bats were better protected than play.

More than half of councils rarely or never inspected new developments to check compliance with flood risk, the Public Accounts Committee was told. Gove even tried to exempt housebuilders from having to worry whether developments produced toxic run-off. But this bid to end 'nutrient neutrality' was scuppered in the Lords after public indignation at yet more filth pouring into English rivers. As it turned out, building schemes were on hold because they could not be connected to the energy grid, which 'lacked capacity'. In Oxford, 90 new homes were due to have heat pumps, but the National Grid told them there was not enough power to connect them, so half would have gas boilers instead.

The preferred form of inflation

Though more people told pollsters housing was important, it never reached high up an agenda dominated by the cost of living and the NHS. After all, most people most of the time felt well enough housed. In Whitehall, its unimportance was underscored by the rapid throughput of 15 housing ministers in 14 years. Yet housing also had veto power. Homeowners had stymied reform of social care for decades: any decent, functioning scheme of care involved the assets of the old themselves, but politicians backed off saying granny's house would have to contribute to the cost of her care. Labour in 2010 and May in 2017 were punished at the polls for suggesting it.

The Tories, like their predecessors, sought political reward in inflating values. Average UK house prices rose from £171,000 at the 2010 election to £292,000 in spring 2023. Owners could continue to feel smug. But something was going awry. More and more couldn't afford it. Ownership among the under-35s halved. The ratio of house prices to earnings shot up. In the 1980s, it would have taken a family headed by a 30-year-old three years to save for an average-sized deposit; by 2016, it was taking the same family 19 years. Now the government began to fear that worried homeowning parents and their stressed children paying outrageous rents were turning against them. Cue Help to Buy.

From 2013, a large chunk of scant spending subsidized first-time buyers with offers of 5 per cent deposits and zero interest for the first five years of mortgaging. But the beneficiaries were the more affluent buying expensive homes: a third of them would have bought regardless of the subsidy. The aim was to stimulate new-build, but there was no sign it did. Instead, as predicted, it was a cocaine hit for the housing market (the phrase coined by geographer Danny Dorling). Prices were pushed up, obeying the logic of finance: the more money was available, the more prices rose. People scrambled to buy to exploit these government gifts: during the first COVID lockdown, when the market might have dipped, prices increased by a mighty 8.5 per cent largely because of a 'holiday' on paying stamp duty. Help to Buy was eventually quietly shut down in 2023.

Striving to own

Aspirations towards owning stayed strong. Of course they did, since the alternatives were lousy and owning was the path to lifetime capital gains. Only 14 per cent of people didn't want to own, compared with 42 per cent in Germany. So families scrambled, scrimped and saved, trying to get a foot on that fabled ladder. Over the years we followed the fortunes of Emma Percy, who showed what remarkable fortitude and determination it took.

Her family were model tenants in Folkestone's private rented sector, never in arrears. But time and again they were pushed out. In tied housing above a pub where they worked, the landlord evicted them for having their first baby. They landed in a desolate Salvation Army hostel. In another rental flat, with no boiler all winter, half of husband Rob's after-tax pay went on rent. No chance of social housing, said the council: reaching the top of the waiting list would take more than a lifetime. Evicted again by a landlord wanting to sell, they moved on several more times, now with three children, sometimes having to move schools. Emma started to train as a teacher while caring for the children and working part-time in a supermarket. They bought nothing, their clothes second-hand, and for their holidays they would camp out in the grounds of the school where Rob worked as caretaker. Once trained, Emma got a teaching job and for a few years they saved every penny she earned for a deposit, never letting up on the spending, hard on the children, she said. Eventually they made it and bought a home, 'a fairy tale come true', she said. Was this the exemplary 'striving' ministers kept extolling or a mountainous ascent few could ever survive?

New housing was available, with 234,000 new dwellings added in England in 2023, of which 213,000 were newly built, the rest conversions. Go to Corby in Northamptonshire, or Andover or Redditch, places where the population increased dramatically at more than 2 per cent a year between the 2011 and 2021 censuses. These were places where developers could buy land, the farmers sold with pleasure and the disappearance of green fields went unopposed. Perhaps in time raw new-build estates on the edge of these towns will become 'community', though now it looked like little thought had been given to providing public spaces or for transport other than cars. Weakened regulation allowed unsustainable building in valleys where water levels were rising. In 2017, Gove began offering grants to local authorities to pay for the roads, schools, clinics and everything else needed for new developments. But some councils (among them his own Surrey Heath) had little inclination, others had no money, and too few planners were left now for anything ambitious. By January 2024, only a third of the Housing Infrastructure Fund had been spent. The party of property, but not leaseholders. Gove had called ground rents for flat owners 'feudal', but then reneged on a pledge to abolish them after investors objected.

Another wheeze was the government's invitation to developers to convert spare office space without planning permission. But its 2020 survey found that barely a fifth of the buildings converted, totalling about 100,000, met normal size and space standards. Amazingly, some flats lacked windows, in defiance of the government's own Building Better, Building Beautiful Commission. New rules on quality were brought in. After COVID, offices had emptied and Gove made further extravagant promises about converting them into homes. Kate Henderson of the National Housing Federation – she'd spoken to us despairingly some years previously when she was at the planners' institute – said regulatory standards were essential to ensure safety and accessibility. The Parker Morris Committee's minimum standards for the size of rooms and height of ceilings were way in the past, abolished by Thatcher in 1980. Many new homes were now so small that IKEA brought out a new range of diminutive furniture to fit them. The Deregulation Act 2015 had even stopped local planners from judging the construction and layout of new dwellings. Substandard housing would of course deteriorate quickly, with indeed no future. Lofty architectural aspiration met penny-pinching low standards.

Intentional tents

Lack of dwellings plus cuts to benefits forced more people into homelessness. Johnson said he would 'work tirelessly' to end it. It grew. Councils in England registered 298,430 homeless households in the year to Easter 2023, on a rising trend. The cost was horrendous: Liverpool city council's bill for homeless accommodation had risen from £250,000 to £19 million in three years; its grant of £1.7 million 'in no way reflects need', said council leader Liam Robinson in an understatement. More households in England were living in temporary accommodation; they contained 131,000 children. Many more young people aged between 16 and 24 were at risk of homelessness, often ejected from families. Bed and breakfast accommodation was now costing councils £1.7 billion a year.

Rough sleeping rose to an estimated 2,900 per night in June 2023 in England amid a total of some 4,000. Over 300 were aged under 25. Homelessness charity St Mungo's said it was now coming across more people who did not have a history of trauma or poor mental health: some even still had jobs but simply could not put a roof over their heads. During the Thatcher years, rough sleeping had come to symbolize Tory government. Ministers had complained because they were tripping over bodies as they came out of the opera in Covent Garden. This time they found homeless people's tents an eyesore. Sleeping in the rain under a plastic awning was 'a lifestyle choice', according to justice secretary Suella Braverman. She proposed legislation to make sleeping in tents a civil offence. (Scouts and young people doing the Duke of Edinburgh's Award would become outlaws.) Charities providing tents would also be penalized. The resulting outrage forced her to beat a retreat without a scintilla of contrition. On a cold night in February 2024, we counted 19 people sleeping outside John Lewis in Oxford Street.

No plan for planning

Braverman would deploy state power to harry the homeless, but otherwise keep government small and weak.

Tories had once believed in planning: Joseph Chamberlain in Birmingham, Harold Macmillan celebrating Stevenage New Town. Michael Heseltine deployed the most statist of instruments, the development corporation, with powers of compulsory purchase, to revive London's Docklands and Liverpool's Albert Dock. For him, vigorous as ever, his ideological deviation wasn't just belief in planning – he had been ejected from his party for opposing Brexit.

Don't plan. May offered hair-raising proposals to allow developers to avoid councils altogether and instead go to an 'alternative provider' of planning permission – excluding the wider public interest or any local say. That went nowhere. Do plan. Gove urged councils to zone land for housing, with firm targets. But then he backtracked, Tory MPs' WhatsApp groups awash with protests at his plan to 'concrete over the green belt' and 'ride roughshod over communities'. The original target of providing land for 300,000 homes a year was reduced from mandatory to merely 'advisory'. Wiltshire immediately rescinded permission to build in Westbury and Melksham.

Right-wing think tanks hated green belts as an incarnation of Attleean socialism, new towns ditto. Under Labour, there had been talk of acquiring land and masterminding the development of seven eco-towns with sustainable and fully green housing. Partly due to local opposition, this plan never even reached the drawing board. Gove appointed a Tory supporter to run a new Office for Place to advise on planning for aesthetically pleasing new communities, amid deep confusion about its sincerity and purpose. Nicholas Boys Smith then bit the hand that fed him. Lack of building resulted from sociopolitical malaise: 'As a society we have fallen out of love with the future.' His beautiful design codes for the councils' housing were somewhat beside the point. Design was irrelevant when councils weren't building.

It wasn't just buildings. New wind turbines, solar farms and micro-hydroelectric schemes faced even longer waits, after a deluge of new connection requests. Planning as a function was 'probably at the weakest it's been since its creation', pronounced the former chief planner for the corporation of London, who had been godfather to the Gherkin and other ornaments of the City skyline. Where was the 'can-do' spirit of professional planning? he asked.

AWOL because of ideology, ambition killed by ministers' attacks, amplified in the Tory press, on 'red tape'. Town hall planning departments were emptied; planners decamped to join the housebuilders they had previously sought to control for the public good, gamekeepers turned poachers. What was lost was defence of the public interest, to ensure not only good buildings, but urban layouts balancing tarmac and greenery, residence and employment, services and transport. Planners had once been trained to hold the ring between the rights of those alive now and those of the yet-to-be-born, between markets and the public interest, between climate and commerce, between beauty and survival, between one neighbour and another. We had talked to Steve Birkinshaw, then head of planning and regeneration for Erewash borough council, the Derbyshire district centred on Ilkeston, and heard a tale of woe. 'We are always getting the blame for the lack of building. If only the planning laws were relaxed, there would be plenty of houses built, ministers say. That's just not true. It's the fault of developers refusing to build. We can't force them to build. We don't own the land, so if they just land bank the sites we nominate and refuse to build, there's nothing we can do.' He couldn't insist that sheltered housing be included. What's more, ministers would routinely overturn local refusals for low-quality, unsuitable developments if appealed to by friendly developers.

Grubby favours

The most notorious example of the mentality was Robert Jenrick, secretary for housing, communities and local government, who in 2020 overruled a planning decision against a £1 billion luxury housing scheme on the Isle of Dogs. A government inspector said it was unsuitable for the area and made no contribution to the lack of affordable housing in Tower Hamlets. Jenrick hurried through a permission for the developer, former owner of the *Daily Express* and a donor to the Tory party, at a speed that helped him avoid paying a £30 to £50 million levy to Tower Hamlets council. At a judicial review he admitted his sign-off was 'unlawful by reason of apparent bias'. Here's a vignette on the Tory party during this period. Ideology was strong (Jenrick later became a hardman, tough on the expulsion of refugees) but always malleable when grubby favours could be proffered. Pelf before principle, when required. That was the plan.

Planning had always to rest on a subtle combination of national interest and local detail. When, in January 2024, Gove announced a grand plan for the expansion of Cambridge in a version of a UK Silicon Valley with an additional 150,000 homes, he hadn't bothered to consult local council leaders, who immediately pointed out that the plan was nonsensical because of a chronic lack of water supply in the area. That was down to lack of investment by privatized Anglian Water. If Gove had bothered to ask, he would have discovered that the Environment Agency, experts from a different Whitehall department, had previously ordered the postponement of all new urban development in the Cambridge region because of water and sustainability concerns.

An even grander project had been floated, with huge implications for science, productivity and modernization. This would link Oxford and Cambridge via Milton Keynes with a new rail line, creating a grand arc joining the research hubs in the two university cities through growth nodes in between. It would require public and private investment, the creation of new communities with transport interconnections, avoiding flood plains, adding stations, linking local authorities who would have to be pushed to work together. Ambition required active deployment of state power over the long haul. It wasn't there.

The only way is up

- Build, build, build more homes
- End Right to Buy
- End no-fault evictions
- Allow councils to borrow prudently
- Align council tax with property values
- Incentivize construction of smaller older people's homes
- End land banking and time-limit planning permission
- Reinstate minimum space standards
- Plan the next generation of new towns

5

Health: Waiting and Waiting

IT WAS AN occasion so bizarre you had to be there to revel in its perversity. That day in summer 2023, the seventy-fifth anniversary of the birth of the NHS was celebrated with monumental pomp and circumstance in Westminster Abbey. A mighty gathering of 1,500 staff of all ranks prayed, sang hymns and alleluia'd along with royalty and hosts of notables. A nurse processed down the aisle with a cushion bearing the George Cross recently awarded to the NHS for its work in the pandemic.

Among the guests was 91-year-old Enid Richmond, one of the first people to work in the service, along with 17-year-old Kyle Dean-Curtis, St John Ambulance cadet of the year. Faith leaders stepped forward to add their blessings to those from the Dean of Westminster. The 1948 creation of the NHS was 'building Jerusalem', the Dean intoned. 'This is more than history today, more than ambition. Today is all about our hope, about our belief.' Tory chancellor Nigel Lawson once sneered that the NHS was the closest thing the English had to a religion, with those who practised it regarding themselves as a priesthood, but today among the votaries was prime minister Sunak. His speechwriters had superlatives at the ready: 'The NHS has been there for all of us, taking care of us through the toughest times but also through moments of joy and hope.'

Who would have guessed that the Royal College of Nursing had just called its first ever strike? They eventually settled, but still left nurses' pay 10 per cent less in value than in 2010. Consultants had followed them on the picket line, their salaries down 35 per cent, along with the pay of junior doctors, who were still in bitter dispute on this celebration day. On just about every measure, the NHS was down. Most visible and alarming were the waiting lists. And safety. The Care Quality Commission (CQC) rated two thirds of London hospitals inadequate or requiring improvement; these one-word judgements were superficial, but the underlying deterioration was plain. The Tory manifesto had promised to make the NHS 'the best place in the world to give birth', but after a series of scandals and deaths, the CQC found two out of three maternity services were not safe enough and one in seven were inadequate.

I'll cut the deficit, not the NHS

It's incontrovertibly a story of decline. Other health systems faced pressure, through ageing, workforce shortages and striking clinicians. But they usually started from a much higher base. Take the A&E (*urgences*) in Nantes, which was reporting a patient flow of 280 per 24 hours in January 2024, at the height of winter. A comparable A&E was Nottingham, a city of the same size, where the Queen's Medical Centre was dealing with 520 every day. In 2010, the Tories had inherited an NHS in reasonable health after years of investment, annual increments in funding and uplifted pay. The year they took over, waiting lists were the lowest since 1948. Tory spin doctors were well aware of the trust differential between the parties, plastering Cameron on posters promising, 'I'll cut the deficit, not the NHS' .

In fact the Tories did the opposite. That's to say, the deficit wasn't cut but the NHS was, though the calculation isn't straightforward. For the sake of accuracy: by the time Cameron left office, the budget deficit was less relative to GDP but not in absolute terms. But there was more Toryism to come, and by 2022–23 the deficit relative to GDP was higher than in the last year before the financial crisis. As for the NHS, spending had been on an upwards curve since the mid 1950s, so budgets need to be compared with a long-run 3.6 per cent per year real-terms increase. Under Cameron, total cash increased at around 0.8 per cent a year. Because the population was growing, that meant per capita spending rose only marginally. Subsequently, real annual spending increased by 2.8 per cent on average, but between 2022–23 and 2024–25, spending was projected to increase by only 0.1 per cent a year.

So a real-terms increase can be recorded, just. Over the 12 years from 2010, UK health spending per head rose from just over £2,000 to £3,400. But factor in COVID, along with the ageing of the population, and that increase looks less and less. The Health Foundation, a research charity, notes that if UK spending per head had kept up with the average in the core EU countries, we would have spent £40 billion a year more.

Surviving?

Sitting halfway up (or down) OECD tables for doctors, nurses and disease did not matter to the public, more concerned with the likelihood of being treated and not dying. Cases of cancer went on rising but mortality went on falling. Half of those diagnosed in England and Wales now survived for 10 years or more. That was twice as many as 50 years ago but lagged well behind comparable countries. Take colon cancer, one of the commonest: the UK came last among seven similar countries. The UK ranked twenty-eighth out of 33 similar countries for five-year survival for both stomach and lung cancer, twenty-sixth for pancreatic cancer. Early diagnosis was crucial, plus access to the best treatment. And speed. By 2023, only two thirds of patients were starting treatment within the target 62 days.

Austerity had been visited on training, the results of which were all too evident 14 years later, with shortages in virtually every NHS specialism, from podiatry to psychiatry, speech therapists, nurses and doctors. Of all OECD countries, the UK now had the highest proportion of doctors over the age of 55. Shortage of nurses was aggravated by the crazy decision to abolish their training bursary, seemingly based on a misunderstanding of how student nurses work in wards while they train. The Royal College of Nursing said, 'they are being put off by the prospect of astronomical student debt, low salaries and poor working conditions'. Brexit caused many Europeans to flee, and when, later, after the damage had been done, the government promised to recruit 50,000 more nurses, it reached the target only by importing them from Zimbabwe, South Africa, Nigeria and the Philippines. Many came from countries the World Health Organization had asked rich countries not to poach from – 3,000 coming from these in the six months to October 2023, including poorest-of-the-poor Nepal. Half of new nurses registered in 2022–23 were educated overseas, outside Europe. Recruiting was competitive: in Lagos or Manila recruiters from one hospital would bump into another from a next-door trust, fishing from the same pool instead of organizing it nationally and rationally.

Insouciant, indifferent, uncurious

Cameron's other pre-election promise had been no top-down reorganization; he had apparently learned just how much the NHS had been plagued by ministers pulling eagerly on levers in Whitehall, convinced they could 'reform' the system in miraculous ways. We reported on one public health director who had the nameplate on his door changed seven times under Labour's restless shufflings. But nothing had prepared the NHS for what was perpetrated in 2012. It's extraordinary in retrospect how any prime minister could have been so insouciant, indifferent, uncurious. When he appointed Andrew Lansley as health secretary, by his own admission he barely glanced at his man's plan, which was so extensive that Sir David Nicholson, head of NHS England, labelled it 'a reorganization so big you can see it from outer space'. He was not being complimentary.

Lansley hacked at the carcass from top to toe, seeking to hew it into segments to compete with each other *and* with private providers. This was straight from the New Public Management playbook, which had been favoured under Labour without much supporting evidence, but now was further extended. 'Any willing provider' could tender for hospitals or community services, with the Competition and Markets Authority making sure the NHS was not favoured in the new market. Using Lansley's law, Virgin sued to get a contract it thought was unjustly retained by the public sector.

Coincidentally, the year of Lansley's great re-disorganization saw the opening of the London Olympics, showcasing Danny Boyle's emotional evocation of the founding of the NHS with children bouncing on beds among old-fashioned starched nurses, drawing roars of approval from the crowd. Embarrassed, Cameron slapped down a Tory MP who had damned a 'leftie opening ceremony'. In private, in think-tank conclaves, Tories were with Lawson in instinctive antipathy: the NHS, like the BBC, was a public institution they regarded as essentially socialist that should be privatized. They knew better than to speak this blasphemy out loud. In code the NHS was deemed 'unsustainable', needing (that word again) 'reform'. The rumbling often broke surface: talking to the

Telegraph in 2024 on 'unconstrained demand', the private equity maven appointed deputy chair of NHS England asked, 'At what point do you say' it should be 'a mixture of social insurance or some sort of private solution?'

Amid half-hearted objections from the Liberal Democrats, Lansley's plan fell apart under the weight of its own impossibilities. Without extra funds the NHS was unappealing to the private sector. Only one company tendered for a whole hospital. Circle Health (now owned by the Emirate of Abu Dhabi) took over Hinchingbrooke hospital in Huntingdon with extravagant promises of improvements and shareholder bonuses: they handed it back after less than a year, badly burned by the strain of demand. Labour, pumping money in, had contracted with private hospitals to shift NHS waiting lists; not to take over services but to provide hip, knee and cataract operations at NHS rates. Some companies did profit from the Tory scheme: Virgin was making £2 billion from 400 local NHS contracts by 2019, details hidden by 'commercial confidentiality'. But overall, Lansley's hope of serious private intrusion was dashed. By 2023, the NHS was spending a pretty much unchanged 6 per cent of its total on private and non-profit contractors. The figure excluded expensive PFI schemes inherited from Labour that continued to cost 2 per cent of the annual NHS budget.

In the Lansley fantasy GPs would take charge of commissioning services, but it immediately became clear they had neither the time nor the inclination. Many practices were small businesses and wanted no part in his bureaucracy. In their absence, the system relied heavily on expensive management consultants, retreating behind a wall of jargon and unaccountability. When we visited his Ipswich hospital, chief executive Nick Hulme told us he had had to hire 30 specialists to code every item, from bedpans to scanners, to make sure he received due income from the commissioners. (Such time-consuming exchange of invoices is typical of the huge admin costs of the American and other insurance systems – a fact that never stopped incessant chatter on the right about replacing the NHS with private insurance.) Meanwhile, commissioners hired their own armies of accountants to challenge the invoices sent to them. Hume said the payment system warped treatment. 'We got £1,500 if we admitted someone overnight from A&E but only £800 for a day treatment, so the finance director wanted us to fill the beds overnight.'

Reintegration and empty pledges

The public hadn't a clue. They just saw waiting times grow, exhausted staff and increasingly threadbare services. Concessions made to the Liberal Democrats had made the legislation even more dysfunctional – handing public health to councils was a recipe for decline, given the mounting cuts in local spending. Lansley was fired, but the most significant change was the appointment of Tony Blair's former health adviser, Simon Stevens, to head NHS England. He used his huge influence in a Downing Street by now alarmed at, if not contrite about, the chaos and set about dismantling the grotesque Lansley structure piece by piece. It was impressively counter-revolutionary. Collaboration became the mantra. The public none the wiser, new integrated care boards were supposed to bring hospitals, GPs, mental health and other services closer, with a role for local authorities, though without any adjustment of finances. It was yet another disruptive reorganization, all very bureaucratic, but a necessary repair. Meanwhile the NHS never got that £350m a week extra emblazoned on the side of the Brexit bus. Stevens did manage to lever in more money with threat, blackmail and promises: Theresa May paid up more in exchange for a long-term plan containing politically useful targets.

Services survived through financial legerdemain. NHS trusts were told to use their capital budgets for day-to-day spending, which pushed yet more dilapidated buildings into disrepair and hindered the replacement of ancient IT. Decrepit systems that still often didn't communicate with one another left doctors and nurses complaining they waited ages for computers and laptops to fire up. Nearly half the NHS buildings in England had been built before 1985, and by the end of 2023, the maintenance backlog had jumped to £11.6 billion. That year, seven hospitals were found to be unsound and in need of urgent replacement because they had been built with RAAC, with buildings at a further 23 trusts also infected.

It was typical that so much time and attention was devoted to Johnson's empty pledge of 40 new hospitals. The figure had been plucked out of the air, unfinanced, no delivery plan attached. When the NAO investigated, they found that the list released by the Department of Health and Social Care was a mishmash of rebuilds and new wings. At the very best, 32 new hospitals might conceivably be constructed by 2030, none of them for mental health.

On hold

On a daily basis, well over half the contact the public has with the NHS takes place in GPs' surgeries, yet primary care gets barely 7 per cent of the overall budget. Labour had started to address that huge anomaly but didn't get far. Since then, little or no effort had gone into rebalancing between GPs and hospitals; many practices were too small and operated out of cramped premises.

The right-wing press took to GP-bashing, egged on by ministers looking for people to blame for lack of appointments and even attacking the COVID-era innovation of online consultations that speeded up treatments. Though public satisfaction with the NHS fell to its lowest recorded level, at 29 per cent, in 2023 in England, GPs remained popular, three quarters of patients still rating their own practice as good. That was despite the GP-to-patient ratio falling since 2010, with the perverse effect of improving measured productivity. In Stevens' long-term plan, primary and community services were supposed to grow faster than the overall NHS budget, but by 2024 the number of full-time qualified GPs was fewer than in 2019. In poorer places GP practices had proportionately more patients and less funding. England would have needed 16,700 more GPs to match the OECD average. Medical deserts were a problem elsewhere, for example in France, though in that much better-funded system, the government was more willing to offer financial inducements to doctors to move.

Dr Shankland's surgery

Here's a snapshot of how GPs' workload had mushroomed. It was hard to generalize, given the heterogeneity of practices, but this felt typical. In Tower Hamlets, Dr Ben Shankland's day began at 8 a.m. and ended at 8 p.m. The day we were there, his morning clinic overran as usual: few consultations can or should be restricted to the regulation 10 minutes. At a staff meeting, GPs, pharmacists and nurses pored over the difficult cases until 1 p.m. A nurse feared a frail older person was deteriorating. Autism and ADHD cases were soaring, with the referral wait two years. A patient was angry at being refused a drug the NHS did not prescribe: it had been recommended by a private doctor, but he wanted to avoid having to pay private prescription rates.

Shankland's afternoon clinic also overran. He stayed on late, having to fit in two hours of admin, with test results, consultant referrals and replies all needing patients' notes to be checked. Easy to see why at this intensity so many doctors burned out or worked fewer days. During a single shift, Shankland had spoken directly to 40 patients in person, online or by phone; he considered many more patients' case notes. Frequently a junior trainee would ask for advice, as did nurses and pharmacists. As often, there was a drama: a family with no appointment brought in an elderly man who had collapsed in distress, unable to move. 'I've known him a long time', Shankland said. He calmed him down and called an ambulance, which took two hours, the patient not deemed a priority because he was in a safe place.

GPs complained of hospitals offloading work they used to do. Shankland had referred a patient to oncology who was still in pain two years after breast cancer surgery. The hospital bounced her back, saying she should be seen by neurology. She had waited a year for a neurology appointment while Shankland cared for her. Then, a week before this long-awaited appointment, the neurology consultant decided to triage his overlong list and bumped her off it, sending her back to be 'managed in primary care'. This was another instance of how waiting lists got massaged down. In any given GP practice, four out of ten patients had mental health problems.

Missing from that list was poor housing. The little boy who died in Rochdale due to damp and mould in his home gave his name to 'Awaab's law', which demanded higher standards for social rented dwellings – but not for rentals from private landlords. A law without funds attached was unlikely to make much difference to worsening housing conditions causing more respiratory illness.

Waiting and waiting

Waiting for new hospitals, waiting for new recruits, waiting to be seen. Cancer waits were the worst on record. Tory ministers and their attack dogs in the press and think tanks tried to make something of the fact that latterly NHS budgets had been improved, relative to the austerity years. Staff numbers had gone up, but numbers of patients treated did not rise commensurately. Given the level of statistical illiteracy in the British media, it wasn't surprising that these articles and postings had forgotten about both population and what medics call acuity: more people wanted treatment and more of them were sicker. Not factored in also was the huge impact COVID had on staff. Many had been exhausted, morally as well as physically, and they had had no chance to recuperate.

The reasons for increased demand were sometimes simple, much due to austerity; and sometimes complex, to do with families, expectations, ageing and people's working conditions. Taking her cue from unhinged US Republicans, Truss had tried in a self-exculpating way to blame the 'deep state'. She would have done better to look for deep society, at households and places off her limited radar. For all the often positive indicators of well-being, many more people seemed depressed, sick, more prone to resort to the NHS for assistance. Some of the causes were obvious: the persistence and intensification of poverty, demanding but badly paid jobs, bad food, inadequate community support and loneliness. Some causes of expanded demand were less clear. Were people less stoical, less self-reliant, more dependent on professional advice? No, said emergency services we visited. For example, at the new ambulance callout centre in Gillingham, where we listened to incoming calls in April 2024, staff and managers said there was no sign of any change: as ever, nearly all their calls were from people genuinely in urgent need. There were just more of them, often with multiple problems.

Time out of mind

Tory ministers deserved some credit for increased recognition of mental health. Demographic facts pressed in. In hospitals, one in four beds were now occupied by people with dementia. Hospital was often not the right place for them, but social care was in increasing chaos.

Royals, influencers and musicians started to refer publicly to their mental health, their anxiety, depression and stress. Parents, especially after COVID, were more conscious of their children's state of mind and problems with eating and behaviour. One of the era's buzzwords was 'neurodiversity', a spectrum of conditions from learning disability to autism and attention deficit hyperactivity disorder. Some fell within the province of psychiatry, others were aspects of personality; yet others were disabilities that demanded social and community care.

For years mental health had been promised parity of esteem with physical health. It did begin to get a bigger share of NHS funds and recruited more staff. By 2023–24, mental health services in England had seen an 8 per cent increase over the previous six years: by 2024, mental health spending amounted to just under 9 per cent of the NHS budget. But the NHS itself estimated that eight million people needed treatment and they were not even on waiting lists. The pandemic had pushed referrals from 4.4 million in 2017 to 6.4 million by 2022; that year the NAO reported 1.2 million waiting for treatment. In 2023, the Care Quality Commission found four out of ten mental health providers were either inadequate or required improvement in terms of patient safety. Lack of community care put a strain on A&E; in one hospital, 42 mental health patients were each found to have waited over 36 hours in a single month. Contrast these figures: between 2016 and 2023, the number of children referred to mental health services rose by over 350 per cent but the number of doctors to treat them rose by 19 per cent.

There were still not enough mental health beds, with patients sent far from home, jeopardizing treatment and costing a lot. High mental health nursing vacancies meant too few caring for too many patients, which contributed to overuse of restraint, seclusion and segregation. The May government commissioned a report from the former president of the Royal College of Psychiatry, Professor Sir Simon Wessely, after scandals over cruel treatment. On the basis of his work, a new act was drafted, more respectful of patients' rights – but then silently dropped.

Under Labour, a new scheme of psychological therapies had been introduced, prompted by the work of LSE professor Richard Layard and Oxford's David Clark, which demonstrated the economic gains from helping people deal with depression and stress in informal and online settings, inexpensively. It expanded and secured further investment, renamed NHS Talking Therapies. But in 2023, the NAO said only a quarter of people with diagnosed need were getting such help.

Unhealthy nation

A point we've emphasized is the government's failure to recognize links and consequences. Poorly paid, backbreaking jobs as a delivery driver or in an Amazon 'fulfilment centre' affected health. Two million people were now receiving benefits related to their poor health, two thirds of them judged unfit for work even by the Department for Work and Pension's tough inquisitors. Their problems were primarily mental and behavioural disorders, followed by back and joint pain.

Prevention being better than cure was always cited as the only remedy for soaring NHS demand, but that maxim was in diametrical opposition to most Tory MPs' non-interventionist, individualist stance. It was the nanny state, aka public health measures, that had cut smoking from something that 70 per cent of men did in 1962 but only 15 per cent now. COVID showed how, in an emergency, vaccines could prevent millions of deaths. However, by 2020, just £49 a head was being spent on prevention compared with £1,742 on treatments after people were ill.

One reason was that prevention is inescapably about politics, about collective choices and socioeconomic outcomes. An estimated 40,000 deaths a year were caused by polluted air, but carmakers and drivers were a powerful lobby, as we saw in Chapter 3. Prevention was largely the job of councils, but they had to cut their public health spending. By 2023, hospital admissions for salmonella, E. coli and campylobacter infections were at an all-time high. The causes included weakened checks at the ports post-Brexit. It was better detection, claimed the Food Standards Agency, but our own visit to local-authority hygiene checkers in Huntingdon brought home to us the alarming gaps, with fewer environmental health inspectors doing fewer checks, caused by austerity cuts. 'Inspectors', wrote the author Russell Jones sarcastically of Tory ideology, 'who had conned us in to thinking they were just ensuring unscrupulous suppliers hadn't been slipping fetid bits of Shergar into your Scotch egg were actually detestable agents of a bloated liberal quangocracy.' Prevention depended on joining policies up. Low-traffic neighbourhoods saw people walking more, with measurable health economic benefit. But at the top, there were only conflicted ideas of the state and its purposes.

Class makes you ill

Supporting socialized healthcare was difficult enough for the Tories; admitting that income distribution and markets made people ill was something else. If the NHS lagged behind other countries' systems, it was partly because it had fewer doctors, nurses, GPs and beds, but also because of more extreme inequalities in jobs and income. In every aspect of health, social deprivation was an overriding factor. Compare Richmond-on-Thames, where men were living healthily on average to the age of 71, with Blackpool, where men could expect just 56 good years of life, women a bit better for both. Poorer areas had fewer GPs per population, but of some things they had abundance. Four out of every five of the billboards advertising fast food and alcohol were put up in the poorest half of England and Wales.

Tory libertarians had always mocked 'elf and safety' measures, no matter how many lives would be saved; seat belts, smoking in public places among them. These stern critics of public spending waste were unmoved by how habits like smoking, drinking, bad diet and lack of exercise not only accounted for around 40 per cent of all premature deaths but weighed ever more heavily on the NHS costs and on the taxpayer. The government's own 2019 green paper accepted that half of health status is determined by social and economic environment. The health secretary, Matt Hancock, buried it.

Junk

The evidence went only one way. Across the Western world people were getting fatter, and in this league table the UK came near the top. Over a quarter of the population were now obese, according to the Health Survey of England, with another third classed as overweight. Most alarming was the rapid rise in children's weight: by the age of 11, a quarter were obese. Streams of reports set out how to encourage healthy eating and discourage cigarettes, alcohol, gambling and junk food. The Obesity Health Alliance calculated that nearly a third of all food bought by UK households was unhealthy, breaching government dietary guidelines for fat, salt or sugar. Those sales together earned the food industry £34.2 billion, while hospitals admitted over a million people a year for treatment of diseases directly linked to being overweight, the second greatest cause of cancer.

Allegedly chastened by his COVID experience, Johnson announced a strategy that was supposed to ban junk-food television ads before 9 p.m. During her brief reign Truss stopped that going ahead, and her successor, Sunak, prevaricated, claiming that a ban on two-for-one offers on unhealthy products would hurt shops. For years there had been wrangling over cutting sugar and salt, with strong resistance from the food industry. It kept promising to cut back voluntarily, warning that regulation would raise prices for the poor, and nothing changed. However, in 2018 a sugar levy was imposed on soft drinks, cutting sugar content by a fifth. Strong opposition from Tory MPs deterred any extension to milkshakes, cakes, yoghurts, sweets, cereals and biscuits. The lack of dentists contributed to children's rotting teeth, but consumption of sugar was the main cause of tooth extractions in the under-fives.

What was needed, said the IfG, was a long-term plan and collaboration between Whitehall departments. Avoid telling people what to eat, offering instead a vision of healthier diets and more productive lives. The point was arguable. Research had found that taxing and imposing stricter licensing regulations saved lives far more effectively than information campaigns. The precondition for both approaches was active, interventionist government.

Teeth

Despite the sweets, over the decades children's teeth were generally healthier, thanks in part to fluoridation. Oral hygiene had become the social norm and the story around dentistry used to be positive. No longer. Four out of ten children now had no access to regular appointments. Lack of care meant 30,000 children and 70,000 adults arrived in A&E in 2023 with rotten teeth needing urgent attention. Tooth decay had become the single biggest reason for children aged five to seventeen being admitted to hospital: as well as late emergency treatment causing distress, tooth extraction in hospital is a very expensive alternative. Lack of checks meant oral cancers had increased by 46 per cent inside 10 years.

Dentistry had always been an anomalous NHS service. Except for children and those on certain benefits, it was not free. The dentists' contract ordained charges for patients in three bands, from £25.80 for a check-up to £306.80 for crowns, dentures and difficult treatments. Increasingly, many people simply could not afford them, while the rates were too low for most dentists. Some nine out of ten now only did private work, according to the British Dental Association. In some areas even private dentists were not taking new patients. Two thousand left dentistry altogether in the two years to 2023. We began this book in one of the 'dental deserts' where there were no practitioners who would take on NHS patients.

NHS dentistry, the Nuffield Trust reported, was in a perilous state, amid lurid reports of DIY surgery with people in such pain they pulled their own teeth. The *Guardian* talked to a young woman in Devon, where no dentist would take her on the NHS. Would anyone take her children? No, only if an adult was a patient too, but no, they wouldn't take on either parent, so the children could get no check-ups. In pain, Lucy went to a private dentist who would have filled her tooth for £500, but short of money, she chose to have it pulled for £400. Intermittently Tory politicians had called for charging in the NHS: Sajid Javid, briefly health secretary, wanted charges for GP and emergency hospital visits. They were not looking at the evidence of what charging had done to the nation's oral cavity. The government promised a new system: it never arrived, and teeth decayed.

Getting fit

After the pandemic, the number of people taking exercise returned to its pre-COVID level – but that level was low. Though nearly two thirds of those aged 16 and over in England did 150 minutes or more of moderate-intensity physical activity a week, a quarter were inactive. The government admitted 'stubbornly high levels of inactivity', but its own policies were responsible for the mass closure of sports grounds, leisure centres and pools. Children were couch-bound; half of them did not meet the Chief Medical Officers' guidance of at least an hour of activity a day. A third did less than half that.

In the Lansley re-disorganization, public health – smoking cessation, sexual health, vaccination and so on – had been removed from the NHS. Hard-pressed councils were tempted to use their public health money for other things, such as potholes. By 2023, there were only 2,000 school nurses left in England to cover 24,413 schools, fewer than one to every ten, leaving the nurses with no chance to make relationships and build trust with children needing help. More health visitors were promised, but the House of Lords reported there were 40 per cent fewer, and large numbers of under-fives were missing out on statutory checks, 25 per cent of them in London. The number of babies taken to A&E rose. Specialist nurse numbers fell by nearly half, leaving people with a learning disability and their families bereft of support. Here was the dismantling of the front line, the best chance to help people early before problems turned serious.

The UK lost its measles-free status in 2019, as rates of children fully vaccinated fell from 95 to just 85 per cent, for a disease with risks of pneumonia, meningitis, blindness and seizures. What was politely called vaccine hesitancy grew as social media conspiracy sites pumped out false claims that the MMR (measles, mumps and rubella) vaccine caused autism, backed at the time by a vigorous *Daily Mail* campaign. The government website warned that current vaccine levels could mean an outbreak of up to 140,000 cases in London alone: an outbreak in early 2024 hit Birmingham hard.

Sex and disease

HIV treatment was a success and the UK hit international targets due to a wide take-up of pre-exposure prophylaxis. But syphilis cases rose to their highest level for 75 years in England, with gonorrhoea diagnoses up 50 per cent, the worst since records began in 1918. Sexual health budgets fell steeply, and we went to see the effects in Leicester.

Ivan Browne, long-time director of the city's public health service, took us to his sexual health clinic in a former TK Maxx outlet in the middle of a bustling shopping centre. From brightly coloured, welcoming premises, his staff dispensed free contraceptives and treated infections, with counselling and tracing of contacts in sexually transmitted infections. 'All my services are pinched', said Browne. This centre had the capacity to take 1,000 calls a week, but he wished his staff could do more. He worried that unanswered callers might be permanently lost to his tracers, spreading diseases further.

He took us to a centre for the homeless, that morning providing free breakfasts for some 50 rough sleepers. There was controversy when he first set up a wet room, a place where street people were allowed to drink alcohol in monitored and safe conditions. We met Lee there, knocking back a beer. This was progress. The beer was less strong than before, so he was causing himself less harm and saving the NHS money. During the previous year he had been to A&E 29 times; but only twice since starting at the centre. A rationale for the new NHS integrated systems was indeed integration, so money saved in hospitals should benefit public health. 'I wish!' said Browne, who saw no money ever flow back to him from the NHS. Lee waved his beer can at us cheerily as we went.

Smoking and drinking

In England, around ten million people were estimated to regularly exceed the Chief Medical Officers' low-risk alcohol guidelines, among them nearly two million drinking at high risk. Alcohol consumption had peaked in the mid 2000s and trended downwards since. Health Survey England found 21 per cent of people reporting that they had not drunk alcohol during the previous year, with the young cutting intake more than other age groups. This was wholly welcome, even if deaths from conditions attributable to alcohol had risen since 2001, and more steeply since 2019. Treating the effects of alcohol cost the NHS in England around £3.5 billion per year; that ran to £21 billion overall in crime and productivity lost through unemployment and sickness. Add in the effect of alcohol abuse on the children and families of drinkers; the Children's Commissioner estimated nearly half a million children lived with a drug- or alcohol-dependent adult.

But drug and alcohol treatment services had been cut by around a third. Attempts to deter drinking by imposing a minimum price per unit were strongly resisted by business, and Tory ministers were easily lobbied. The Portman Group, a trade body, said a crackdown on alcohol would be 'disproportionate and inappropriate'. But Sunak did propose a ban on candy-flavoured disposable vapes, which were drawing children into smoking. Astonishingly bold was his planned ban on anyone buying cigarettes aged 15 or below, rising each year, so that no one born after 1 January 2009 would smoke in future. Truss led opponents, calling the plan 'profoundly unconservative', Johnson calling it 'nuts'. Sales of harmful products (tobacco, excess drink, junk food) were estimated at £81 billion, earning the tax authorities £29 billion. But smoking caused about 459,000 people to be unable to work, and the wage penalty from unemployment and lost productivity due to smoking, drinking and obesity was £31 billion a year. Did tobacco industry proceeds of £24 billion justify the fact that sales would eventually kill half of its consumers?

Free marketeers, at least those who stand for election, can suddenly get squeamish about their own core beliefs. Free markets in alcohol and tobacco, yes, but not in cannabis or other drugs on a list of proscribed substances put together as much by accident and history as medical judgement. Some three million people in England and Wales were believed to take drugs deemed illegal. Tories at Westminster said, on the one hand, there would be no change in the law, yet on the other, they would do less to mitigate the harm of drug abuse. Spending on adult drug and alcohol treatment services decreased by 40 per cent in real terms between 2014–15 and 2021–22. Local authorities' funding of drug and alcohol services peaked in 2014–15, but by 2024 had fallen by 27 per cent.

COVID

When the pandemic struck in spring 2020, the NHS was in a weakened state – but cope it did, as did public services at large. It was a time of great heroism by those who kept working at risk to themselves and their families, in the NHS and in food, delivery, energy and water industries. Clapping on the doorsteps for a while recognized that everyday selflessness, but sentiment didn't carry over into better rewarding it afterwards.

Inventing then rolling out an entirely new vaccine was a great success. But other COVID stories of venality and corruption, ministers' cronies given mammoth contracts, took the shine off. Ivan Browne in Leicester was bitter. Local public health systems had for decades run infectious-disease tracing and they were ready to take in the COVID tracing work. But the Johnson government ignored local expertise and created a super-expensive new national system, starting from scratch, with battalions of untrained tracers on national phone banks. What the Public Accounts Committee called unimaginable sums of money were wasted.

Leicester had been allowed to set up its own system, building on deep local knowledge. Browne had a heavy caseload, but being Leicester born and bred, and of West Indian heritage, helped him navigate the complexity of contacts among the city's dozens of diverse communities. When the pandemic was over, he wrote a report on lessons learned. At first he was full of optimism about the rapid coming-together of people and services, out of their silos, out of their professional rut, sharing data. Here was a model for tackling many other health problems, from childhood immunizations to screening for cancer, diabetes and high blood pressure. But by the time we met him, he was disillusioned. 'Everything we learned in COVID is gone now, everyone is back in their silos, professions back in their boundaries, nothing has been learned for next time.'

Other lessons too were rapidly forgotten. The old were in most danger, the young and those of working age at little risk but making great sacrifices to keep the elderly safe. Schoolchildren lost most, cohorts who would be behind for the rest of their education, for lack of extra tuition. Yet there was no surge of national concern for children, no determination to change priorities and put them first. The interests of the old prevailed.

Going home

Except they didn't. One service on which older people particularly depended was social care. Its relative lack of pull in the policy arena remained a puzzle, since one in seven people over the age of 65 now faced lifetime care costs topping £100,000. Its condition went from bad to worse as council provision shrank and more expensive private care became the norm. Experts reckoned an annual shortfall of £7–8 billion. The King's Fund health think tank said the number of adults requesting care hit a record high of two million in 2024. Total spending in England on adult social care had been over £24 billion in 2010; by the end of 2022 it was £27 billion. So had things improved? Not when you factor in the increased number of older people, their expanding needs and average weekly fees on a steep rise.

Reports were published then ditched, for the simple and central reason that their recommendations would cost money and require muscular, imaginative state intervention in markets that were patently failing. Social care had become big business, employing 1.6 million people, or nearly 6 per cent of the workforce – in addition to the estimated 4.7 million mothers, daughters, siblings and other relatives who cared unpaid. The Department of Health and Social Care had no overarching programme, the NAO concluded, and seemed especially at sea over the social care workforce.

It surely knew there was a chronic shortage of staff, their pay among the lowest, with no NHS-style career structure, working in a haphazard mix of large and small private homes. The government had to relax visa qualifications to let more foreigners in, to the anger of anti-immigration Brexiteer MPs, who, typically, were unwilling to square the circle and calculate what a 'domestic' workforce would need to be paid. Social care mounted as a proportion of shrunken council budgets, while social workers, who did all-important assessments of need, were in free fall.

'Nothing has changed', May had said frantically in the middle of her disastrous 2017 election campaign. Nothing did change. Her social care plan requiring people to pay more had frightened the horses and she ran away from it. On the steps of Downing Street her Tory successor swore to fix social care, but his indolence took over. What was left was a promise of a cap on the maximum anyone need spend on care, to be introduced, later, in 2025. Any feasible scheme has to address property and savings as well as pay and migration, none of them subjects of Tory enthusiasm or unity.

In many areas the social care system was anything but; rather a maze of charities, public authorities and families, who were often both confused and avaricious about inheritance. The pandemic showed how much social care capacity mattered. The NHS was locked in a symbiotic but toxic relationship with care homes – in 2024, some 13,000 hospital beds were blocked each day in England, occupied by older people who would be better off in their own home. But they often needed care of a kind their relatives could not provide. Councils had long ceased to be able to send in their own staff to help: strict tests of means were applied. Fewer people were cared for, and as the CQC reported, often not well. The mass closure of day centres left many bereft.

In 2019, we had witnessed the last days of the Isabel Blackman Centre for the elderly in Hastings as it closed its doors, seven other local centres having already shut. The centre's bus used to take people out for a spin, visiting the sights; it had been decommissioned. There would be no more art, music, singing, yoga, quizzes and games, nor visits from a chiropodist to keep them mobile or a hairdresser to keep them happy. As the packing cases were being filled with pictures from the walls, we talked to Rose, Mary and Sal, old friends sitting together at a table as they always did, but now for the last time. The 60 people here, some with dementia, others recovering from strokes, most infirm, would be separated. They would probably now go out less, perhaps joining the estimated 200,000 lonely older people who never talked to a friend or relative in a given month.

At several points in this book we might appear to be complaining about the old, their tendency to back Tory governments, their unwillingness to support necessary levels of taxation, the growing disparity in their housing space and the lack of it for the young. But the old too were victims of the prevailing ideology and poor stewardship of services. That's what increasing numbers of the elderly discovered in their last years when they and their families found the state was not there with the care they needed.

The only way is up

- Prevention first, with vigorous public health programmes
- Levies on junk foods, salt and sugar
- Pooled charges on property to pay for social care
- Bursaries for all who stay in the NHS after training
- Focus on GPs and polyclinics to take on hospital tasks
- Remake a public dental service
- Press on with equality for mental health services
- Rebuild decaying hospitals
- Grow community care to ease loneliness and health visitors for families

6

Misgovernment

IN THE LEXICOGRAPHY of the era, no word resounded more than 'control'. That vacuous but supremely successful cry of the Brexiteers, 'take it back', implied they knew what to do with it when they got it. We're assuming that by and large prime ministers and cabinets had levers to pull and choices to make. So it's fair to judge them on whether they did indeed control what they declared as their objects in politics. One of them was Steve Barclay, in and out of senior positions, including chief of staff as Number 10 crumbled under Johnson, then back again as a Sunak pick. The Tory aim, he wrote in the *Daily Telegraph*, keeper of their flame, was cutting back the size of the state. So did they?

When Labour lost power, the UK public sector had 6.4 million employees, and as of September 2023 (when Barclay was health secretary), it had 5.9 million. Remember the population of the UK grew during those years, so more people needed healthcare and other services. More people, more shopping but fewer trading standards officers (see below), fewer environmental health officers, fewer inspections of every kind, even by the Border Force. The total workforce grew, but as a proportion of that, public sector employment fell from 22 to 18 per cent. The lowest point, before COVID, was in 2017, when the figure was just under 17 per cent. A Tory aim accomplished?

Public spending is another index, with a surprising result. In the throes of the financial crisis following the bank crash, total managed state expenditure was 46 per cent of GDP. In 2022–23 it was ... 46 per cent. Apply the political test that Osborne had bandied in 2010, that Labour was entirely responsible for spending despite the global financial crash. On that basis, you have to attribute parallel responsibility in 2024, so shrinkage of the state amounted to zero. They could plead COVID. Before the pandemic they had managed to cut spending to 39 per cent of GDP, which testifies to the effectiveness of austerity. As the statisticians say, it's all about the denominator. GDP hardly grew. The population did. The cuts were real enough. People's needs increased, not just because we were getting older. A higher proportion of spending went on debt servicing, leaving less for public services. The shape of the state changed. Pensioners were favoured through the triple lock. Public investment was heavily cut. As schools, roads and hospitals crumbled, sooner or later revenue spending increased to cope with the day-to-day fallout from dilapidations.

Given their political salience, taxes are a prime measure of performance. When Labour left office, the tax take was just under 33 per cent of GDP; by 2022 it was 36 per cent. That put UK tax revenue around the average for the G7 countries, higher than Australia, but lower than European neighbours. Again, it's what didn't happen to GDP that matters: it stagnated, so COVID, furloughs, pensions and the rest had to be financed out of a barely growing pot.

Constitutional spoliation

If the Tory record on the sum total of tax and spend is surprisingly small, they also altered the mechanics of government. It's hard to put numbers on or assess the longer-run consequences of their constitutional spoliation, but it feels like damage has been done. Nominative determinism inverted: these conservatives did the opposite to the conventions by which we are governed.

Think Lebedev, loadsamoney donors, lying, putting pals in high office, party hacks, undermining the law: from Cameron to Sunak these would-be state-shrinkers packed an already bloated House of Lords, which with 784 members ranks as the world's largest legislative chamber bar China's National People's Congress. Not a thought to parliamentary efficacy. Partisanship ruled as the Tories failed even to think about replacing an oligarchical second chamber with something that looked a little more twenty-first century or acknowledged devolution within the UK. Another fault line was courts and judges, checking and balancing the prerogatives of the party that controlled the Commons. The *Daily Mail*'s mob attack on judges during Brexit set the tone. So senior judges sniffed the wind and pulled back from active invigilation of how ministers used and abused their power.

After Cameron hoodwinked his Liberal coalition partners over moving to fairer elections, Tory MPs abandoned any consideration of the legitimacy or effectiveness of Parliament.

The Commons abdicated its supremacy by allowing the Brexit vote, surrendering to demagogues such as Nigel Farage, Russian trolls and the slim majority of those who voted in the referendum. MPs then allowed first May then Johnson to trample over their sacred rights and duties, which allegedly included holding executive power to account. COVID posed a specific test of their will and capacity to handle real-time analyses and information about ministers' performance, especially Johnson's. The havoc wrought by the pandemic forced the establishment of a ponderous judge-led inquiry afterwards; its very existence underlined the weakness of parliamentary committees and oversight.

MPs' biggest failure was to prevent ministerial lying, which became commonplace. Kemi Badenoch told MPs she was holding trade talks with the Canadian government, fulfilling a Brexiteer fantasy. The Canadian high commissioner denied any such talks were taking place. Penalty? There was none. A silly parliamentary custom forbade MPs the word 'lie'. Ministers did it; it was obvious they did it; MPs chose powerlessness. Ejecting Johnson for extravagant lying only happened because by then his party had calculated the electoral odds. MPs (not just Tories) were implicated in a string of disgraces sparking by-elections, fuelling the public's perception of parliamentary squalor.

And yet. We have relied on successive reports from the secretariat servicing Commons committees and from the NAO, which was exemplary during and after COVID, keeping tabs on the billions spent and misspent in often highly critical terms. Its head, the C&AG, said it was crucial as the pandemic receded 'that we don't forget and move on, but instead reflect on what we have learned'. To date no such reflection has happened. During COVID, the civil service had panicked (and partied) while ministers lined up mates for cosy deals. The auditors acknowledged there wasn't time to use lengthy tenders to buy protective equipment or apply rigorous checks. But safeguards could have been applied and they weren't. Government delayed publishing details of contracts awarded without competition. Conflicts of interest went unstated and unchecked.

Earlier the OECD had complacently observed that austerity had had little effect on the ethos of UK public service: it had not increased corruption or led to misappropriation of public resources. But COVID found us out. When the opportunity arose, peculation proved to be as tempting here as anywhere else. Perhaps culture was just catching up with the behaviour of the bankers. They had gone unpunished. Why not, like

Cameron texting rabidly on behalf of Greensill Capital, join them at the trough? The doctrine of maximizing personal and corporate gain at public expense had long been displayed in water, energy and other sectors where the public should have had a large claim on decent and honest behaviour.

Bamboozled regulators

The apparatus set up by Thatcher and John Major to regulate the power of the privatized monopolies had been tested to destruction. Cameron and his successors made things worse by appointing political pals with no interest in identifying failings, let alone remedying them. A Tory peer became chair of Ofcom, lauding biased GB News and its disregard of neutrality rules as 'innovative'. Lord Grade was not even first choice; Johnson had fought to line the role up for the former editor of the *Daily Mail*. Imagine, the protagonist of the daily hate given a quasi-judicial role over the BBC, ITV and the internet. Ofcom's capacity to regulate online communications let alone get to grips with streaming and the fragmentation of broadcasting would have challenged an expert and professional body free from political influence. Ofcom could not lay claim to be that, even if it had been spared the appointment of Paul Dacre. Perhaps his failure to pass what sniff tests remained showed that the public interest still had some protection.

Could that be said based on the performance of Ofgem, Ofwat or the Office of Road and Rail Regulation? What exactly had the chief inspector of constabulary been doing when police numbers were cut, the Metropolitan Police fell into disrepute, then police numbers expanded at huge cost to efficiency, asked an interviewer. The article described someone with 'naked obsession with their public image', without much to show for it. How much did this powerful group of regulators and inspectors, often far too close to the ministers who appointed them, understand what was happening in their sectors? In water, energy and communications, they were bamboozled by financial re-engineering; consumer protection was secondary and neglected. And woe betide regulators who asserted their independence. The chief inspector of immigration found his remit was entirely conditional on political approval: embarrass a minister and you're out. David Neal, a former military policeman, so no softie, dared to voice his concerns about lack of inspection of private planes and conditions at migrant reception centres. He was sacked.

During these years, the Premier League had swollen with television rights and match-day revenues; witness the new interest of Americans in grabbing some of the action. But this was still English football, which depended on a dense undergrowth of minor clubs and codes applicable to all players of the game. The public had a deep interest. Tory ministers hesitated and procrastinated over allowing the Premier League to avoid what the rest of the game considered a fair distribution of its profits. Anti-intervention instincts prevailed despite the game's significance in English culture and community: why else would Cameron have felt it necessary to pretend to support a club with which his prior connection was invisible? Only late in the day was a regulator proposed, one of the panicked proposals emerging suspiciously close to the 2024 general election.

Whitehall, inexpert enemy within

Regulators are part of the state, which operationally speaking is a chain of command starting with ministers and the civil service. This was not Whitehall's finest hour. The COVID fines and karaoke parties were one sign of a falling-off in standards of behaviour, or maybe just officials' inability to resist aping their ministers' mores. More serious were repeated criticisms in auditors' reports of 'generalist leaders who lacked expertise', especially in managing the opportunities and threats of digital technologies. (Only 4 per cent of civil servants were digital professionals, compared with an average of 8–12 per cent in big commercial firms.) Many aspects of training and expertise were within the competence of permanent secretaries to improve. Little happened. A state that can't do IT is going to be ineffective – and the same can be said about engineering, science and professional public administration. The low number of permanent secretaries who had degrees in STEM subjects was indicative. Perhaps it wouldn't have mattered so much if their ministers were knowledgeable and scientifically trained; they were the opposite.

An ethic of disinterested public service is one thing, damaged but recoverable. It must be married to capacity. If you recruit Oxford classicists, at least require them to undergo rigorous postgraduate training in systems, management and the opportunities and perils of information technology. Johnson's hatchet man, Dominic Cummings, harangued Whitehall about its knowledge gaps, especially around science and technology. He was broadly right, but his standing was destroyed by dishonesty over Brexit, his own lack of professional credentials and, crucially, his cowardice when it came to criticizing those in charge of the system, starting with his patrons, Gove and Johnson, the very personification of amateur, know-nothing government. The line followed by Cummings and right-wing think tanks was completely undercut by their unwillingness to confront the facts of Toryism. They were confused. Their instinct was to disparage government itself, preferring markets; why then worry about making government more efficient and effective.

What organization could function properly when, like civil servants, its staff were publicly savaged as enemies within and forced to suffer visitations by the likes of Jacob Rees-Mogg pontificating about their hours and the ratio of face-to-face and at-a-distance work they should do? Like Cummings, Rees-Mogg had never come close to running a complex organization in his life. Priti Patel not only harassed her officials; like Truss, Johnson and others, she went in for public condemnation of the very people who were meant to be carrying out her impossible policies. Yet all the while the permanent secretaries kept silent. Some of them were dangerously complacent, allowing Whitehall press offices to become partisan mouthpieces.

Where was the outcry when Truss aggressively dismissed Sir Tom Scholar, in an 'ideological purge' made all the odder since the victim was a dry-as-dust Treasury austerian? Senior civil servants were happy, publicly speaking, to get on with the job of delivering partisan and hugely damaging policies, a kind of human shield for the Tories. Some succumbed, abandoning the capacity to think straight and speak truth. Others signed on and attempted more or less enthusiastically to deliver extreme policies.

Discontent, however, ran deep and wide. Pay had fallen, median pay decreasing for most staff after 2013; this hit morale and Whitehall's ability to recruit and retain staff. Strikes rippled through one department after another. Here's a niche group of civil servants: driving examiners. We talked to Steve and Mike, examiners of many years' standing in one of the 270 Driver and Vehicle Standards Agency (DVSA) centres around the UK (transport had been devolved, but not driving tests). Pressure was on, the public angry at delays in test appointments, 19 weeks on average.

'Tests are dangerous and very stressful', Steve said. Examiners did seven a day, each lasting 38–40 minutes, back-to-back with little time between. 'You have to keep your wits about you every second, you need to concentrate hard, it's demanding.' When the DVSA raised the number of tests, examiners balloted to strike: eventually DVSA backed down. As for pay, Mike said he earned £24,900 in 2009, which was just about the median wage then. 'We're now on £26,900, not much more despite inflation.' Weekends used to be paid over-time, but no more; they were now part of the working week.

No surprise, they both say, that the churn of staff is high. When trained examiners leave, new ones are hard to recruit and it takes a year to train them. 'It's the same everywhere in the public services: do more for less, they cut the numbers of us, they can't recruit, and the service gets worse.' There were also the potholes, more and more of them: 'They jolt your fillings out!' Steve laughed.

Civil service numbers recovered after Brexit, but often in the form of temporary staff. Some 245,000 of these were employed in the year to March 2023, against 87,000 five years earlier. Ministers such as Gove had a habit of harangu-ing councils for employing consultants, yet during that period from 2018 to 2023, Whitehall's consultant numbers increased fivefold. Coping with Brexit and the pandemic, ministers needed more civil servants; as with the police, the holes left by austerity cuts had to be filled.

Devolving the axe

If success was enforced shrinkage, the Tories succeeded with local government. The watchword had always been 'devolve the axe'. By cutting grants, they would force councils to spend less but, master stroke, force them to take the opprobrium for slashing services. In 2022, control of Westminster council, a Tory bastion, where once a leader had tried to force out council tenants for the crime of tending not to vote Tory, passed to the Labour Party. But, as elsewhere, Labour councillors had no choice but to make cuts. For example, the council had supported charities based at St Martin-in-the-Fields to reach out to the homeless and rootless who flocked to the centre of the city. Grants were cut; night-time patrols ended.

When eventually that ploy ran out of steam and even Tory-controlled councils began falling into bankruptcy, ministers allowed local authorities to make inflation-plus increases in council tax to keep them afloat, knowing the town hall was more likely to be blamed than Whitehall. While all this was going on, first Osborne, then May and Johnson sought kudos for their variously labelled northern and levelling-up strategies. They pushed new mayors, even outside the conurbations where the office made some sense. Through a multiplicity of 'deals' – doling out pots of money from the centre – cash-strapped councils were trained to sit up and beg. Levelling was destined to fail when simultaneously councils in poorer areas were suffering disproportionately larger cuts in their budgets. It was a funny sort of equalizing to force councils, many in the north, to shrink and shrivel. Liverpool suffered much deeper cuts than Dorset.

Unlevelled

The facts of uneven development within England, let alone the UK, were stark. Life expectancy, years spent in ill health, and labour market inactivity were all higher in northern and disadvantaged postcodes, attainment in school and college lower. A study across the European Economic Area put the UK top for women and second highest for men in measured health inequality between regions – hugely different from such countries as the Netherlands but also the Republic of Ireland. Whole cities were deprived, such as Birmingham, along with parts of cities (Bristol) and pockets within other-wise affluent counties and boroughs. Here were concentrated the homes that fell below acceptable standards of poverty and under-attainment at school. For most people living in

Oldham, Skelmersdale and Sandwell, life was harder than in Christchurch or Cumbria, though it was as easy to find tracts of poor housing and deprivation along the south coast as it was in Carlisle and Workington. Economic trends had their impact locally, too. The Centre for Cities calculated that the average person in Milton Keynes had by 2023 lost £21,000 compared to where they would have been if pre-2010 trends had continued; for Burnley residents the figure was £23,000.

Levelling up was an empty slogan as long as the government ignored fundamental facts. One was the movement of people: older folk were leaving cities for the coast and rural areas, least well served by buses and nurses. Huge differences in the distribution of wealth across the country were not even considered let alone dealt with. The extent of England's lopsidedness was shown in a study of gains made on property sales. It looked at Notting Hill, setting for feel-good movies, barely yards away from Grenfell Tower. In the four years to 2019, its residents made more in capital gains than the entire combined population of Liverpool, Manchester and Newcastle-upon-Tyne – remembering that 97 per cent of the population never received any capital gain for the good reason they did not have assets to sell. (The tax was not payable on selling your own home.)

The unfairness of council tax grew. Incredibly, it was still based on the property values of the early 1990s and its bands failed to capture the huge distortions in house prices. An average property in the London borough of Westminster paid as little as 0.06 per cent of its value while in, say, Hartlepool, the average property paid 1.3 per cent. The Hartlepool householder, living in a house worth £150,000, paid £200 a year more in cash than the Westminster resident living in one worth £8 million. All parties knew it required complete reform; at the very least, extra bands were needed to make it a bit fairer. No changes were made.

Sleight of hand: we believe in local autonomy, they said, we'll let you councils keep business rates; we'll cut your grants pro rata. The ploy ran up against the growth in inequality – not least in property valuations – between rich and poor districts, Westminster's business rates income so much higher than the Wirral's. It's hard, in retrospect, to judge whether Gove and other ministers were stupid or merely cynical; we can leave Johnson in the latter category.

Levelling up had to contend with a deliberate shift of available money. Sunak had boasted of his plan to an audience of Tory members in far-from-deprived Tunbridge Wells. 'I managed to start changing the funding formulas, to make sure areas like this are getting the funding they deserve. We inherited a bunch of formulas from Labour that shoved all the funding into deprived urban areas and that needed to be undone.' In fact, giving more to them that already hath began in 2010. 'Over the last 14 years', the Barnsley council leader Sir Steve Houghton complained, 'the method of allocating funding has been moving further and further away from a needs basis.' Less priority was given to deprivation, more to 'rurality' and numbers of older people, tipping funds from Labour to Tory councils. Hardly levelling up. The funding systems for schools, councils, public health and the police were 'not fit for purpose', did not properly reflect differences in needs, were not set up to tackle inequalities and worked against the government's own agenda, the IFS concluded.

Municipal mayhem

By the 2020s, councils in England were £8.4 billion a year worse off than before 2010. Their spending power – their grants plus what they were allowed to raise in taxes – had fallen by 29 per cent. But the number of people aged over 65 expanded by 14 per cent, the numbers of children looked after (in the care of councils) grew 11 per cent and households entitled to temporary accommodation increased by over a third. At the same time councils had to cover increased pension contributions, the National Living Wage and the apprenticeship levy. Because funds for schools were distributed directly from Whitehall, council cuts fell on social care, which absorbed half their spending. Children's departments were badly affected, which did not prevent ministers or the *Daily Mail* criticizing them for failing to stop child abuse.

Councils cut buses along with youth services, halved planning departments, housing and libraries, chopped highways and roads maintenance by a third. Don't get caught short in Woking: £2 billion in the hole thanks to Tory councillors' dealings, it permanently shut its lavatories. Birmingham had historic problems over equal pay for its female workers, but it had also lost £1 billion in grants. As in other bankrupt councils, the government installed commissioners: they demanded cuts, lopping £52 million off the budget for children and families in one year, with a further cut of £63 million the year after, plus sales of council assets to the tune of £1.3 billion, irretrievable civic treasures gone. Its 30 public libraries were to be cut to under 10, some of them established by the nineteenth-century Tory mayor Joseph Chamberlain. 'We have not the slightest intention of making profit', he had declared. 'We shall get our profit indirectly in the comfort of the town and in the health of the inhabitants.' No longer, it seemed.

Some Victoriana survived. After a four-year restoration the Grade I listed town hall in Rochdale reopened in 2024, allowing visitors once again to glimpse the Magna Carta mural and Great Hall, paid for in part by a grant from the National Lottery Heritage Fund and in part by the council. Which proves a point about places. They are different; if all councils cut, some still found ways for civic pride to flourish.

But some were incompetent and ideological at the same time, trying to maximize the number of contracts they let to private companies without ensuring they delivered. Tory Northamptonshire was the first to go bust. The government responded unconservatively by overnight abolishing a county that had existed since Saxon times, replacing it with two new councils oddly named North and West Northamptonshire, inspiring no loyalty and, born into austerity, cutting services from day one. Some of the local anger fuelled the Tories' later by-election losses, as in Wellingborough (North Northamptonshire) in 2024.

Who's checking?

Pretty much everywhere you turned, public functions were disappearing. In Enfield in north London, three of the council's already depleted team of four trading standards officers (TSOs) faced the sack. Their professional institute said that England-wide, 2,500 highly skilled professionals had gone, leaving half as many as in 2010. Theirs was vital work, on weights and measures, including all scales; from airport check-ins weighing your bags to baby scales in clinics and butchers' scales to weigh your mince. No one else checked packet sizes, counterfeit goods, e-cigarettes, gas appliance safety, fireworks, sunbeds, mineral water, car tyres and brake linings and calorie counts. TSOs are responsible for checking personal protection equipment for infection control and the safety of children's toys. You assume a litre goes into your petrol tank because someone checks, but that's vanishingly rare. The Chartered Trading Standards Institute did a spot check in Salford and found bows and arrows with 100 times the legal limit of phthalates – and fashion dolls 300 times over the permitted amount of these chemicals, which have been linked to cancer.

When the Liberal Democrats took control at Somerset council, the Tories bequeathed them a £100 million gap between the cost of services and funding. Leicester city council ran out of options to cut and faced bankruptcy in 2024. Thurrock, where the Tories had been predominant since 2014, had been badly mismanaged, with a 'lack of corporate focus and paucity of capacity in the finance team'; presumably because it had been Tory, the government refused a public inquiry. It would take four decades to pay off its accumulated debt. Derby, where no party had been in overall control, faced an overspend of £6 million in 2023–24, after reserves were exhausted. In Coventry, Labour said care demand had consumed the budget. Schoolchildren in Newcastle-upon-Tyne would have to eat less or at lower quality after the council cut its contribution to school meals. Havering, where Tories and residents' parties had been in control for decades, admitted it had run out of money. In Labour Southwark, 63 pence in every municipal pound was now being spent on older residents. In 2020, Croydon issued an official declaration that revenues did not meet spending. Public amenities were shut; libraries closed. The government had encouraged councils to find ways to make money, but some, like Croydon, came adrift over property investments: the commercial heart of the borough, the Whitgift Centre, was losing its shops.

The government rewarded friends, provided they kept shtum. We met David Hodge, leader of Surrey county council. He was very rare, a Tory council leader who raised his voice. The county had more children but no money to build new schools. His social care costs were rising by £254 million a year, as Surrey had proportionally the most over-85s in the country. They live long in the Home Counties. He was indignant about Surrey's MPs, who included the then Chancellor Philip Hammond, Gove, Hunt, Raab and Grayling: they had the bare-faced nerve, he said, to send him mountains of letters begging for special favours for their constituents, for school places, help with care, housing – which they themselves were responsible for cutting. In 2017, he rebelled and declared he would put the dire state of the county to a citizens' referendum, proposing a council tax hike of 15 per cent. If then other Tory leaders had stood up and been counted, the public would surely have stirred and the government would have had to back down. But no. Surrey was pacified with a private bung disguised as a pilot scheme that let the council keep more of its fat business rates. David Hodge CBE stood down a year later and his protests were heard no more.

Places

Places could be their own worst enemy. Decades of European support had enabled Cornwall and the Isles of Scilly to upgrade roads, improve the airport, provide space for start-up businesses, expand broadband connections and become home to several universities. Those 'foundations have helped our economy to diversify, our people to develop skills, and local wages to increase', said the council's New Frontiers report. Despite that, most of the residents of Cornwall and Scilly voted Leave. As elsewhere, despite promises, the old EU grants were not replaced.

Labour councils were none too vocal, and the councils' national voice, the Local Government Association, was muffled. The government's ploy worked; councillors faced a political dilemma in declaring they were doing badly when soliciting for votes. There was also something in municipal culture, where councillors often defer to officers, who blithely assume what they do is never 'political'. Councils often hide the fact of their party make-up as if it were a dirty secret. There had been a watchdog on council finances, the

Audit Commission, but one of the first things the incoming government did was abolish it, along with the regional development agencies, instruments in Labour's bid to level up. Not unequivocally successful, they were popular with businesses wanting a local focus and did stimulate investment. The Tory alternative was local economic partnerships, weak assemblies with few resources and staff, which excluded councils. Their ragbag of duties and powers included things often forgotten, such as careers services for schools. As predicted, they made scant impact, which is why 13 years later they were given the last rites and their residual powers transferred ... to councils, who would swallow their little money and forget their duties.

Without the Audit Commission, council accounts were often delayed and went unaudited. Ten authorities, including Slough, another bankrupt council, had not had their accounts checked for at least five years. The crisis reached such a stage that lo and behold, the government had to create the Office for Local Government (Oflog) to carry out many of the commission's functions. Its chair, the former C&AG, Lord Amyas Morse, admitted there was 'systemic pressure on local government, not least in the areas of social care, SEND, homelessness and asylum'. However, 'Oflog has not been given the remit to judge the right level of funding from central government.' No prizes for guessing why.

Ministers hid deficiencies with special regeneration funds, which they would dole out piecemeal, such as the Shared Prosperity Fund. Only a third of projects under another such scheme, the Towns Fund, went ahead. When the NAO investigated, the fund was found to be haphazard, unlikely to be effective, jeopardizing billions of pounds. Barely any of a vaunted 71 'shovel-ready' projects due to be completed in spring 2024 were on track: only a tenth of the promised £10.5 billion had been spent. Gimmicks such as free ports, touted as a benefit of Brexit, would depend for their success on planning and coordination with local government. Instead, councils were sidelined. On Teesside, Ben Houchen was lauded and given a peerage, though it turned out the huge public investment the Tory-elected mayor was making in Teesworks, a big brownfield development, could leave local councils with massive financial exposure.

It wasn't just the north that might have benefited from levelling up. In the past, Swindon had grown fast alongside the Honda factory. But the plant finally closed in 2021 with the loss of 3,500 jobs. Even before then the town had fallen into decline, no longer attracting foreign companies such as Intel Motorola, victimized by Brexit, investment uncertain. Under Tory control the council had sacked planners and business development staff. 'If Swindon was better resourced within a coherent UK economic strategy for growth areas, we wouldn't lose those opportunities and jobs', said Matt Griffith, director at Business West. Labour took control of the council for the first time in 20 years in May 2022, but the task was huge. In Swindon's town centre, as elsewhere, shops were shuttered and sites lay vacant.

Box-office blues

Amid council penury, spending on arts, culture, heritage and tourism took a huge hit, with at least £500 million cut from spending of £1.6 billion in 2010–11, according to the County Councils Network. The budget of the Department for Culture, Media and Sport had proved an easy target, along with allocations to Arts Council England. Similarly at local level. What chance had museums and libraries, let alone travelling theatre companies, when budgets for social care and special education were under such pressure? Special measures were brought in during COVID, preventing widespread cultural collapse.

But the arts suffered dual opprobrium. Artists were perceived to be woke and un-Tory; the arts struggled to produce the sort of linear data to convince policymakers of their benefit and impact. This was in part due to a general failure to grasp the dimensions of an economy increasingly powered by the service sector – in which leisure and culture were not just important domestically but export earners. The arts found it hard to land the value of experience, to prove that music, theatre and books not only had intrinsic value but underpinned well-being. In the wider scheme of things, arts funding was minuscule. After 13 years, central grants and lottery funding for the arts had fallen in real terms by £178 million. Theresa May, MP for Maidenhead, was not the only Tory MP accepting no fiscal responsibility for what they voted for in Parliament while complaining about councils deciding to do away with all arts support.

That support dwindled. Public funding for the arts per head of population – including the National Lottery, councils and central government – fell by a third after 2008.

Business sponsorship was also down by over a third. But a bright spot: earned income (box-office sales, venue hires, catering, etc.) rose by nearly half. Cuts in Arts Council England grants hit the south of England hard, London facing a £50 million cut over the three years to 2025. Support for the University of Cambridge museums was halved. But the Arnolfini in Bristol and the Towner in Eastbourne were among galleries that gained from a shake-up supposedly emulating the levelling-up economic agenda.

Find donations, arts groups were told. Easier said than done. The artistic director of the New Wolsey Theatre in Ipswich pointed out that a third of young people in the town were living in poverty, that this part of Suffolk had no 'high net worth' individuals to tap and there were no longer any substantial local businesses to offer sponsorship. However, new ventures did take off. Paid for by Bristol council (Labour till 2021, then Labour and Green), with help from the Arts Council and lottery money, what had been Colston Hall was transformed into Bristol Beacon, with a 2,200-seat auditorium and smaller hall plus rehearsal rooms and vaults.

Libraries in East Yorkshire and northern Lincolnshire were given a share of a £33 million fund. Every little helped; it would have been more rational and sustainable to have prevented Hull and other library authorities falling into penury in the first place.

In his gesture to literature, Johnson made the romantic novelist Nadine Dorries culture secretary. (Some might mock her literary style, but most writers would envy her three million in sales.) She ordered the Arts Council to pivot northwards, and one immediate result was a cut to the grant given to Glyndebourne for outreach, which meant it had to abandon its autumn touring to places, some in the north, otherwise without opera. In the 1970s, English National Opera at the Coliseum had put on 244 performances a year; now it could only mount 82. Its huge auditorium in St Martin's Lane with 2,359 seats cost £3.7 million a year to run, before even a single opera had been staged. ENO had had a recent troubled history, but now it was to abandon the capital altogether for somewhere in the north. The Arts Council forgot to consult Opera North, based in Leeds, or Welsh Opera, which toured in the vicinity of Liverpool. After a fuss, ENO was reprieved, granted six years to make a move.

There is a case for dispersing arts funding – Manchester has long been a centre for music and would make a fine home for an opera company – but the decision was made capriciously and without any apparent regard for the infrastructure needed to support the arts, including buoyant local council assistance, funds for educating musicians and, above all, prosperity allowing patrons to afford the price of a ticket for *Das Rheingold* or *The Merry Widow*. The ENO debacle might have been avoided if the government had not wasted upwards of £120 million on a mindless scheme to 'celebrate Brexit'. Its emptiness soon obvious, it was renamed the Unboxed festival and took place in 2022 without anyone being aware of it. Some coverage was given to the conversion of a disused oil rig in Weston-super-Mare into 'See Monster', but that was about it. Audience engagement data were not available, the NAO noted sceptically.

Having ordained arts austerity, shameless Osborne became chair of the British Museum and an overnight advocate of better funding. He had, to be fair, faced down those Tories demanding the abolition of free entry to the national collections, some of which (we mentioned the National Portrait Gallery in the Introduction) did find money from donations and grants for essential capital works.

The rest of the UK

The *National* Portrait Gallery, but whose nation? In Queen Street, Edinburgh, the Scottish *National* Portrait Gallery houses a fine collection of paintings, busts and photos. Brexit aside, the ambiguity surrounding the identity of the UK probably deepened during the Tory era. That cliché about the British Empire describes it: devolution proceeded in a fit of absence of mind. For a while a sort of institutional momentum carried Labour-era reforms forward, the Welsh assembly gaining legislative powers and Scotland (some) tax. The thing couldn't be undone but Tory cabinets did not want to think about its constitutional and parliamentary ramifications, and nor did many residents of the constituent nations. Devolution had, however, created asymmetries that raised profound questions about the functioning of Westminster, which deserved a considered and bipartisan answer. It wasn't forthcoming, beyond Cameron's knee-jerk promise of 'English votes for English laws'. This was on a par with levelling up, a gesture to backbenchers with little follow-up.

Northern Ireland was always the most special of cases, made more special by Brexit. As for Scotland and Wales, a grand opportunity had not been taken before 2010 and was even more out of sight after. Devolution was a natural experiment giving Westminster, Edinburgh and Cardiff a wonderful chance to measure, contrast and learn ... about hemicyclic parliaments, different taxes and multi-party ruling performance. But the door to this laboratory of democracy was kept firmly shut. No running tally was kept, no rigorous studies commissioned; parliamentary Tories were deaf, dumb and blind, often to their own devolved colleagues.

Nationalism in neutral

There ought to be more to say about an era when the Tories were so weak in Scotland. Three reasons for this gap suggest themselves. One is that the Scots allowed themselves to be hoodwinked. Cameron's approach to the 2014 independence referendum was of a piece with his Brexit behaviour – palliate his party first, put the interests of the UK second. Gordon Brown saved his bacon by making strong promises about further devolution of powers, Scotland in Europe and public services, much of which turned out to be nugatory. After Brexit, Westminster wrested back some powers and largely ignored Holyrood during COVID.

A second might be that Scotland was not the northern social democratic paradise fantasized by some. Right to Buy was ended; more social housing built; the harsher edges of austerity smoothed. Then the nationalists seemed to get lost in a maze of gender. A degree of fiscal conservatism had underpinned the majority choice in 2014, and though the

SNP government did increase marginal income tax rates, inequality in Scotland remained pretty much on a par with the UK at large, landed estates, grouse shooting and all. The third reason might put our criticism of Tory competence in context. Despite higher levels of public spending and higher proportionate numbers of health and education staff, even allowing for disadvantage, sparsity and demography it was hard to spot differences in social outcomes.

Devolution had only ever been partial. Despite the Scotland Act 2012, which gave Edinburgh some rights to set income tax, four out of every ten pounds spent in Scotland were still managed by Westminster. Of UK tax revenues, 8.6 per cent was generated in Scotland, which included North Sea oil and gas (tax take at record levels in 2022–23). Public spending there amounted to 9.2 per cent of the total. Scotland's population was 8.2 per cent, cueing Tory ministers to mutter to the *Daily Mail* (English edition; it cynically made sure to junk bad headlines in the Scottish version) about grasping Alba, where each resident netted an extra £1,500.

Most of these figures were contested. Scotland's needs and costs were higher (because of a sparse Highlands population, more disability and faster ageing), so arguably it deserved more. Curiously the Tories seemed to accept this, officially at least. But the same argument applied to the north-east of England, to Wales and to deprived urban areas, which not only lost out but were actively discriminated against. Remember Sunak's pledge to the burghers of Tunbridge Wells. The Barnett formula, the Treasury mechanism used for distributing the UK total, continued to have an unfair drag effect to Scotland's benefit. This was partly because Scotland's population was barely increasing, partly because Scotland had become much more relatively affluent since the formula calculated deprivation and need in the 1970s.

Scotland did have deep social problems, with more workless households and big gaps between better-off (Newton Mearns in the Glasgow suburbs) and disadvantaged areas (Newton Stewart), though rural regions compared favourably with those in the rest of the UK. Life expectancy at birth was a good two years less than in England for both women and men. One cause was death from drug abuse, three and a half times higher than in England and Wales. But control of drugs was not devolved, so what might have been a test bed for, say, decriminalization of certain drugs was lost.

Patterns of crime in Scotland largely followed the general trends. Nobody checked whether creating a single force in Police Scotland made any difference. Ditto moves to integrate health and social care rather than fragment as in England. As for drink, the Scottish government introduced a minimum price for a unit of alcohol in 2018. As attested by the World Health Organization, consumption fell, though alcohol-related death rates remained high, and in 2024 Edinburgh planned to raise the minimum by a further 30 per cent. There were lessons here, and some English local authorities, among them Sunderland, petitioned to apply them. Scottish residents were not much fatter than those in the rest of the UK, but no thinner either, and the proportion of the population that smoked was about the same, too – the pattern here as elsewhere showed marked improvement before 2010 and slowdown since.

Across the socioeconomic landscape, difference emanating from partial Scottish self-government wasn't easy to spot. Salmon fisheries suffered from Brexit; they weren't alone. Scottish water, though public, had its share of shit. Rents rose in the central belt, though by less than inflation in Argyll, Ayrshire and Dumfries and Galloway. The end of emergency rent caps and eviction protections for private renters during 2024 was expected to cause problems: housing campaigners were seeing cases of tenants being served with notice of rent increases of as much as 60 per cent.

Central Glasgow became a tourist mecca, but the arts did not obviously fare better under devolved administration. Edinburgh was still as crammed during the festivals. Pollsters found Scottish residents a bit more concerned about inequality but not that much. Specific efforts were made to mitigate child poverty – a £10-a-week payment for under-sixes – but they still left one in four in poverty against one in three in the UK. The adult poverty rate was slightly less, too.

In 2015, academics had concluded that Scotland's distinctiveness in health, income and gender inequalities was more rhetorical than substantive. That didn't seem entirely fair, given the lowering of sugar in soft drinks (well before Sunak's initiative), banning smacking children, and young people's voting. Since then, leadership styles were seen to differ markedly – Sturgeon vs Johnson – but COVID death rates were not much different. The IfG did stout-hearted work in trying to spot the differences. Scotland spent more per school pupil and person on health and social care, paying for more teachers, clinicians and care workers; personal care for people over 65 was free (but not 'hotel' costs, which were means-tested; these arrangements extended to under-65s in 2019), as were prescription charges. In England, around 5 per cent of people aged 65 and over received state-funded care in March 2020, and in Scotland 8 per cent. But discharge from hospital did not seem to have been any faster, and what is called treatable mortality moved at the same rate as elsewhere in the UK. The IfG concluded that it simply wasn't possible to say which social care system performed best.

Should Scotland's higher spending have translated into higher educational attainment? Recall the international evidence in Chapter 1 saying government focus had more effect than spending levels. If that's so, the SNP failed on two counts: it spent proportionately more and results declined, in a country that had once prided itself on its schools. In the OECD's 2022 student assessment survey, Scottish pupils' mean maths scores fell, certainly relative to England and to Wales. Science scores similarly fell. Some blamed the big curriculum reform that started in 2010 (and which originated before the SNP took power).

Short commons in the west

If levelling up had meant anything at all within the UK context, Wales would have been a focus and benefited from a more generous share of total spending. And to some extent this was accepted, even before Johnson's PR blitz. Per person public spending in Wales in 2022–23 was £13,967, 11 per cent above the UK average. But Wales's social and geographical profile was demanding: the country was ageing, pupil attainment was historically low and disability rates high, though life expectancy was only a year less than England's, and connections north–south were rugged.

An expert commission had declared that Wales was underfunded relative to estimated need, and the Tories accepted the Barnett distribution formula needed adjustment. From 2016 Wales was to get a higher share of any general spending increase, to reach 115 per cent of English spending. With short commons, policies followed by the Welsh assembly government were 'challenging and radical', according to Mark Drakeford, the second of the three first ministers in the period. His proposal for making council tax fairer by bringing payments closer to property values merited the adjectives. Right to Buy went; affordable housing was promoted; plastic bags were penalized. But elsewhere, differences from England were slight. Theatre and music, for example, after Arts Council Wales cut budgets by a fifth.

The Welsh government was more generous with social care, capping payments even for people with assets above a threshold considerably higher than England's.

In health, the emphasis was in the opposite direction to Lansley, in favour of collaboration, councils having a legal duty since 2014 to promote health and social care integration. Better health outcomes were however hard to spot.

On OECD comparisons, Wales had long had a big problem with schooling. From 2010 it combined early years with the first two years of school to provide a new foundation for learning, and sought to improve teachers' professional development. School performance was assessed but on wider criteria than applied by Ofsted. The IfG pointed out that Wales continued to have a high proportion of low achievers and a low proportion of high achievers: 'the starkly lower performance of secondary school pupils in Wales is notable and consistent over time'. Pupils in Wales seemed to do less well even when controlling for socioeconomic factors.

British no more

Conservatives might once have conserved and unionists united, but not the contemporary Conservative and Unionist Party. It could not comprehend that the state was a guarantor of nationhood, sustaining the diminishing number of institutions with a genuinely British or UK identity. The NHS and the BBC came top of the list, followed by the Post Office, its reputation incinerated. Other symbols of a united kingdom such as Royal Mail had been privatized; it was now fighting residual commitments to delivering letters on a common tariff to Padstow, Pwllheli, Peterhead and Portadown. Carriers of collective identity, such as the Royal National Lifeboat Institution and the climate-concerned Royal Society for the Protection of Birds were subject to assault because their values were deemed too liberal. The same went for Justin Welby, who even though he was primate of all *England* was the man to put the crown on the head of the king of the UK; the Tories had not much use for the gospels and they weren't too sure about Charles, either.

Instead there was GB News, murkily funded, along with a shop-soiled, foreign-owned right-wing press that spent as much time hating the British as it did claiming to speak for England. When it came to media, it wasn't market ideology or some theoretical belief in competition; it was something visceral, a sort of cultural paranoia that fixated on the BBC, though ITV and Channel Four were targeted. Culture secretary Lucy Frazer tore up every convention and tried to instruct BBC staff as if they were civil servants. In an extraordinary example of synecdoche, the BBC's entire output of music, drama and mass entertainment was forgotten because it sought to report politics fairly. Even before the Tories put a former Number 10 director of communications on the BBC board with a remit to disrupt it from within, BBC editors had run scared, appointing journalists who, given their antecedents and reporting styles, could be considered moderately sympathetic to the government. It would never be enough. BBC funding was cut – the licence fee prevented from rising in line with costs. Of course the BBC faced existential challenges, from streamers, social media and the anachronism of the licence; a well-disposed government would have helped it think through solutions. Instead, Australian-American Murdoch was in and out of Number 10 as if it were a second home, and don't forget Cameron's cosy kitchen suppers in the Cotswolds with Rebekah Brooks: hence continuing attacks on the BBC in the mogul's media. The BBC had tried to win favour with ministers, making a commitment to levelling up by shifting production to Cardiff, Glasgow and Salford. It would never be enough. Leave national culture to Netflix, successive culture ministers said, symbols to Sky and British values to Amazon Prime Video.

The only way is up

- Crack down on lobbying and contracts
- Fair elections to the Commons
- Governments forced to follow NAO recommendations
- Strengthen regulators
- Retrain and strengthen civil servant expertise
- Base council tax squarely on property values
- Recreate regional development agencies in England
- Base funding on measured social need
- Reconvene the Leveson inquiry into media
- Secure BBC funding

7

Security: Criminal Neglect

A COUNTRY WHERE Gavin Williamson can be appointed defence secretary was not taking national security seriously. This specimen of Tory incompetence illustrated just how far the defence of the realm had slipped: his qualification for overseeing the army, navy and air force had been keeping a tarantula in his office to show he was boss as chief whip. His response to the Russian poisoning of the Skripals, father and daughter, in Salisbury was breathtakingly embarrassing. The Russians 'should just shut up and go away'. No Aeroflot flights were grounded, no significant freeze on Russian finance or energy operations.

The underfunding of defence? We could buy tractors and 'put really expensive guns on them'. Another wheeze was 'paintball ships trespassing in Gibraltar's waters' to humiliate the Spanish navy. Theresa May is regarded as a sober prime minister, her reputation flattered by the contrast with her successor; it was she who appointed Williamson.

Yet the hapless minister also symbolized the era's confusion, especially over the inter-penetration of home and abroad, between domestic security in the broadest sense and national defence. Historically, generals tilted to the right; after all, Wellington became a Tory prime minister. But now they deviated. The head of the army, General Sir Patrick

Sanders, called for national mobilization to form a citizen army. How could a consumerist society like ours, fragmented and marketized, ever put itself on the war footing that international conditions might now demand? A society moreover where so many children were obese and poor, where school PE had been cut and food industry lobbyists populated ministers' WhatsApp groups? Wellington's playing fields had been sold off.

The lightweight Grant Shapps, another in the long string of defence secretaries, claimed we were in a 'pre-war' period, the forthcoming opponent presumably Russia. His colleagues ignored him. In his 2024 bid to the Treasury he demanded defence spending at 2.5 per cent of GDP, saying it would re-establish our leadership in Europe. A post-Brexit joke. He was refused; those who celebrated austerity had to live with its consequences.

Shapps might have quizzed those colleagues about their attitude towards Putin. Truss, spinning like a top, had hobnobbed with American enthusiasts for the Russian president, including Trump, for whom she said she wished to vote. The voters of Epsom and Ewell who had for years returned the omni-incompetent Chris Grayling now had the Tories' next selection for the constituency, a right-wing fantasist, Mhairi Fraser, another Trump fan, unconcerned by Putin, whose register of risks to the UK seemed to start and end with spending on welfare benefits. Someone might have pointed out to her the forces' chronic inability to recruit, which might have something to do with squaddies' families resorting to food banks. Or it might be related to the doubling of forces personnel seeking mental health support, with long waits for treatment for veterans of Iraq and Afghanistan, the leftovers of wars the UK wished to forget.

However, despite Putin, despite Ukraine, there was little sign of an increased public sense of insecurity. At home and

abroad, safety ranked low in the polls. For all the buccaneer-
ing rhetoric of the Brexit debate, the public showed scant
interest in foreign affairs or national defence. Public appetite for foreign adventures, if it ever existed, had evaporated
after Iraq. MPs refused to back Cameron over intervention in
Syria, but allowed the brief engagement in Libya, helping to
create another failed state in the Islamic world. So disengaged
had the public become that polls showed only one person in
thirty knew the UK had forces in Estonia, ominous as Putin
whipped up war rhetoric on NATO's borders. The invasion
of Ukraine brought public sympathy and generosity but no
recalibration of security. Perhaps ignorance and indifference
served the government well, so voters didn't clock an army
with just 227 battle tanks against Russia's 20,000, give or
take those floundering in the Dnipro mud. By 2023, barely
157 UK tanks were available to undertake operations within
a 30-day period.

On the home front, cyberattacks targeted the NHS, water
companies and nuclear installations, many directed from
abroad. Ministers were curiously ambiguous. Proponents of
national sovereignty, so vocal over Brexit, proved torpid in
investigating let alone prosecuting Russian domestic aggres-
sion. Parliament was told the Star Blizzard group, linked
to the Russian FSB, were behind the leak of official papers,
phished from ministers' emails. Russian spies had targeted
MPs, peers, civil servants and journalists for years: they were
behind a hack that may have influenced the 2019 election.
You did not have to look hard to join the dots between
Johnson, Tory party fundraisers and Russians, which made
Foreign Office protests and summoning of ambassadors
sound somewhat hollow, at least until after Putin's invasion
of Ukraine. And then there were the Chinese ...

Big defence = big state

The land war on European soil sharpened defence conundrums. How was the UK to pay for a 'presence' to keep punching above its weight? Or cope with the Trump-era unreliability of the US? Or meld its defence with that of the Europe it had exited so rudely? The dissonance between the UK's military ambitions and its capability detected by Sir Richard Barrons, former head of the joint forces command, at the end of Cameron's premiership was even more obvious during Sunak's. Truss, garbed like Thatcher in a tank, had not thought about closing the gap. The generals, marshals and admirals tried frighteners. They protested that the UK had more hairdressers – 185,000 – than soldiers. As an election ploy, Sunak offered half-baked service for a handful of 18-year-olds; the generals, desperate for thousands of professional recruits, laughed. The threats to the UK might be diversifying and proliferating, among them Pyongyang and the Houthis. But the collapse of the western presence in Afghanistan wasn't enough to persuade foreign secretary Dominic Raab to cut short his lounging on a Greek beach, leaving inexperienced Foreign Office staff to cope. The formula for effective defence against guerrillas with old AK-47s, improvised explosive devices, drones and landmines did not look like the UK's expensive aircraft carriers and nuclear subs.

From around 2018, the government started panicking. Austerity had done huge damage; reviews promised recovery, but not till the end of the 2020s at the earliest – and that was before the Russians bombarded Kharkiv and Kyiv – leaving what the analysts euphemistically called a 'trough', which even the most obtuse of Chinese, Russian or terrorist planners could see maximized vulnerability. As we will see with the police, the Tories seemed determined to relinquish their historical claim to cherish men and women in uniform. Recruitment had been outsourced to a private firm, which missed its targets for six years in a row. Alarmed, army chiefs openly considered buying in private security companies – mercenaries – to cover for the lack of manpower. In a scathing report in December 2023, the NAO reported that the equipment budget for the forces was an unaffordable black hole, the shortfall between military aspiration and provision costed at £17 billion and growing; budgets were tilted by the cost of commitments to the navy and nuclear weaponry. Defence analyst Malcolm Chalmers said it felt as if the government had lost budgetary – key word – control. It appeared that Johnsonian braggadocio had won: the UK aspired to remain a great power but the government was not going to pay for it. By 2020, the army had 82,000 regulars, 8,200 short of target. Even if there were enough soldiers, they would find it hard to communicate with HQ. Already two decades old, the army's battlefield communications system saw its life being extended into the 2030s, joining the long list of procurements hit by delays and budget overruns. The army was proposing to fight with 'ancient technology', according to Francis Tusa, editor of *Defence Analysis*.

Big defence implied a bigger state. Or big choices, like abandoning the army to concentrate on the navy, or running down nuclear deterrence for the sake of a functioning air force and army. But Tories were tepid, procrastinators, doing nothing to alert let alone change the view of voters, who put defence well below health and education among their spending priorities. Defence austerity had more or less ended by the 2020s, given their commitments to boost spending as a proportion of GDP; that should mean no more cheating by stealing from the international development aid budget to add to the defence budget. But where were the ships and munitions to be made, given the run-down of UK ports and factories? For navy sonar and missile launchers the sovereign UK depended on French firm Thales. Foreign capital and foreign suppliers no longer looked appealing. In 2021, the United Arab Emirates pledged

SECURITY: CRIMINAL NEGLECT

to invest £10 billion, targeting energy, tech and infrastructure, to whoops of joy from Brexiteers claiming it was evidence that Britain was open for business. But within months Tory ministers had rushed to legislate the National Security and Investment Act 2021. The Cabinet Office intervened to halt the Emirates government building up its stake in Vodafone. It wasn't safe to put your defence assets in the control of a Gulf state.

The long decline in the navy's strength was now to be reversed, but support ships and tankers were still being mothballed – and the big question of what for and where lay unanswered. HMS *Queen Elizabeth* needed foreign navies to provide escorts to form a carrier strike group, once it was able to leave port. A broken propeller meant it was late in joining NATO exercises in February 2024. In the months before HMS *Diamond* was deployed to the Red Sea, new recruits to the navy were down again on the previous year, which itself had seen a 27 per cent shortfall. Maybe the new frigates would arrive, but till then it was 'muddling through', said Tusa. The nuclear deterrent ('not fit for purpose', said MPs) was owned and could only be operated at the behest of an increasingly unpredictable and unreliable US. Shapps suffered the embarrassment of being on board HMS *Vanguard*, a British nuclear sub, off the coast of Florida when a Trident missile the UK leased from the Americans misfired and sank in the sea nearby. The mantra remained the same: 'The US and UK are very close allies with a uniquely broad and deep defence and security relationship, and a shared understanding of the challenges we face.' Both parts of the sentence were untrue before Trump entered the White House and became even less credible afterwards.

A more or less arbitrary basis

The purpose and capacity of each arm grew more uncertain. Ceremonial fly-pasts continued, just, though the Red Arrows were shamed by revelations of sexual harassment and bullying. What was *national* defence when French planes were needed to shield our aircraft carriers and foreign forces for our beach assaults? Defence relied entirely on allies and alliances, which were deteriorating. Inter-operability meant close industrial collaboration, but post-Brexit cross-border tariffs would be an obstacle. Sovereignty after Brexit apparently meant depending on other sovereign states. Were British forces going to die in the ditches on the Estonia–Russian border? In official papers the government said the UK remained unconditionally committed to the security of Europe; it wasn't a view expressed on Brexiteer platforms.

It was as if government and nation had closed their eyes and blocked out the crashes and bangs in Eurasia and the Middle and Far East, Trump's dangerous talk and the all-too-visible cracks in what wonks called the rules-based order. If the world was a more dangerous place why make reductions in defence capability 'on a more or less arbitrary basis', asked Sir Jeremy Blackham, former deputy chief of defence staff. The government said the UK was a world-class military partner, with the full spectrum of military capacity at our disposal to 'reinforce Britain's place in the world'. But that capability was paper-thin, a village without General Potemkin, and no one, certainly no Tory minister, could convincingly say what the UK's place was, or could afford to be.

Knives out

There's a parallel story to be told about security at home, featuring the same ambiguous attitudes about the size of the state. Cameron had been surprisingly unafraid to cut police numbers in England dramatically after 2010, by 22 per cent, often losing the most experienced officers. Later the absence of a local police presence started worrying people. The IfG said public awareness of bobbies on the beat reached its lowest recorded level by 2023.

But crime was falling down the list of concerns, with people more upset about not getting a GP appointment and erosion of their household's spending power. Feelings about safety and security may be intensely local, too. The Crime Survey of England and Wales found people's perceptions completely out of kilter with reality, always believing crime was on the rise despite it steadily falling from a peak in 1995. They were better attuned to locality; residents in places with the highest crime were (accurately) most likely to perceive crime rising.

Certain kinds of crime provoked alarm. Young people in towns took to carrying knives when out on the streets, for self-defence they wrongly thought. At the police station in Milton Keynes, we visitors gasped as two large crates of knives dropped with a heavy clatter on the table. Some had been confiscated, some handed in on a no-questions-asked amnesty. Machetes, combat blades, bowie knives, carving knives and very ordinary kitchen vegetable knives, easy to imagine their grisly use. Crimes of violence among the young might be falling, but the heartbreak of mothers weeping over the loss of their boys became a regular TV news item.

Milton Keynes had had a serious knife problem. Thames Valley Police launched Operation Deter with a fanfare of publicity and zero tolerance of knife-carrying. A sculpture was brought to the city, a towering 27-foot 'knife angel' made of 100,000 bladed weapons collected from amnesty bins around the country. The aim was to alert and frighten, while police targeted areas where young people congregated and fights broke out. Boys often only carried knives out of fear of others. Police showed them the facts. Knives did not protect, quite the opposite: the chance of becoming a victim soared if they carried a knife themselves. At the station an officer talked of the 'raw pain of telling families their child has been killed. The hardest thing I've ever had to do.' Operation Deter had worked well: in just two years knife crime here had fallen well below the national average.

Despite the reports, the death rate involving knives was not rising nationally, with 261 homicides by stabbing in 2022. Higher figures for knife crime were partly due to more reporting. Reliable figures come not from police but from hospitals, where the trend was down. The proportion of young people in trouble with the law continued its long-run downwards trend. First-time entrants to youth justice fell from 45,000 in 2010 to 10,000 in 2020. Even thefts of bikes more than halved between 2010 and 2023. There are always fashions in new offences and public anxiety: there was a rise in street racing with cars and attacks by uncontrolled and probably uncontrollable American XL bully dogs.

Untough on the causes

Amid mixed evidence, overall crime did decline: the growth in police-recorded crime was explained by administrative changes. As measured by the Crime Survey of England and Wales, crime fell by a fifth (allowing for the pandemic lockdown, which cut the number of interviews undertaken).

Beneath Tony Blair's 'tough on crime' slogan had lain awareness of its interconnectedness with social conditions. Tories disliked exculpation. The Centre for Social Justice was founded by former Tory leader Iain Duncan Smith on the axiom that whatever the problems of the poor, more money wasn't the answer. 'Dependence', i.e. welfare benefits, was a cause not an alleviation of poverty. His commendation of contraceptive-less marriage clashed somewhat with removing benefits from larger families. Yet eventually even right-wing think tanks have to confront reality, and by 2023 the CSJ was saying the UK was 'deeply divided'.

This blinding discovery was all the more original since the very same think-tankers had led the chorus when Cameron discovered 'Broken Britain' leading up to the 2010 election. In 2023, the CSJ's Social Justice Commission found 'the nation unwell, with deep systemic problems facing those at the bottom of society in danger of becoming entrenched'. Presumably, if broken Britain had been the fault of incumbent Labour, then now this socially divided Britain had to be the fault of the Tories. Apparently not. As for security, the commission quoted a Teessider saying: 'There are no police here. There are no laws or rules, you just do what you want.' Unmentioned went the fact that the police and crime commissioner for Cleveland (which includes Teesside) was Tory. It somehow escaped the report's authors that the government, of which Duncan Smith was a loyal member, had not only cut police numbers but severely damaged the capacity of law courts to deal with offenders.

Still, the social roots of crime were not straightforward. Abundant crime drama and serial killers on screen contradicted the statistics showing a downward sweep since the 1990s. Possible explanations included the removal of the lead from petrol that made brains more antisocial, and a rise in abortions, which reduced the number of unwanted and badly parented children growing up to a damaged life of crime. Since homicide is well reported, its volume was a guide to trends in serious violence: it kept falling. As across Europe, property crime, theft, robbery and burglary all fell.

Policing in crisis

But within the total, specific crimes increased – or were better reported; either way the public was alarmed. Such as sex offences, sharply up. In the year to March 2022, one in fifty adults (an estimated 1.1 million people) experienced sexual assault. #Metoo encouraged women to come forward and report, for example, unwanted sexual touching, previously tolerated but now taken for what it was, assault. During COVID, the murder of Sarah Everard at the hands of a police officer focused public attention on women's safety. One in two felt unsafe walking alone after dark in streets near their home – compared with one in seven men. Reports of violence against the person (a less serious category) also rose. As with unwanted touching, perhaps this reflected a change in culture, which goes some way to explain the discrepancy between finding that crime was decreasing and the one-third increase recorded by the police between 2010 and 2023.

Social norms change, often for the better. The number of traffic officers was halved, resulting in fewer roadside breath tests, down by two thirds from 2009. The chance of getting away with drink-driving must have increased. However, 2021's drink-driving deaths were the same as 2009's, perhaps reflecting shifts in attitudes towards both alcohol and road safety.

More reports to the police didn't lead to more charges and convictions. Maladministration was behind the fall in charging, halved between 2009–10 and 2021–22. HM Inspectorate of Constabulary said the gap was a sign of inefficiency, insufficient supervision of officers and lack of digital forensic capability. The party in power, erstwhile custodians of law and order, oversaw an 'unacceptably low number of crimes solved following investigations'. Prosecutions for sexual assault fell dismayingly. In 2014, 11 per cent of offences ended up with a charge being laid, but by 2021 that had fallen to 3 per cent. Just one in every hundred reported rapes was charged. Police officers did not understand sexual violence and, according to an official 2022 report, 'disproportionate effort' went into testing the credibility of victims' stories. Outbursts of indignation led to promises to improve followed by further reports of disgraceful behaviour and attitudes within the police, especially the Met. Theresa May's long tenure as home secretary had no effect on the misogyny deeply embedded in police culture.

Public confidence had been sapped, then fell sharply after 2020 on the back of high-profile cases of police misconduct. Louise Casey was scathing in her review of the Met. Once the Tories were hand in glove and at ease with the boys in blue. Thatcher, the chief constables and the right-wing press formed a powerful coalition, notably during the notorious confrontation between police and striking miners at Orgreave, noted author Tom Harper. Things fell apart under Cameron. A symbolic moment was the evening in 2012 when chief whip Andrew Mitchell exited Downing Street on his bike. Officers on the gate said he insulted them with the word 'pleb'. The veracity of their evidence was challenged, Mitchell absolved, but the story underneath this fracas was resentment over pay and cuts, which counterintuitively hit Tory areas.

Like the Lansley health deformation, Cameron created police and crime commissioners in a fit of absence of mind, possibly just something to put into the manifesto. He left 30 per cent of police funding to be levied from the increasingly iniquitous council tax – even though councils had lost responsibility to these new arrivals. If the commissioners were meant to reform and discipline the police, their failure was palpable. A decade after their creation, five forces outside London were in 'special measures', under supervision from the constabulary inspectors – who themselves had a case to answer. Voter turn-out for this novel elected office was derisory; nowhere ever above 15 per cent, most people having no idea what they did or why. The NAO found they were not checked and balanced since the panels set up to scrutinize them lacked powers.

Special measures

Later olive branches were proffered to the police, May abandoning the second part of the Leveson inquiry, which had been going to look at corrupt relations with the press. Johnson started a mad scramble to recruit more police, to replace the 20,000 axed. It would have been hard to devise anything less effective. Appointing 46,504 new officers, approximately a third of the total workforce, led to a force bigger than since 2002–03, with the highest ever proportion of women, but proper vetting arrangements were bypassed. Hundreds had joined who shouldn't have, said inspectors; over a third of officers now had less than five years' experience. Nor could they all communicate with each other: the Home Office spent £2 billion on a new comms network for emergency services; eight years later, it had not materialized. Police productivity may even have gone down, given the need to tutor new recruits, some becoming sergeants after only two years. Not surprisingly, the Home Office did not evaluate the impact of the decrease or the increase.

The police were courted with the Police, Crime, Sentencing and Courts Act 2022, which gave them more powers and less accountability, but the effect was nullified when home secretary Suella Braverman went to war, using a Tory conference platform to berate them for 'virtue signalling', by which she meant following modern norms on race and gender. Modernity was an issue. On the streets opportunities for theft and mayhem change. A good police service will both anticipate and plan to deal with emerging threats. Thieves discovered ways of breaking into allegedly secure top-of-the-range vehicles, which were then exported by criminal gangs. Carmakers complained about a lack of police surveillance at ports, and Jaguar Land Rover chief executive Adrian Mardell departed from the usual script by demanding the government delay tax cuts to spend more on police. But carmakers themselves weren't innocent: when they were forced to update security systems, thefts of Range Rovers were a fifth less in 2023 compared with the previous year.

What the police recorded varied with public and media interest – and the cost of living. In the year to September 2023, shoplifting offences rose by nearly a third, the highest level in the two decades with comparable records. Supermarkets began security-tagging baby formula, mothers unable to afford it. These were not just crimes by the poor. Shops were targeted by organized gangs not only after wines and spirits, but also selling on stolen steaks and cheese. Co-op Food complained that police officers turned up at only a fifth of the incidents its staff reported.

There needed to be greater clarity over the police's role in society, said HM Inspectors vainly. The police don't just do crime, yet how little public and policy discussion there was about their role sweeping up and social-ordering. Antisocial behaviour was on the rise, though fewer bothered reporting it: half of people surveyed said the police were not taking it seriously enough, and more reported personal encounters with it. Academics, saying levels had never been so high, blamed austerity for the collapse in youth clubs and youth workers. 'Prior to 2010', according to one, 'we were really good at managing it. But that capacity has been stripped away, not only within policing but in local authorities and youth work.'

A couple of years ago we visited the Bedfordshire Police control centre. We noted how many calls concerned suicide and psychosis. Pressed on staff and budgets, forces started saying they would no longer answer calls concerning psychiatric cases, which chief constables said used up millions of hours of their time. In Bedfordshire, private children's homes had mushroomed. Councils, especially in London, were unable to maintain their own and were increasingly sending children out of area. The police were getting more calls about children absconding from these private homes, sometimes sucked into gangs. 'They arrive here, no one is told, the local authority here knows nothing about it', one officer told us. Local pupil referral units were becoming a magnet for child groomers, paedophiles and recruiters to 'county lines' drug gangs.

Scams and fraud

Among crime growth areas was online fraud; 2023 was a peak year for scams, according to accountants BDO. Only in 2017 did the ONS start including online fraud among the statistics of crime, immediately adding an additional five million offences a year. Anyone online, young or old, has nowadays to be intensely conscious of higher risk: cybercrime now accounted for half of all offences reported by victims. Anxiety was well placed when, as the Police Foundation said, officers' interest seemed oddly slight. Charges for cyber fraud fell and only a tiny fraction of all reported incidents resulted in a charge or summons.

Of course the public are perpetrators as well as victims. In 2013, the last year before the paper tax disc for vehicles was abolished, 0.6 per cent were found to be untaxed. By 2018, that rose to 2 per cent, falling back to around 1.2 per cent in 2023. Here is an example of the state using new technology to cut costs, the unintended consequence a decline in revenues, the Treasury losing at least £120 million a year. People are more honest about paying taxes if they think they will be caught.

COVID was a crime fest. The NAO said billions were stolen. Fraud publicly acknowledged rose from £5.5 billion in the two years before the pandemic to £21 billion in total in the following two years. Of that, £7.3 billion related to pandemic relief schemes. The statutory inquiry, fuelled by some dogged investigative journalism, made public the extent of waste, extravagance and possible fraud in procuring masks and equipment: criminal investigations continue. Tory ministers were complacent, blind or merely willing to give their mates access to a quick buck; these are the same ministers who were so avid to extend no mercy to benefit 'scroungers'. Public bodies 'do not know how much fraud they face' and had not adequately mobilized to counter it. Meanwhile £10 billion a year was being lost to criminal evasion of tax, which was additional to the scores of billions lost to avoidance of tax. The Tories established a new Public Sector Fraud Authority in response to concerns about COVID fraud. It reported that in 2020–21 there was between £33 and £59 billion of fraud and error in government spending and income, unrelated to the pandemic. Ten pence in every pound of the £608.8 billion collected in tax was being lost. If you sincerely wanted to give the NHS an extra £350m a week you only needed to tighten up by a modest amount. Counter-fraud is exciting and rewarding work. Our personal experience with the Audit Commission and the NHS convinces us this type of work attracts dedicated and enthusiastic accountants and officials; remobilized, the government counter-fraud function could potentially win extra billions.

Illegal aid

Security and order depend not only on the police, but on courts, prosecutors and those who administer sentencing. Justice shrank. Protection of rights weakened; access to tribunals and courts was deliberately narrowed. Legal aid had been one of the cornerstones of the 1945 welfare state, intended to make the law accessible to all. No longer. Funds for legal aid dropped from £2.5 billion in 2012 to £1.8 billion in 2022. If the law as a profession had once tilted rightwards, the Tory party and its tabloids now turned against it. Fat cat and leftist became their adjectives of choice for the wig-wearers, not least over asylum.

We visited an evictions court in Chapter 4; people no longer got help in cases against landlords, nor redress when benefits were unjustly withheld. They were now left alone in cases of debt, clinical negligence or infringement of their immigration or education rights. No help for parents in life-changing disputes over custody of children. After aggrieved employees were forced to pay high upfront charges in 2013, cases taken to industrial tribunals dropped by three quarters. The Resolution Foundation has noted that the UK relies heavily on tribunals to enforce the rights of workers, elsewhere uniform and statutory. Needless to say it was the lowest paid who were and are least likely to make a claim when cheated of their earnings.

The 2012 Legal Aid, Sentencing and Punishment of Offenders Act slashed funding for law centres and legal aid solicitors. Those wrongly charged and found innocent were no longer repaid their reasonable costs, so the innocent could lose everything, fall into deep debt even bankruptcy, just to pay for their defence. Cut off your nose to spite your face. Judges found their courts full of people who would not be there if they had been able to instruct a solicitor. Without legal aid, litigants were trying to represent themselves in court, taking more time and burdening judges and court staff. Unresolved housing disputes meant councils spending more on temporary accommodation for evictions. Tenants unable to challenge housing conditions ended up sicker. The C&AG's verdict: ministers 'could not demonstrate a spending reduction for the public purse' overall from those legal cuts.

Justice had not been particularly expensive pre-austerity. Differences in legal regimes within the UK accepted, the country was about in the middle of the range of comparable jurisdictions for the overall cost of justice. On barristers' pay, the government made hay with a few high-profile cases where large fees were levied. Criminal barristers were not well paid and went on strike, with fewer young lawyers choosing crime as their specialism. Even in the higher echelons, disquiet broke out. The head of the Bar Council, Sam Townend KC, feared the legal system would prove less attractive to lucrative foreign litigants once they spotted the stains on the carpets at Southwark Crown Court. His more serious point was that judicial systems are whole, the higher jurisdictions depending on the quality of recruits and lower courts. Here was yet another example of the Tories' inability to think and join up. If you squeeze and constrain opportunities lower down, the pipeline of talent constricts; there are fewer future judges. 'You can't put one part of it in a gilded cage and let everything else fail and still expect to maintain [an international reputation]', in Townend's words.

Injustice

Justice did not prevail. We visited the Colchester call centre run by the children's charity Coram. Desperate parents were ringing in from all over. Staff were under pressure, phones going non-stop: a thousand calls unanswered. A mother was in a state of panic. The court had given her ex-husband visiting rights, but she feared he planned to steal the children away to his home country, Iran. What made her so desperate was the fact that he had taken possession of the children's passports. It was the sort of emergency where legal aid previously would have paid for a solicitor to take urgent action. 'I went to the police but he hasn't committed a crime yet. I'm supposed to go to mediation with him, but it's in London and I can't even afford the train ticket, or to take the time off work and the extra childcare. I'm a nurse and I can't change shifts.'

Coram could only advise: go to mediation or you will look obstructive. You need to go to court to seek an order. You are giving him reasonable access but there's no cast-iron definition of reasonable. You will only get legal aid if there is domestic abuse. The case was complicated; life, families are complicated. If she did get to a family court, she would find herself with forms to fill, procedures to navigate and laws to understand all by herself. After the legal aid cuts, by 2017 only a fifth of family court cases involved parties who both had representation; in a third of cases neither party had a lawyer, and in many it was the woman most likely to represent herself, up against men with barristers.

Hundreds of crown and county courts, tribunals and family courts closed, and the plan was to halve the number of magistrates' courts, vital local symbols of justice. Defendants, plaintiffs, victims and witnesses had to travel further – only to find the swollen backlog of cases meant hearings were postponed or transferred. Justice at a distance, after long delays, undermines any sense of timely connection between offence and adjudication, let alone punishment. Justice delayed fuels a sense of insecurity and loss of control. That epochal word once again.

Suspend sentence on his culpability for a moment. Here's AJ, found guilty in October 2023 of harassing a young woman. Sounds like he deserved punishment. But when he travelled from his home in Morecambe to Blackpool magistrates' court – no mean feat when the 40-mile journey involves either three trains or two buses taking at least two hours – he found a note on the door saying the court was shut. It had been closed because the builders had used RAAC. Blackpool magistrates had translated to Blackburn, where the magistrates' court was also dealing with Preston remand cases, as Blackburn remands had been transferred 15 miles away to Burnley. Judicial mayhem. One Blackpool case involving an Albanian accused of cultivating cannabis plants was called off for the fourth time when an interpreter failed to show up. 'It's happening all the time', said one lawyer. The accused 'have their phones confiscated on arrest, so it's difficult to let them know what has changed – assuming we have been told, which often isn't the case. Some are homeless, so can't receive letters. Most are on benefits so will have borrowed money to get to their nearest court, let alone another one miles away.' The Association of Prison Lawyers complained about access to those convicted or on remand; of the 87,000 in prison at the end of September 2023, 16,000 were awaiting trial or sentencing. Appointments backed up, lawyers having to wait months for video calls despite the Ministry of Justice saying the number of such calls had increased 16 per cent in 2022.

Still locking more up

In austerity, the Ministry of Justice had taken the hardest hit. Self-assured secretary Kenneth Clarke promised to reform ever-lengthening sentences to reduce prison numbers. But when he tried, Cameron surrendered to the hue and cry led by the *Daily Mail*, sacked Clarke and prison numbers went soaring upwards again. In his place came Chris Grayling, brandishing stiffer sentences and banning books for prisoners. Disaster followed.

The UK already locked more people up. France and the UK have the same size of population; in 2023, France had 75,000 prisoners, the UK 95,700. The 123 jails in England and Wales housed double the population of 30 years ago, bursting their capacity; built for 500 inmates, Pentonville had 1,000. Amid overcrowding, prisoners spent more time locked in their cells, with less education, training or treatment, pushing suicide rates up along with higher turnover among overstretched staff. Staff were less experienced, reducing prospects for rehabilitation. Crime might be falling long-term, but there was no evidence that more prison was a cause.

Along with policing, prisons had long been a site of Tory psychodrama. MPs and ministers wanted to be seen to be tough but without spending more. Unlike health or social services, prison is one of the few services where the state has immediate control over demand: by fiat it can change sentencing guidelines and cut numbers. Instead, the government chose to expand the list of crimes punishable with prison and to lengthen sentences. There was one improvement. The number of incarcerated children dropped, the Howard League for Penal Reform together with the Sainsbury Foundation having persuaded chief constables to keep most out of the criminal justice system, where they risked lifetime recidivism. The Howard League has no relation with Michael Howard, whose 'prison works' mantra still echoed, appealing to that hard, atavistic strain in the Tory psyche.

The prisons the Tories inherited were nothing for Labour to be proud of. Things got considerably worse: real spending fell by 16 per cent and prison officer numbers at one point dropped by 26 per cent despite numbers of prisoners being at an all-time high. Assaults on staff tripled. A new generation of synthetic drugs, spice most common, were lethal, psychosis-inducing and harder to detect. The UK might be behind the curve in drone technology, but criminal gangs were already adroitly flying packets of drugs over prison walls. Successive inspection reports said prisons had become very dangerous places, forcing the government to reverse and to re-recruit several thousand staff. In 2021, ministers committed to spending £3.75 billion for 20,000 new places by the mid 2020s. But refurbishment costs had risen. Planning permission for new prisons was slow in coming, and even with expansion at big city jails, for example Birmingham and Liverpool, inmate numbers were set to rise to over 106,000 by 2027.

The system was choked. Cells were blocked by remand prisoners waiting for the blocked courts. So back to Clarke, as the Tories were forced after all to legislate to cut sentence length, suspend short sentences and bring in community orders. Justice minister Alex Chalk said jails would start releasing low-level offenders before the end of their sentences. It was a huge and little-publicized turnaround. Tough on crime had given way to moderate toughness on the causes of bursting jails.

The public service ethos persisted, a kind of miracle. Despite austerity, despite *Mail* and *Telegraph* fanaticism, despite ministerial incompetence, the state was able to retain excellent, dedicated people. Their stoicism astonished us. We visited HMP Woodhill in Milton Keynes. Its governor, Nikki Marfleet, had the courage and imagination to say, 'Start at the beginning. It's Sure Start we need, to help families from the day a baby's born or before. Damage is done so young, that's where I'd put all the resources. That's what makes most difference, saving people at the start.' She had researched youth crime, identifying reasons why gang membership was attractive; her vision also included overstretched social services, schools and mental health.

Here she was, at the very end of the line, when everything else had failed. At Woodhill, as elsewhere, overcrowding meant two prisoners in cells built for one, barely space for two men to stand up at the same time. An inspection report noted deterioration in safety and activity, chronic staff shortages and inexperience. Yet the governor's effort and commitment to a positive culture won praise and admiration. She told us that more staff had at last been recruited, though nothing could make up for lost experienced officers. She had even resorted to urging the residents of nearby Milton Keynes to join. Little wonder the NAO concluded that the Prison and Probation Service did 'not provide sufficient activities to prepare prison leavers with a significant deterioration in the quality of release planning and rehabilitation services in recent years'.

No previous experience

One man bears most responsibility for that. This Tory typified many of the era's never-mind-the-facts, ignore-the-experts style of government. 'Sometimes', he said, 'we just have to believe something is right and do it.' This was of course Grayling. If anyone tries to argue Cameron was some sort of enlightened moderate or May an efficient prime minister, think Grayling.

So he spent heavily on consultants biased towards privatization, and contractors replaced the probation service. Because even he could see that markets would have a built-in incentive not to deal with high-risk offenders, he had to retain a skeletal public body – to which, of course, the contractors immediately tried to pass on all cases likely to cost them money. Four out of ten offenders were being supervised only by telephone calls every six weeks instead of face-to-face meetings. Many of the escalating numbers of the homeless were ex-offenders, released unsupervised with £46 in their pockets and nowhere to go. Payment by results collapsed because keeping people out of jail demands accommodation, employment, social support, precisely the public services being shrunk. It was all, a senior civil servant said ingenuously after the event, a bit more complicated than they had thought. If Ministry of Justice officials knew so at the time, they either kept silent or were ignored.

Little wonder that author Ian Dunt found Grayling the most compelling example of the reasons for probation failure. Ignorance was bliss; chaos was no accident. 'He'd demonstrated no previous experience of the criminal justice system. He'd shown no evidence of having studied it, or worked in it or researched it. So without any expertise or experience, Grayling made a decision. He would privatize probation. He would burn the existing probation model to the ground and start again from scratch, using market mechanisms.'

Determined to make no admission of guilt, the May government poured extra money in, hoping the companies would come good. Eventually they gave up and recreated a public probation service for England, re-recruiting staff sacked or transferred to contractors, desperately trying to recover offender records. By the end of 2023, thousands of orders forming part of community sentences had not been completed, years after being made. Without community sentences, the government's own ambitions for cutting prison overcrowding could not be realized. Michaela Hall, murdered by a serial offender wrongly graded as medium risk, was one of the victims of the failing attempts to mend the failed privatization, her inquest heard.

Another example. In 2012, in the government's dislike of expertise, the Forensic Science Service was abolished, pushing DNA analysis and sample examination out to a miscellany of private laboratories. An official regulator was retained, who promptly warned that financial pressures were compromising quality and jeopardizing justice in serious criminal cases. Again and again, it's that notion of system – understanding that ill-considered, often anarchic decisions here will have knock-on consequences there.

The only way is up

- Restore legal aid
- A new plan for rehabilitation to reduce prison numbers
- Rebuild and restaff the courts
- Make national security central to company takeovers
- New norms for reporting and dealing with sex offences
- Better policing of cybercrime and fraud
- Clean up Russian influence in UK politics
- Abolish police and crime commissioners
- Improve incentives for criminal lawyers

8

Equalities: Unjust Rewards

'WE'RE ALL IN it together', said George Osborne, before falling from heaven (HM Treasury) to cushioned patronage and preferment. He landed plush and flush in the City plus a bonus chairing the British Museum despite having pillaged the arts in successive budgets. He was spot-on if the 'we' who were in it together meant the coterie, wearers of the same old school tie, fellow members of the Bullingdon and graduates of Oxford University.

Being in it together meant chums looked after you in the way of his Russian mate, son of a KGB goon, who received a peerage – and made Osborne editor of the London *Evening Standard*. Or Cameron, whose Australian pal paid him handsomely to ransack his contacts list on behalf of Greensill Capital. And so on. Johnson's buddy paid for his wife's exclusive wall coverings. Truss's sponsors ensured that despite the most egregious political failure of modern times she was well supplied with lucrative speechmaking gigs around the world. No wonder the Glasgow bra queen looked at them and wanted a piece of that upper-class action when COVID contracts were being handed out. Osborne did his plutocratic duty and left behind a country where the rich were richer.

Company directors proved immune to public shaming. We sat through annual meetings where the directors on the platform clearly found that subjecting themselves to one day of mild embarrassment at a shareholders' shindig was worth the millions in pay and bonuses nodded through by distant mega-institutions that never turned up to hear rebellious small-timers' objections. That's income: we will come to the extraordinary acceleration that saw the wealth of the top 1 per cent multiply 31 times since 2010.

For millions of others, low pay became endemic while austerity did great damage to the infrastructure of solidarity: leisure, youth, art. Day centres, children's centres, all places where you meet, sites of social belonging, now shut, along with libraries, community halls, post offices, local bus services, parks, sports clubs, museums and galleries. The collapse of the high street accelerated, meeting places for friends, mothers and daughters in familiar old department stores in retreat, replaced by charity shops, slot machine parlours, nail salons, vape shops or often sad gap-toothed vacant shopfronts. Rising fares and cuts to benefits for young families and those with disabilities isolated more in their homes. The number of people living alone went on rising, reaching 8.3 million by 2022. Theresa May, desperate for a gimmick, appointed the first ever minister for loneliness … whose role lasted barely months.

Solidarity presupposes we know who we are. Pundits pontificated about identity politics. On the ground, Louise Casey, serial leader of inquiries, found a lack of coherent identity across urban England, groups and entire places isolated, cut off from one another by race, age or sheer inability to reach out to others as council services withdrew. She blamed culture and religion as well as government inaction. Communities were 'not only holding citizens back but run contrary to British values and sometimes our laws. Time and time again I found it was women and children who were the targets of these regressive practices.' Foreign events amplified divisions at home. Street disturbances in Leicester echoed politics in India and Pakistan; the Hamas attacks on Israel in October 2023 showed how international allegiances shaped and exacerbated domestic difference.

So 'we' were a puzzle. The heightened sense of belonging among those whose will was supposedly expressed by the Brexit vote was evanescent. Sentiment stirred inchoately, Englishness and Britishness shape-shifting and confused. The UK central bank, though also Scotland's central bank, continued to be called the Bank of England, albeit having to recruit a Canadian (Mark Carney) to run it. (He, incidentally, ended up warning that inequality was the greatest threat to economic growth.) If 'we' was more readily felt in Scotland and increasingly in Wales, Brexit sandpapered the old divide in Northern Ireland. Like Pep Guardiola and Sarina Wiegman, Carney belonged to an elite class of welcome immigrants. The others formed an anonymous, threatening mob on tabloid front pages. Yet the very same front pages might the next day describe one of them as a life-saving neighbour, a pioneering NHS doctor or a necessary barista. So did 'we' include Muslims, black people, Romanians, asylum-seekers? Leave, UKIP and Reform were driven by coded and all-too-explicit references to 'them', bearded, burka'd or Bulgarian.

Despite austerity, despite Brexit, despite policies deliberately to divide, a stock of social capital remained, which could still be a foundation stone. We'll illustrate that shortly, through support for hugely popular charities that defied meaner instincts. But first it's necessary to record a great disappointment.

The COVID dividend that wasn't

Through the pandemic washed a great surge in social concern, expressed in volunteering, delivering medicines and food parcels to neighbours and clashing pots and pans for the NHS on

Thursday-evening doorsteps. Many thought a corner had been turned and a new era of national unity had begun. Polls found a heightened expectation that people would stay together as we recovered. According to Andy Haldane, head of the Royal Society of Arts, the crisis had 'reinforced values of community purpose and social solidarity'. The great contemporary historian Peter Hennessy heard echoes of the Attlee era and its ethos of mutual obligation and solidarity. But it wasn't to be.

With recovery, attitudes reverted. Even during the pandemic, social explorers consciously setting out in the footsteps of Orwell to savour the mood of the nation found plenty of disharmony and discord. It was citizens of the world (i.e. of nowhere, said Theresa May) vs Ashfield, Ashington and other bricks in the fallen Red Wall. Before becoming head of a right-wing think tank, the writer Sebastian Payne gleefully recorded the negativism of the north. His interviewees grumbled resentfully, refusing to join the dots, complaining about schools and the NHS but parading their new allegiance to the Tory party that had caused them to collapse.

Fellow feeling

Proxies for solidarity and mutual obligation are charitable giving and volunteering. Time dropped by about 15 per cent, in terms of hours offered. In 2022, the National Council for Voluntary Organizations found fewer people taking part in sponsored events and a big drop in campaigning. Cameron's vaunted Big Society – was it ever any more than ad man's flatulence? – looked smaller: cuts weakened the voluntary sector while increasing demand. Calls on Citizens Advice rose sharply, up by a fifth in the two years from October 2022, especially about housing and debt.

Charity income fell in real terms, with less money in people's pockets. Yet those on the lowest incomes have always given away a higher proportion of their money than the rich, the north-east the most generous. Here was an example, from Hartlepool. Frances Connolly and husband Patrick were living in a rented terraced house when, on New Year's Day 2019, they won the EuroMillions jackpot of £115 million. Since then they have given away huge sums. When we talked to Frances in Hartlepool, warm, funny and deeply engaged with solving other people's misfortunes, she spoke of her natural repugnance for pointless luxury and waste: 'I'm never going to be part of the jet set', she told us. Their charities donated hundreds of tablets and laptops for young carers, schoolchildren and care-home residents whose relatives could not visit. Frances packaged clothes, pyjamas and toiletries for the destitute, especially refugees and asylum-seekers. Finding small charities struggling, she pulled local soup kitchens and food providers into working together.

And yet the couple's phenomenal win amounted to barely twenty years' salary for a far-from-brilliant corporate chief executive. Their generosity of spirit stands out, but also Frances's observation that charity is not the answer to inequality. She knew so much more than the top dog we met on a high floor at Canary Wharf for our book *Unjust Rewards*, who had hyped up philanthropy, promising 'tax us less and we'll see the money well spent'. In fact the very rich give randomly, according to whim, and not very much.

Austerity reduced income, including that of the Royal National Lifeboat Institution. But the 2019 onslaught launched against it by the *Daily Mail* and Tory MPs for saving lives on the high seas – those of migrants – gave a fillip to donations, which in 2022 shot up to £66.5 million. Either the attackers had lost touch with Middle England, or that mysterious land was bifurcating. It did unite over animals: the RSPCA's total income in 2022 was £152 million.

The wellsprings of belonging, sharing and caring had not run dry. The era's most emblematic charity had to be the Trussell Trust, which supported local food banks. Its total income in 2022–23 was £58 million, with donated food worth additional sums. The 420 or so local charities running 1,400 banks across the UK provided three million food parcels during 2022–23, involving 12,000 churches and 36,000 volunteers. In low-wage Knowsley, the Big Help Project was running 10 banks handing out food parcels to 10,000 people each year, with baby boxes for newborns and paint for decorating homes. Like others, it depended on a dynamo individual – Peter Mitchell, a former private-sector finance director. He observed astutely: 'People do say to me we're letting the government off, we're filling the big holes they've made in the welfare state. And that's true but what can you do?' In 2010 there had been no food banks in the whole Liverpool region: the first opened in 2011.

Hardship wasn't a northern phenomenon. Follow the yellow Cotswold paving stones and even in Witney, Cameron country, you found evidence of his government's depreda-tions. Here the food bank had crammed into a garage. On the day we visited, the woman in charge was crying after a man had come with bags of food as thanks for what he'd received when he had been left destitute waiting for delayed benefits. Tories were embarrassedly ambivalent. In 2013, the prime minister angrily blocked a £22 million grant from the European Union to help finance food banks. Nothing to do with benefits, snapped Lord Freud, work and pensions minister. Confronted with armed forces families resorting to food banks, defence minister Johnny Mercer tried the line that queuing for food parcels was a lifestyle choice. In February 2024, the DWP stopped issuing benefit claimants with referral slips to take to food banks, verifying their need. A spokesperson said coldly that it was up to food banks to decide who should receive their support. While deputy chair of the Tory party, before defecting further rightwards, the MP for Ashfield, Lee Anderson, implied the existence of food banks was somehow a plot against the government. By then, however, the official tune had changed. The cameras rolled when Duncan Smith was filmed helping Christmas collections for a food bank at a supermarket: Conservative Central Office urged MPs to tweet pictures of their food bank efforts.

Decade of disconnections

In 2020, we characterized the prior decade as a time of mutual disrespect and distrust. The common centre was besieged by the right laying claim to a Britishness strictly defined by its own tribal (Tory) identity; from the left came grievance and encouragement for a sense of diversity that pushed people further away from collective belonging. Being trans was one example of people seeking to label themselves as separate and specific in their victimhood. The intense individualism that sometimes lay behind the new politics of gender could, philosophically and perversely, turn oddly close to the Thatcherite impulse that put the singleton before the collective. That didn't stop the Tories trying to exploit culture wars, the tag imported from the US, to beat up the left and the 'woke', as a way of diverting attention away from the consequences of austerity, class, poverty and inequality.

They succeeded, for most of their years in power. The work was started by Osborne and Cameron, their successors following on. They tightened the screws on benefit claimants, despite very low unemployment, smearing them as idlers, skivers and scroungers, in bed with the blinds down while others went out to work. This wasn't just a UK line of attack. In its rightwards phase the Macron presidency tightened the (more generous) French system, cutting out-of-work benefits for workers over 55 to pressure them back into employment, ministers coining the phrase *chômeur profiteur* – the free-loading unemployed.

In the UK, work was decreasingly valued in both a financial and cultural sense. Jobs remained available almost everywhere, just not good, secure and well paid. Employees on high pay, defined as one and a half times the median hourly rate, formed only a quarter of the workforce. Pay levels rose after the pandemic, helped by increases in the minimum wage and shortages of staff, notably in health and social care, leisure and sales. But even so, they did not return to pre-crash levels.

Low pay

The poorest households were hard at work, their low-paid jobs accounting for two thirds of employment growth. Tories who had always stoutly opposed Labour's introduction of a minimum wage did an about-turn and started to push it up when they realized they could gesture without the state paying. The Resolution Foundation called this a policy triumph. Up to a point. The proportion in work paying them less than the poverty threshold hit a record low of 8.9 per cent in 2023, but 334,000 employees were still being paid under the legal minimum. And poorer working families lost 63 pence in Universal Credit for every pound extra in their wages. Overall, real pay was not forecast to return to 2008 levels until 2028.

Rights a century in the winning had all but vanished for those in the gig economy. Managers' arbitrary whims kept the work-force in a kind of servitude, where half of those on shifts got less than a week's notice of their forward schedules, a torment for parents with childcare or those with second jobs. Competing for much-needed extra hours, complainants risked falling out of managers' favour. To restore decent pay, employees needed to rebalance power in the workplace by joining unions. But they didn't or couldn't. Only a quarter of the workforce were now unionized compared with half when Thatcher became prime minister, amid a drumbeat of anti-union propaganda from the right-wing press, not just when strikes were in the offing.

Cameron's pal Adrian Beecroft told him in a report to scrap existing workplace protections. He didn't dare, but employers exploited the opportunities they had. So *Financial Times* reporter Sarah O'Connor found shops in Leicester's garment district paying as little as £3.50 an hour, less than half the then minimum. Clothes for brands such as Boohoo and Missguided were produced in sweat shops, where staff got no sick pay, many of the jobs taken by recent migrants, often from Asia. In this twilight world, taxes and National Insurance weren't paid, safety standards ignored. The balance could only be redressed by an active state. Instead, there was now just one labour market inspector per 35,000 workers, three times fewer than the International Labour Organization standard. We kept asking HM Revenue & Customs (HMRC) for an interview with a minimum-wage inspector. They prevaricated, probably embarrassed at the paltry number of criminal prosecutions for failing to pay the minimum wage. In only half of cases pursued were arrears ever awarded.

Tribunals were the only recourse, but as we saw in the previous chapter, the government imposed huge fees. After rebuff in the courts, in 2024 the government said it was going to reintroduce these charges. Note the continuity between Cameron and Sunak, one supposedly liberal, the other supposedly pragmatic. They said they believed in fair competition; they tilted the odds in employers' favour.

Migration

Immigration was and remains the wickedest of issues, partly because, in the UK, it meant looking inwards rather than out, querying the economic free-for-all set in train under Thatcher and sustained by her successors. This was something the Tories simply could not do, so migration policy was fatally undermined.

Migration was inseparable from diversity and ministers oscillated between acceptance and regret. By the 2020s, the UK's foreign-born population was approximately 14 per cent, a share similar to the United States and Spain but smaller than in Australia or Canada. The related figure that alarmed the right was the 28.8 per cent of UK births to non-UK-born mothers (largely because non-UK-born women were more likely to be of childbearing age). Embracing the far right was a constant temptation, whether to out-UKIP UKIP or because the Tory party semi-consciously sought racists to balance its recruitment of the illiberal progeny of non-white migrants. In 2018, the UN's special rapporteur said austerity and immigration policy had made the UK more racist, citing the hostile environment policy adopted by May, who sent trucks out and about in urban areas with 'Go Home' emblazoned on their sides. That set the context for the Windrush scandal, with officials working on the crude assumption that removing as many people as possible was policy, regardless of law or justice.

Mismanagement of the conjoint issues of race and migration rested on a refusal to confront the public with hard facts and choices. The gulf between public belief and fact was allowed to grow. Migration was a statistical minefield; exits from the UK weren't properly counted; the public did not believe official figures. The Tories could have picked up the baton dropped by Labour and brought in identity cards to make the counting easier and illegal employment harder, but that was anathema to the anti-statist right, who often paradoxically were the same ones who abhorred immigration.

The public believed the untruth that three out of five people who came to the UK were asylum-seekers when, in

2022, refugees (including 114,000 Ukrainians) were just 316,000 out of a total of 1.2 million migrants, the rest of whom came with visas. Right-wing media, their lies and distortion amplified in cyberspace, claimed welfare pulled people in. But benefits here were meaner than in France and the rest of the EU, and the Home Office itself had concluded that the 'role of welfare policies, economic factors and labour market access is limited, as many asylum-seekers have little to no understanding of policies and the economic conditions of a destination country'.

The UK was not alone. Stricter measures to deal with migrants arriving in Germany were agreed by chancellor Olaf Scholz, and NGOs criticized Italy's plans to create centres in Albania to accommodate asylum-seekers. For the government the fantasy solution was Rwanda. Sunak enthusiastically took up a bogus plan proposed by home secretary Suella Braverman based on a deal to send undocumented arrivals there. At maximum the central African country could take a few hundred, nowhere near the 36,704 'irregular arrivals' in 2023, at a probable cost of £230,000 per migrant. The government responded that it would only be £170,000 per person. Viewers of *Match of the Day* were bemused to see Arsenal's hoardings flashing 'Come to Rwanda': an increasingly problematic tourist destination. The scheme's legality was serially challenged, prompting calls to abandon the European Convention on Human Rights, to the stupefaction of the millions who had believed propaganda saying it was connected with the EU, which the UK had exited. It wasn't just callousness – an immigration minister ordering murals of Winnie-the-Pooh and Mickey Mouse to be painted over in a child migrant reception centre in Kent. This was willed myopia about the causes of refugee flows across countries and continents and small-state incapacity in accommodating and processing the arrivals.

Migration into the UK was the much bigger phenomenon. The flow of plumbers, builders and fruit-pickers after EU enlargement in 2004 stopped abruptly in 2016. But Europe, despite Farage and Johnson, had never been the whole story. Non-EU workers receiving official employer-sponsored visas increased steadily from 2012 and again after Brexit. There were 968,000 non-EU long-term arrivals in the year ending June 2023: that was over two and a half times more than recorded in 2019. This surge in immigration from further afield certainly wasn't something the Brexit campaigners had plastered on the side of a bus.

We looked at the reasons in Chapter 2. For many the prime attraction was openness – lots of low-paid, unskilled jobs together with minimal levels of inspection and ineffective domestic identity controls. Four out of ten of those moving to the UK for at least a year said their main reason for moving was work; for dependents and others it was an important indirect reason. Tories were reluctant to own up to the contradictions. Simply put, the UK was failing to train its own people and to pay them enough. Towards the end of 2023, the Sunak government panicked, introducing tougher curbs on family dependants and increasing the earnings threshold – except for care workers. Some 146,000 visas were granted to the latter in 2023 because, Unison general secretary Christina McAnea said, the system 'would implode without migrant care staff'. Controlling migration would require radical changes in socio-economic policy. The government's own independent adviser, Professor Brian Bell, spelled it out: if you cared about net migration, then pay home-grown care workers properly.

Class

Care workers didn't belong to the 'fortunate few' whose advantages were not going to be entrenched, said May on entering Number 10. 'We will do everything we can to help anybody, whatever your background, to go as far as your talents will take you.' Everything short of addressing income and wealth inequality and structured disadvantage. Perhaps she was prompted by evidence that two thirds thought it government's responsibility to reduce the gap between people with high and low incomes, similar to opinion in Sweden and Germany and substantially higher than in the US.

This followed the Tories' odd dalliance with social mobility. Ironically, no sooner had the Bullingdon boys arrived in Downing Street than reports proliferated on how few people from working-class backgrounds were getting into the arts, theatre, law, journalism, finance – or any other high-paying desirable jobs. Future Hamlets were going to be Harrovians at this rate; already virtually no player of the bassoon in major orchestras had been educated in a state school. But when Tory ministers talked of mobility they always meant up, choosing to forget that without downward mobility – perhaps their own children falling down the snakes – the ladders could not carry others up, up and away. Mobility was a euphemism. The social truth that dared not speak its name was class.

By 2017, the members of the Social Mobility Commission established by Cameron could stand the contradictions no longer and resigned en masse, blaming austerity for making wealth and property ownership even more influential. The facts were incontrovertible. Michael Marmot, professor of epidemiology at University College London, revisited his own 2010 report after a decade to find disparity between the classes growing in life chances, health and chances of dying early. More than ever, birth was destiny. With typical vehemence, education secretary Damian Hinds said 'more was to be done' to close the eleven-month gap in attainment at the age of five between poor children and their contemporaries, a gulf that grew as they advanced through their school years.

The government couldn't – didn't – dispute the facts, but the response was piecemeal, limited. Disadvantaged students qualified for some subsidies. Employers were exhorted to take more people from lowly backgrounds in 'opportunity areas' and various bungs came from transient ministers. But here was the verdict of their own Centre for Social Justice: 'Those at the bottom of society barely feel these benefits amongst the general experience that life has become more difficult, challenges have become more complex, and poverty has become more entrenched.' That's one of those words you keep coming across in the social reporting of the era. Entrenched.

Look at an initiative to address the acute shortage of housing for military families (another consequence of austerity). The Ministry of Defence told the army that units should be allocated according to family size, not military rank. A platoon of officers' wives went on the attack: how could a colonel be put in a poky two-bed semi while some private with a horde of children got the garrison mansion? Officers and men would mingle! Squaddies might inhabit the best homes! Rosie Bucknall, wife of a captain, accused the ministry of utter betrayal, while General Sir Patrick Sanders (son of a lieutenant colonel, boarding-school-educated) said the plan jeopardized 'the social fabric of the army'. The government struck its colours in panic.

Taking the knee

But the social fabric of the UK was in the throes of change, whether the generals liked it or not. England and Wales went on diversifying: 18 per cent were recorded as ethnic minorities in the 2021 census, compared to 14 per cent in 2011. The Tories didn't dare dislodge Labour's 2010 Equality Act that made it unlawful to harass or victimize those with the 'protected characteristics' of age, disability, race, religion, sex or sexual orientation or those who underwent gender assignment. (What consequences might have flowed if class had led that list.) The act was enforced by the Equality and Human Rights Commission, which hung on despite repeated assaults from the Tory benches.

A wave of popular indignation followed Black Lives Matter. Football teams took the knee as part of the pre-match ritual, and attention turned to British history and, since the sixteenth century, the centrality of colonialism and slavery. The *Daily Mail* was aghast at the National Trust rewriting captions on statues and paintings. In English schools, under ministerial edict, terms of reference for a history curriculum panel omitted the word 'colonial'. But history is never static and culture warriors' attempts to stop Britannia sinking beneath the waves were doomed: no government censorship could still the tumult of questioning and rethinking about the imperial past. After the statue of Edward Colston, slaver and magnate, was toppled into Bristol harbour in 2020, attorney general Suella Braverman referred aspects of the case to the appeals court, hoping to make political capital. The fact that she was non-white but extremely right-wing was perceived as a win-win. Her forensic skills were demonstrated later when, with typical moderation, she wrote, 'The truth is that the Islamists, the extremists and the anti-Semites are in charge now.'

Despite brown and black faces around Tory cabinets, a survey of 10,000 black Britons found 88 per cent reporting racial discrimination at work, with similar proportions saying the police unfairly targeted black people and that racial identity was the biggest barrier in schools. Another inquiry found that more than a third of people from ethnic and religious minorities had experienced racially motivated physical or verbal abuse. Ethnic minorities were poorer; gaps in relative earnings were wide; discrimination in hiring and disciplinary proceedings and promotion were rife; they suffered most in the pandemic. Louise Casey found that black boys were still not getting jobs, white children from low-income homes also doing badly in education; Muslim girls were getting better grades but lacked decent employment opportunities. Inquiries were mounted into school exclusion, race in the workplace, the treatment of minority people in the criminal justice system, deaths and serious incidents in police custody. Yet the UK seemed to have become more at ease with racial difference. 'The UK was among the most comfortable with neighbours who are immigrants or of a different race', according to a 2023 survey.

Tory tergiversation was most evident during the tenure of the 'piccaninny' prime minister. Johnson felt he had to respond to the Black Lives Matter upsurge. The inquiry he ordained whitewashed well, denying the existence of institutional racism. Its findings were heartily welcomed by the equalities minister, Kemi Badenoch, who presumably did not think she fitted the black stereotype so crudely etched by Johnson. With her strong doctrinal dislike of state intervention, the Equality Hub she created in the Cabinet Office was fated never to be heard of again, ditto the Office for Health Disparities in the NHS.

Sunak, of Indian origin, liked to boast of a racially diverse front bench. But how they twisted and turned. Senior Tories could now smear Muslims with impunity. And black women. When a big Tory donor and major beneficiary of NHS contracts was caught saying the MP Diane Abbott made him 'hate all black women', Sunak simultaneously dithered and acted decisively – refusing to return the tainted £10 million. Health secretary Stephen Barclay ordered NHS managers to stop recruiting to roles promoting equality, diversity and inclusion, oblivious to problems of racism and discrimination affecting staff as well as patients. It had to be explained to him that the NHS depended critically on non-white staff and that regulators had demanded fair promotion of ethnic minorities.

The cynical truth, manifest in the behaviour of Gove and May, was that the Tories weren't sure whether race offered a political opportunity or a policy challenge. The Home Office's own log of hate crimes in England and Wales showed an upward trend, driven partly by better police recording of incidents. Gove's Brexit campaign was a clear cause: an Opinium survey found the proportion of people from ethnic minority backgrounds saying they had been targeted by a stranger was increasing, from 64 per cent in 2016 to 76 per cent in 2019. Hate crimes increased again following a spate of terror attacks – Finsbury Park mosque, London Bridge, Westminster and the Manchester Arena. Gove intervened ham-fistedly in Birmingham. Schooling in mainly Muslim areas provoked clashes, parents objecting to sex and relationship syllabuses that had been approved by inspectors and were widely used in other schools. Get (Muslim) religion out of schools was the implicit cry; not religion, since a third of English schools were still run by Christian churches, extraordinarily divisive in an essentially atheist country. Remember how Gove, backed by the hate-fomenting *Daily Mail*, had sent a bible to every school.

Poverty

He had not underlined Matthew 19:24 and Christian doctrine on riches and poverty. On the latter Gordon Brown put it well in an article in February 2024. It was as if the government had put a D-Notice– a legal silencer – on the issue. The very word had been banned: civil servants referred instead to 'low income'.

The government relied on both public ignorance of the complex benefit system and a distinctly English censoriousness about the moral failings of the poor. Brown's point touched on a sort of conspiracy. It suited the right-wing media either to ignore poverty or, along with sensationalist television producers, to seek out bizarre characters and freak cases to feed a narrative about skivers living the life of Riley on benefits. Sleight of hand: the government played with different measures, especially absolute poverty. *Daily Mail* and Murdoch journalists were fixated on poor families owning mobile phones and smart televisions. The assumption was that if you could get by in 2010 on a certain income, you could do the same in 2024. Logic suggested that by that standard, year by year as the economy grew, fewer should be poor. But come 2024, the number officially recorded as in absolute want had risen to 12 million, including 3.6 million children. It's worth pausing on the enormity of that figure. Those people, our fellow citizens, were trying to live on less money than they had relied on 14 years previously. This wasn't some abstract condition. Perhaps as many as 3.7 million did not have enough money regularly to buy food.

The true picture is worse. As GDP and living standards rise, so any reasonable definition of poverty must also change. Back to those mobile phones and televisions. Poverty is relative to society's norms. Mobile phones are a necessity of life. The DWP demands all benefit claims are now made online. In March 2024, research found that nearly half the families with children fell below basic digital living standards, lacking internet access, laptops and fundamental skills, many unable to send a simple email. No wonder educational gaps were widening.

Every year the Joseph Rowntree Foundation asked the public what were the bare necessities of life then calculated a Minimum Income Standard (MIS) – the government itself forsook any official measure of what was needed for survival. The sum naturally changed over the years. A couple with two children where one parent worked full-time on the minimum wage were found to be living on three quarters of the MIS. The main measure of poverty is that used by government statisticians around the world, income relative to the average. To be in poverty is to live on less than 60 per cent of median income. In 2023, the relative poverty threshold for a couple with children aged five and fourteen was £25,300 a year. After housing costs, 14.3 million of our fellow citizens were in poverty. One third of all the children in the UK, 4.2 million, were living in households below that line.

Poor children

Aside from recent migrants, the UK birth rate was in free fall, disquieting some – nationalists tend to be natalists. But in a 2012 speech, Cameron made it quite clear what kind of births were valued. 'Quite simply', he complained, 'we have been encouraging working-age people to have children and not work.' Natalists might instead have worried about the fact that UK children were becoming shorter than their European counterparts. Food banks and baby banks providing basic baby equipment and milk had become a staple of many families' lives.

Tony Blair had made a famous speech pledging to abolish child poverty within 20 years: by the time Labour left office, they had almost hit the halfway mark, a million fewer poor children. Cuts to benefits since, added to the effects of stagnant or falling wages for low earners, meant poverty rates were heading back to the level Labour inherited in 1997. A staggering proportion of all children were now living this kind of life, their parents forced to skip meals to see them fed, going to school hungry. Why no louder outcry; where was the once touted compassionate conservatism? There in 2015 was Cameron signing a UN charter pledging the UK with others to halve their own poverty levels by 2030: experts predicted that ambition would be missed by a country mile.

Children in families out of work fared worse. After 2010, the real value of unemployment benefits fell one tenth; for a family of three children, the drop could be three times as much. There was a brief respite. In the pandemic, families drawing Universal Credit were given £20 a week extra. It showed how close to the edge so many were living when that modest sum made such a difference, pulling 350,000 more children out of poverty for a brief time, only to be plunged back when the £20 was withdrawn in 2022.

Undeserving

Apart from children, single people were singled out for benefits cuts. By 2023, the cost of food and heating alone exceeded 100 per cent of their benefit. Rapporteurs from the UN pronounced benefits of £85 a week for a single adult over 25 'grossly insufficient'. The Resolution Foundation's Torsten Bell was blunt. 'Anyone younger without kids is basically guaranteed destitution if they are forced to rely on the state, with just one-third of the support pensioners receive relative to that minimum income standard.'

Even that old distinction between deserving and undeserving poor vanished. Those in work were treated with the same harshness as those out of work. People with disabilities, once unquestionably among the deserving, now became the butt of accusations of swinging the lead, even leading to physical assaults on disabled people. Duncan Smith pushed disability stories to his acolytes in the media, with no mention of the exceptionally low rate of fraud and error, at just 1.5 per cent of claims. Gruelling work capability tests were made tougher, the DWP calling in people with incurable wasting diseases, making them walk up stairs to interviews. Personal Independence Payment (PIP) was introduced to cut the number of claimants, so over half those with epilepsy who qualified for the old disability living allowance were thrown off. The fact that three quarters of those who challenged the decision won on appeal showed how vindictively the tougher conditions had been applied.

Universal Credit

Despite all that, the British Social Attitudes survey found that empathy with the poorest grew over these years. With so many in the middle feeling pinched, there was more awareness of children going to school hungry. But sympathy easily dissipated in the face of administrative complexity. A longstanding plan was to weld DWP and HMRC computers. The idea was to pay tax credits and benefits through a single sum, which would adjust automatically according to a family's circumstances. If they earned more, their credits would fall, and would rise if they earned less.

The idea behind Universal Credit was sound. But implementation during austerity was a disaster. Duncan Smith, a man of simple conviction and simple brain, had ignored warnings. For ministers guided by ideological impulse, ignorance of administration became almost a badge of pride (think Grayling wrecking the probation service, or anything Williamson did). Mere technicalities: sheer conviction would solve all. Universal Credit burned through expensive software systems. Promised costs of £173 per claim soared to £699 when the system began (late), then settled at £301.

A big problem was how to taper away entitlement as people earned more. The decision was made that for every extra pound they earned, families lost 63p. Imagine the outrage if high earners were charged a 63 per cent top rate of income tax. Meanness pervaded the scheme. By 2024, not all claimants had been transferred, which was welcome since people lost out when moved off the old tax credit system. The NAO reported that large numbers of often vulnerable people vanished down the cracks. One group that stood to gain in moving were those with a disability or illness drawing Employment Support Allowance. For that very reason, the NAO said they were being deliberately held back from transfer until 2028.

Universal Credit was stress-tested during COVID and it stood up well, coping with twice as many claimants overnight. For all the budget overruns and delays, the system eventually did function. Its reputation suffered from the harshness of how its rules were enforced amid benefit cuts. A totemic act of meanness was the five-week wait each claimant had to endure before being paid. Large numbers started out in debt, needing to borrow to cover the weeks before they were paid. Debt cumulated. Making a claim was deliberately made more difficult: online only, and many people did not have IT skills, let alone a computer. The application form was 50 pages long. DWP civil servants were assessed on how many claimants they could remove from the roll. Look out for the weak and feeble, they were instructed: if they are a minute late for an appointment, strike them out. Or trip them up with hard-to-understand instructions, easy if they are not fully literate or don't speak English well. Make them apply for scores of jobs each week, even jobs they have no hope of getting. If they erred, they were 'sanctioned' for weeks or months. This epochal word was the subject of Ken Loach's angry film *I, Daniel Blake*, showing how a brutal system left many with nothing to live on for long periods, tipping them into homelessness.

It was the coalition that did the worst damage. Benefits were clawed back from tenants in social housing if their accommodation was deemed to exceed official norms for family size. The 'spare bedroom subsidy' was immediately dubbed the bedroom tax. A family whose 10-year-old child had recently died suddenly lost income because of her empty bedroom; as did a couple keeping a room for a son in the armed forces

– that one embarrassed even the Tory tabloids. Half a million households were being penalized in 2022. Only 4.5 per cent of those charged the bedroom tax downsized: many wanted to move but there were no smaller homes available to move into. In addition, grants backing council support for poorer families' dwelling costs were cut or, a euphemism, left to local discretion. Councils started employing bailiffs to dispossess their own tenants.

Hard luck

Benefits were only available for two children, which overnight impoverished larger families. The woman with three children recently left by her husband – hard luck. Then came the additional rule that, regardless of circumstances, benefit income was subject to a hard cash limit. Families living in high-rent areas who couldn't find a cheaper home faced severe cuts in support. As of 2024, three quarters of families on Universal Credit with four children or more were in poverty.

Catholic ministers such as Duncan Smith had some confessing to do. Opposed to contraception and abortion but penalizing large families? His great campaign was to reward marriage through the tax system. The allowance, worth £252 a year, encouraged no more couples to walk up the aisle; it would not even cover the drinks at a wedding reception. From a 1970s peak of 74 per 1,000, the marriage rate had fallen to 18 by 2019 (and was barely half that in COVID-hit 2020).

Poor households had to borrow more as their outlays overshot. Some eight million were struggling with debt. Charities such as PayPlan, StepChange and Citizens Advice did their best, but an estimated 600,000 a year who had need of debt advice could not get it. A sign of the times was the rise of loans companies, lending small sums at extortionate interest rates to tide families over. QuickQuid once charged a typical rate of 1,294.1 per cent APR; by 2024 it had moderated its terms to 102.5 per cent. Borrowers were found to have been seriously misled about loan conditions by the Wonga company, which went bust in August 2018, claiming it could not cope with the thousands of claims against it registered with the Financial Ombudsman Service.

Rewarding the old (who vote)

In Tory eyes, the poor became more virtuous the older they got. The old voted and they mostly voted right. Labour had taken a million pensioners out of poverty, a startling drop from 28 per cent to 14 per cent: for the first time in history, the old became less likely than the rest of the population to be poor. The Tories made a strong play for the vote by triple-locking their pension, guaranteeing it would rise by 2.5 per cent a year, by the inflation rate or by the annual increase in average earnings, whichever was the highest.

Generous though that seemed, the proportion of pensioners who were poor stayed at 14 per cent. Come the last days, the government even seemed to have given up on them, the tax and benefit changes in the March 2024 budget knocking several hundreds off the annual household income of older people, though, as expert commentators said, this could have been a bit of an accident rather than an intentional hit. Intergenerational strife hovered in the background. David Willetts made a bid to stir it in his book *The Pinch*, complaining that the young had scant chance of buying a home unless they had rich parents to help them; they also had to repay university fees (which Willetts himself had increased when he was a Tory minister). Perhaps he succeeded in rousing the generations, as barely anyone under 35 said they would vote Tory – as low as only 12 per cent, said the polls – and nor were they turning Tory as they aged, as they once had.

Those born in the 1950s and 1960s were retiring with generous defined benefit pensions – their affluence on display in burgeoning glossy ads for cruises and retirement communities. Millennials born in the early 1980s could reach age 60 with around £45,000 less in their pension pots than those born when the Beatles first hit the airwaves. But the gap between rich and poor became more marked among pensioners than in the rest of the population. The old were more likely to own their own homes, over 78 per cent of them, but again a contrast: a higher proportion of pensioners, mostly poor, were living in private rented accommodation than had been the case for a long time. The state pension of £11,500 (April 2024) was a nice bonus for those with other income, far too little for decency for those with nothing else.

Comfortable old age could be jeopardized thanks to the coalition's 'liberation' of private pensions. From 2015, pension savings no longer had to be used to buy annuities; retirees could draw money to spend on anything they liked, even – chortled the Liberal Democrat pensions minister, Steve Webb – a Lamborghini. He failed to see that many pensioners would underestimate their own longevity and abandon safe company schemes to get hold of a lump sum, ruining their prospects; his own brightened when, on losing his seat, he became a pensions industry adviser. Schemes saw huge withdrawals, and only later did the Financial Conduct Authority start to chase finaglers using high-pressure tactics to sell the old rotten investments. Then came the Truss revolution that instantly wiped an estimated £425 billion from pension fund values, a near quarter drop.

Levelling down

Truss was the last straw, but even before her public unease mounted as, despite the general fall in living standards during the pandemic and inflation in food and energy prices, the rich did better and better. Inequality was something of a closet issue for the Tories. A third of those identifying as Tory regarded equality as their least important value. They were quick to claim that the most unequal country, the US, was also the most affluent. But in political practice, they avoided the subject, the public having no appetite for the massive American problems of bad health, poverty, drug dependency, crime and social disorder. For Hayekians and Thatcherites and their cheerleaders in the think tanks and leader columns of the right-wing press, the standard defence was that inequality created incentives for innovation and growth. 'In the UK, this has been strikingly untrue', noted columnist Martin Wolf. Instead, the UK's fate was high inequality *and* slow growth.

Income inequality had risen remarkably during the Thatcher era and stuck. The financial crisis had hit some high earners, at least until the government responded to the wails of bankers whose bonuses had been capped. The overall distribution of income reflected a complex balance of pluses (increases in the national minimum wage) and minuses (the harsher benefits system) along with burgeoning ways of being rich. The Gini measure of inequality of income did not show much overall change. Inequality between places was as unmoving as between people. Some four fifths of the variation in income between the different areas of the UK seen in 2024 could be explained by the same differences existing in 1997. Kensington and Chelsea, the richest local authority, had an average income per person of £52,500, four times more than the poorest, Nottingham, on £11,700.

That's rich

The rich are good at propaganda. May picked up their factoid that 1 per cent of earners carried 28 per cent of the tax burden, deploring it as the highest percentage ever. Full Fact challenged. The rich did pay 28 per cent of income tax, but certainly not of all taxes. Three quarters of the state's income came from other taxes. Meanwhile, the poorest paid the highest proportion of their income in tax by far (mainly in the form of VAT and council tax). The top tenth of the income distribution paid 39 per cent of their income in tax while the bottom tenth paid 50 per cent.

Top people coined it. Jeff Fairburn of Persimmon was gifted a £75 million bonus, not for entrepreneurial heroism or risking his own money in clever investment, but for milking a scandalously loose housebuilding subsidy. The UK still had more very highly paid bankers than the rest of the EU put together, over seven times more than Germany. That made the 2022 axing of the cap on UK bankers' bonuses particularly unjustifiable.

To have plutocracy personified in the prime minister was a bad look. On the day Sunak's tax return was published in 2024, the front page of the *Financial Times* warned that hard-up voters would not find it easy to accept his capital gains of £1.8 million. Receiving his money from assets, it was taxed at the lower rate of 23 per cent, instead of the top income tax rate of 45 per cent he would have paid if it were classed as income from employment. The entire private equity industry was founded on describing its income as capital gain to get the tax break. As for Sunak's wife: even when she abandoned her peculiar status as someone not domiciled in the UK for purposes of her overseas tax liabilities, it emerged that through a loophole her heirs would pay no inheritance tax on her sizeable fortune. Everyone knew tax reliefs and loopholes abounded for the wealthy, while fiscal foot soldiers had no choice since tax was exacted at source through PAYE.

That's super-rich

Dividends paid by companies in the UK reached a record high of £99.8 billion in 2018. Budget by budget, usually amid resounding silence, wealth continued to accumulate and concentrate. By 2023, the richest 50 families in the UK held more wealth than half of the UK population, comprising 33.5 million people. Age played its part. One in five of those born in the 1950s now owned a second property. The total wealth embodied by second homes, buy-to-let investments and those foreign gîtes, *case rurali* and flats on the Costa climbed to over £1 trillion. Owning wealth had become more influential: the child of a homeowner was three times more likely to own their own home than the child of a non-property-owner when they grew up. In the 1990s that had been only twice as likely. Inequality was regional too. Per capita wealth in the northeast would remain at around half that of the south-east for the rest of the decade. So much for levelling up.

The ONS calculated that the richest tenth of households held 43 per cent of all wealth. The poorest half, by contrast, owned just 9 per cent. Wealth figures are notoriously hard to get – for obvious reasons. Tax authorities did not know or did not want to know. Money got sequestered in tax havens. Within the ranks of the affluent, a gap opened between the super-rich and the wealthy also-rans and it grew. One tenth of the top 1 per cent owned nearly a tenth of all wealth and saw their share double between 1984 and 2013.

The bullying power of the wealthy swells the more wealth they control. The rich and their representatives frighten chancellors with threats to offshore their money. UK businesses, including railway companies, banks and consultancies, used tax 'arrangements', the result of which was to deprive the state of revenue. A government genuinely concerned with fiscal fairness would have squeezed them, along with the Googles and Amazons who played the jurisdiction game, hopping their corporate accounts between countries. Half the foreign profits of US multinationals were booked in tax havens (which included the Republic of Ireland and the Netherlands).

Some 8 per cent of global wealth, $7.6 trillion, was thought to be hidden in havens. A 2016 database leak from Panama lawyers Mossack Fonseca made the fiscal wound gape gangrenously. The Treasury tentatively started investigating the clandestine companies behind the discreet nameplates in St Helier, Nassau and Douglas: those incorporated in the UK were required to declare their beneficial owners as well as their shareholders. Unexplained wealth orders could now be used to force high-value property owners who claimed limited income to explain their mysterious standard of living. Much hinged on enforcement. It was thought some 6,800 UK citizens controlled 12,000 firms from within low-tax jurisdictions. But they were as tax-resistant as ever, with a third of the UK's estimated 93 billionaires having moved to tax havens.

Some backbench Tory MPs collaborated on legislation to force the UK's own offshore tax havens in the English Channel and the Irish Sea to make their registers of company ownership fully searchable. At the very last moment, the May government withdrew crucial clauses. Lobbying by the territories (or their clients) had evidently proved effective. The government then put the fox in the henhouse by allowing banks implicated in wrongdoing to help run a new economic crime board, which would supposedly hold companies to account. Sue Hawley, policy director of Corruption Watch, said that didn't pass the sniff test even to a nose with heavy catarrh. The government chose not to implement a 2009 law that would have banned large political donations from those resident abroad for tax purposes. Tax-exile donors went on giving and went on being given honours and titles.

A burden?

The politics of the era were triangulated by ideology, incompetence and accident. The biggest example of the latter was COVID; it cost money. At the heart of the figure sat tax. Having averaged 33 per cent of GDP in the first two decades of this century, by 2027–28 UK tax was projected to rise by over 4 per cent of GDP (£4,200 per household). However, at 37 per cent, the UK still raised less in tax than similar countries, such as France and Germany. This record had the Tories writhing: how could the low-tax, small-state party be presiding over the highest tax take since 1945? The answer was that chancellors did not adjust thresholds; more people paid income tax and more were pulled up a tax band by inflation. The Resolution Foundation sternly reminded us that average rates of tax on income remained low by comparison with the past. People paid higher rates on some of their earnings, bringing scary *Daily Mail* headlines about marginal tax rates, but the long-term direction of travel on personal taxes was down, not up.

The only way is up

- Create an official minimum income standard
- Recommit to abolition of child poverty
- Improve benefits for single adults
- Expand and support Citizens Advice
- Strengthen labour market inspection
- Crack down on tax havens
- Revisit identity cards
- Encourage union membership
- Improve access to industrial tribunals

CONCLUSION

Up, Up and Away

THE GRAND OPENING was splendid. Royalty, at least of the theatrical kind, trod the red carpet into the restored Oldham Coliseum. An opening-night Christmas pantomime as glitzy as the London Palladium's was to be followed by *The Marriage of Figaro* from ENO, happily settled in its new home a tram ride away in Manchester. Cue tearful speeches from hometown actors commemorating the late Bernard Cribbins, born in Oldham into deep poverty, who was apprenticed to the Coliseum company at the age of 14. *Coronation Street* actress Julie Hesmondhalgh, Maxine Peake and Christopher Eccleston had campaigned to save this fine old theatre, just a whisker away from property developers' clutches back in 2024.

If only activists in the West Midlands could have stalled the destruction of the Dudley Hippodrome. Despite their vigour, it had been demolished in August 2023, when the Tory leader of the council called it an 'exciting day' as they 'leave behind the past'. Conservatism wasn't as conserving as it once was.

Recently, not just for the arts but for the unlevel regions of England and the rest of the UK, the way had been up. Arts Council England began regenerating music, drama and design in schools and community centres. New Cribbins

Apprenticeships helped young people into careers that had become closed to any but those with money. Already its graduates were making their mark in Bollywood as well as Hollywood. Not just as performers; stage hands, grips, lighting technicians and production managers were being trained for the events and venues industry and to staff burgeoning studios in Leeds, Cardiff and Bristol in addition to Elstree and Pinewood. Confident councils were protecting local venues, the breeding ground for bands, some of them able to draw on the surprise Noel and Liam Gallagher Foundation and the generous legacy to popular music left on the sad passing of Sir Paul McCartney.

Naysayers in the *Daily Mail*, its circulation sliding precipitously as the second part of the Leveson inquiry got under way, derided this new wave but they could not deny the boom in enthusiasm and creativity. Musicians whose earnings had been decimated by Brexit were flourishing thanks to new treaties freeing them to travel. The NAO confirmed the cost-effectiveness of the new arts funding regime, accepting that while difficult to quantify, community pride, confidence and reduction in inequality could be given a substantive value.

New dawn

The year is 2030 and we're fantasizing about what might be. Our book has been about what went wrong, what was missing, what got lost, but now … what could be. That was the litany of complaint; here is not so much the remedy as a set of measuring rods against which to judge those in power during the rest of the decade, a ready reckoner if you like. Get your disappointment in early for the victors of the July 2024 general election but be proportionate. They have to govern in the teeth of malevolent media and a daily diet of social media distortion. We've described the dimensions of their financial and policy task. But for a few pages, let's indulge the fancy of a UK that by 2030 looks and feels a lot fairer, more effective and efficient than today. And cleaner.

Let's start with the top people. We already have some, but let's imagine more patriotic millionaires convincing the super-rich about how to live together in a less divided and more fairly income- and wealth-taxed society. Plutocrats aren't going to rush to relinquish their leverage over the media and boardrooms or to stop oiling the wheels of politics, but at some sweet spot moral sentiments, however residual, meet political realism and their fear of what a future rougher and radical government might do. At that point, they accept fiscal concessions.

Maybe that point is when they realize that everyone, including them, is caught up in climate crisis, Putin, China and dangerous trends in American politics spilling out to the wider world. War has become more possible and drones kill rich and poor sons and daughters alike. Might a growing sense of a world in crisis lay the ground for domestic coming-together? Brexit has not altogether played itself out, still rumbling with some voters, yet there's an overwhelming wish for practical rapprochement – the summer Olympics 2024 had kicked off a renewed British love affair with France and Europe. What must lie ahead is national honesty about the UK's modest global status and its oddly asymmetric capacity, with those nuclear weapons and aircraft carriers. Rational rethinking encompasses the imperial past and the diverse present.

The world presses in. No more of that world-class, world-beating guff. The UK is a middle-ranking power with a big history, and lots of 'soft' power – in the English language, reputable law, the BBC and its World Service, the British Council spreading the whole array of lively culture – alongside the residual 'hard' stuff – ships, nuclear submarines and an army. As a matter of geographical fact we're European, and whether the Brexiteers like it or not, we share the fate of our neighbours. Migration will go on heading the national risk assessment, along with terrorism, threats from maverick states, pandemics and technological extremism – artificial intelligence and cybercrime leading examples. European neighbours face domestic neo-fascist insurgencies, disrupting the EU and NATO. As Brexit tensions fade and prospects for commercial and policy agreements with the EU grow, can the UK recalibrate its dependencies on the US and former 'kith and kin' countries, Canada, Australia and New Zealand? A measure of progress has to be recognizing 'over-stretch', in the UK's anomalous position on the UN Security Council, its seaborne capacity (for which oceans?), its land army (for whose territory?). A measure of progress must be an end to denial and braggadocio.

The deep blue complacency of Middle England had been shredding itself for some time. One of us (PT) spoke in early 2024 at a regional Women's Institute gathering in the Midlands, the county high sheriff resplendent in her feathered hat. For members, the status quo was less and less a happy place. Their gathering rippled with anxiety about social conditions, young people's life chances, gender inequality and the climate, instinctively conservative no longer.

Net zero

Realization dawns that the world really is teetering on a precipice. Imagine if the record rainfall of the preternaturally mild and wet winter of 2023–24 were followed by a succession of scorching, almost unbearable summers: it provokes widespread alarm, which morphs into demand for more radical climate action, as potent in the north as the south, among old and young, rich and poor. Public backing for accelerating the transition to net-zero carbon emissions becomes vocal and permanent.

So by 2030 all UK electricity is generated from non-carbon sources, catching up with other EU countries. A new generation of small modular nuclear reactors has generated high hopes, work on them speeded up thanks to a new Advanced Research Fund financing specialists. UK science at last has a grand strategy, funding to match, and state finance to lubricate start-ups and the exploitation of innovation. Hinkley Point has come on stream at last, and though green ultras weren't keen, approval is given to extend the life of EDF's other reactors, based on a new accord between the UK and French governments – spanning defence, Channel crossings as well as energy and the environment. The threat of the neo-fascist candidacy in the presidential elections of 2027 faded after Marine Le Pen's ties to Russia had finally been exposed.

With nuclear electricity providing backup 'base load' for unwindy days, the UK had breathing space to experiment across the range of renewables: tidal, hydro, hydrogen, wind and solar. Scotland and Wales shot ahead, then England started applying Exeter University research that showed how wind and sun exploitation on a sliver of land (3 per cent) could power households two and a half times over. Breakthroughs in battery and storage technology were helping the UK's energy balance of trade and mitigating China's geopolitical heft. New oil and gas wells at Rosebank off Shetland never needed to happen.

NIMBYs still objected to land-based wind farms, but farmers earned money from them and community funds paid locals for pylons. This boosted a rural economy in transition, along with new tree-planting organized by a revamped Forestry Commission. Across the Midlands and the south-west the English national forest was bursting into leaf. The projected scale of flooding meant strict controls on development in vulnerable areas, abandoning buildings in certain riverside and coastal areas.

State-owned GB Energy was gingering up competition, acting as a backstop where companies failed to provide, though private investment was expanding now that companies had long-run certainty on price. Gas ducts were being adapted for hydrogen and the geology of the former coalfields exploited for carbon capture. Obsolete planning restraints on household solar panels were abandoned. Better relations with the EU brought collaboration and more energy trade. Those giant emitters, aviation and shipping, were now being included in internationally agreed carbon calculations. As in France, short-haul domestic flights were banned in favour of the railway.

Accelerating this required reunifying the electricity grid in the age of more dispersed generation. In 2024, Kona was starting to build a giga battery factory near Lancaster and wanted to develop others, but had been warned of long queues for connection to the grid. Now these priority connections were fast-tracked.

Upskilling

The new mood around sustainability and the environment stimulated children's interest in engineering. A national mobilization of past and could-be maths and physics teachers had upped results at GCSE, with a promising increase in likely A-level candidates, and a variety of options in applied maths, stats and science were sprouting in FE colleges, with more vocational and day-release opportunities.

Some six million homes have been insulated, thanks to accelerated training for retrofitters matched to the needs of local insulation companies: everyone on a course is guaranteed a job. New tax arrangements described below have started the better matching of housing space and emissions to the size of households. The insulation programme is spreading better paid work everywhere, with 13 million more homes still needing to be upgraded. Heat pumps were slow to get going, but now, with higher subsidies, sales are picking up and prices are reducing. Understanding that we share a common fate induced public support for measures to make low emissions affordable for lower-income households.

Getting there

The railways are again a genuine network, even if some franchising of lines has been retained for the sake of comparing performance and stimulating innovation; there's regional control of suburban lines in the new integrated transport systems in the West Midlands and West Yorkshire. Connectivity is the watchword, bus and train times coordinated following the Netherlands' example, with special attention to places formerly badly served by both bus and train. Diesel engines are being phased out, and electrified rail freight is shifting more loads off the road. The railways have reorganized and united; ticket buying and pricing became more rational and train services more reliable.

Local authorities now control franchises or run their own bus fleets, mostly electric, with expanded park-and-ride further diminishing car usage in towns and cities. Bus riding is the subject of songs and new public enthusiasm. Municipalities have been getting a grip on the 'last mile' of home deliveries to end congestion and pollution caused by scores of underpaid drivers on impossible schedules criss-crossing streets to deliver parcels to the same houses. Experiments are under way to give a highly regulated Royal Mail a local last-mile monopoly since they visit every house every day anyway:

posties' official role is expanding into social care and delivery of medicines and meals to the frail.

A national roll-out of charging points for electric cars on a common tariff made drivers less hesitant, while scrappage and purchase schemes for low-income drivers pushed EV sales and leasing. Car volumes are permanently down thanks to improvements in public transport and dedicated common travel lanes on the motorways. New codes of conduct for e-bike users have made urban cycling safer and more popular. Rows over low-traffic neighbourhoods evaporated: they had always been popular with locals.

The great clean-up

A great river clean-up began, starting with the Wye, led by a task force of Environment Agency and Welsh government enforcers, funded by a levy on polluters. In their wake followed new enthusiasts for free swimming and canoeing, acting as monitors of water quality. A simple principle – polluter pays – was being widely and rigorously implemented, paying for inspections too. The widely publicized Wye clean-up acted as a catalyst, exposing the river-killing poison of the host of chicken farms on its banks; higher clean-up standards did help push the price of food gently upwards, lowering demand for meat while benefiting sustainable farming. Public disgust at farm run-off fuelled the campaign for meat-free days as the trend to healthier eating gathered adherents. Some compared it to the decline of smoking.

Ofwat, the Office of Water Regulation, has been remade top to bottom and has tightened the licence conditions for water supply and sewage. Letting its shareholders carry the can for Thames Water acted as a salutary warning to other utility investors: a solid and guaranteed income from consumers is the reward for infrastructure investments, with none of the debt-overloaded financial engineering and speculation that brought down Thames. Water companies can profit only if they repair leaks, build reservoirs and maximize recycling of effluent. No more self-monitoring: the regulator and the Environment Agency, funded by the water companies themselves, now have staff to check and teeth to penalize. Licence conditions include open-book accounting, making it clear who owns what and whether any surpluses are justified by the investment record. In some parts of England moves are afoot to replicate the Welsh non-profit model, with water sharing between regions based on new grid connections. Engineers are once more being appointed to the top jobs rather than financial wide boys. Households in the drier but more affluent south-east and south-west of England face paying more for water piped in from the wetter, less affluent zones, which benefit. In 2020 the NAO had sounded the alarm about lack of water planning; at last it was being heeded.

Renewal

Renewal reverses what John Muellbauer and David Soskice called the 'intimate relationship between credit-fuelled property booms, high property prices and diminished productivity growth'. This broadens out into how land is owned, taxed and zoned. Investment and consumption are rebalanced. The UK's problem, exacerbated since 2010, had been saving too little while the stock of capital was being used up or sold off to foreigners, reported Martin Weale. Incentives to save more do mean less spent on clothes and holidays.

But the prize is a great rebuilding, with cranes and diggers everywhere. In Whitehall housing is no longer a political graveyard. Now it's a prime cabinet post, in contrast to the 16 housing ministers coming and going between 2010 and 2024. Economists have long said that freeing up planning and building fast is the best motor for Britain's previously flatlining growth. Policy is striving for the perfect balance between sustainability, affordability and fairness.

Resistance to the revaluation of properties for council tax in England has been overcome, as people are much more aware of how buildings emit carbon: larger properties should bear a fairer share of the burden. Inheritance tax incentives to stay on in large draughty houses was an Osborne-era perversity, but now national planning guidelines require developers, public and private, to include more homes adapted for older people. When they downsize into these, they get a stamp duty holiday as encouragement.

Planning rules are stopping clumps of new homes being thrown up in a peripheral field with no bus services, GPs, schools or walkable shops, let alone jobs. Developers can no longer hoard their land: once planning permission is granted, the clock starts ticking. After six months, unless spades are in the ground, they must resell at pre-planning-permission value. Planning has become an intelligent enabler, redrawing the green belt to permit development where it is more grey and brown, on car parks, disused factories and scrub land. A new planning protocol presumes in favour of equitable development: land should be preserved free of building only if it has an exceptionally high economic, strategic, natural beauty or public amenity value in its undeveloped state. This was bad news for the tiny fraction of the population who play golf. Policy had absorbed the calculation that the 1.5 million dwellings needed in the south-east could be found by identifying golf courses within a two-kilometre radius of railway stations to build on. Some of these lush acres had been turned into public parkland and nature reserves, going a little way to reclaim the two million hectares of publicly owned land that had been sold off since the 1980s, as recorded by Brett Christophers. The National Housing Federation had calculated that upfront spending on housing would soon recoup itself through savings on benefits payments, use of public services and extra tax revenue generated.

Planning had become an exciting, attractive profession again, mixing social science and engineering skills, predicting population movement, employment and social need and aligning them with topography, aesthetic design criteria and management of emissions. Most ambitious were the free-standing new towns, linked to regional growth plans, the land bought at low existing use value without planning permission as farmland or brownfield by development corporations. ONS accepted that this spending scored a nil rating in the national debt accounts since it immediately secured an asset value well in excess of the purchase price. Few were as large as Milton Keynes, but the history and layout of successful previous new towns served as models. The corporations had the power to borrow to build, and then decades on to sell remaining assets, as elected local authorities took over. The new iteration of the model mixes social and private eco-housing, open spaces, public transport, workplaces, shops, cinemas and leisure centres, alongside schools and clinics.

High streets are being remade, little by little. Retailing is adapting to new habits. Shopping has become more presentational, online purchasing and high-street visits working in better conjunction. Some shopfronts have gone for ever and landlords have had to adjust rental expectations to accommodate alternative uses: pop-up shops, artisan studios, catering, health and education, gyms, games arcades, music venues and sports halls. Strict planning rules govern conversion of shops to flats and housing, which can have a deadening effect on business districts and destroy existing retail.

High-street footfall has started to rise again, with the effective end of the car as a viable form of inner-urban transport. Electric buses and lorries have helped improve air quality.

Pedestrianization and new rules for safe use of bikes have introduced a peculiarly British form of the *passeggiata*, with high streets places to see and be seen. Urban crime continues its decades of downward trajectory as police forces re-equip to deal with cyber fraud, now in close collaboration with the EU and other jurisdictions.

Right to rent

Right to Buy has been abolished. Social rented housing is precisely that: affordable rented dwellings where tenancies rotate according to family circumstances and the need to move home for jobs. Housing associations have been recalled to their original purpose, to construct niche developments of housing that is genuinely affordable for people on moderate and low incomes: the ridiculous use of the word 'affordable' to mean an unaffordable 80 per cent of rents has been abandoned.

The old problem was low productivity and an insufficient building industry. But increased land supply has spurred competition. Decent standards for space and light are compulsory: no more windowless rabbit hutches in converted offices. Strict rules now constrain speculators, domestic as well as foreign, who buy but then leave property empty, whole blocks dark and wasting. Councils can now borrow on the strength of future rental income and, where appropriate, on the value of their existing stock: such prudential borrowing was signed off by the NAO as making no net addition to public debt. Councils were encouraged and where necessary forced to swap lending rights, allowing the valuations in less active local areas to be used to fund housing development where needed.

There's still a wait, but housing lists have stopped lengthening. Better supply is starting to have some effect on the private sector, softening demand and rents. Adventurous local authorities, including the mayor of London, have begun buying privately rented dwellings for re-lets on social tenancies, pushing down numbers in temporary accommodation, families with children a priority. Private renters have more security, with longer leases, and no-fault evictions ended, and private landlords now have the same obligation as social landlords to keep properties up to a decent standard. Second-home owners and holiday lets have come under scrutiny, with councils in stressed areas now able to apply strong financial pressure on underused housing and effect a better balance between local needs and those of visitors and tourists. Housing has been a kick-starter for growth throughout the economy.

Our future

Along Water Street in Ashton-under-Lyne straggles a crocodile of primary school children swinging their sports bags. They are heading for their weekly swimming lesson. Every Child a Swimmer is one of the government programmes in what they call 'school enrichment': in spirit it's tied in with the waterways clean-up. The new ambition was for every primary schoolchild to sample and have the chance to do sports, arts, exploring the countryside, visiting London, France and the seaside. Shocking numbers of children had never done any of these things, had barely been outside their own neighbourhood.

These children chattering on their way are too young to know that the wrecking ball was only weeks away from demolishing Ashton-under-Lyne's leisure centre and swimming pool in 2024. Tameside council had not wanted to close it but was desperately starved of funds. At that time Swim England said 2,000 pools were under threat. Now saved, many are refurbished, sometimes doubling up with new GP health centres and libraries, themselves often replacing those that had been shut. They were often rebuilt in tandem with private and non-profit developers using sites for housing and offices, cafés and cinemas, now enjoying a revival as people tired of only streaming at home. Groups of mothers run cafés in many of them, often a ferment of volunteering and local activism.

The biggest shift in the lives of children, starting at birth, was the reinvention of Sure Start children's centres, offering early education, childcare and a host of services from health visitors and midwives through to speech and language therapy and mental health support. IFS research had added weight to evidence proving the benign effects lasted right through to better GCSE results. This time round they are sited mainly in primary schools, which often have empty space because of falling numbers of young children. They are becoming community hubs: every family knows this is where the council has a desk for registering new babies, introducing them at birth to all the facilities.

Secondary schools too are being enriched as music, art, drama and sports, design and technology are restored; local employers are being encouraged to offer pupils a better sense of what jobs are on offer and what training may be needed. Inspectors – Ofsted having been thoroughly renewed – now incorporate children's own descriptions of their school life and their well-being as well as academic attainment. School nurses are back and mental health support staff too. Parents, themselves signing up to new codes of conduct and respect for educational professionals, are being invited in, catching problems earlier, reducing the distance between home and school, with mothers and fathers giving talks about their jobs and being helped with their children's learning at home. Most exams are becoming open book, children having mastered how to find reliable sources at the click of a mouse, well schooled in the scams, fakes and dangers of the internet. The big media companies have been shamed into supporting new schemes for IT skills and children are gaining new confidence in quantitative work, a basic understanding of everyday statistics a key threshold as they move through the secondary years. Critical thinking is a course that all take.

Skills for life

Further education is reviving as, after years of tinkering and ill-judged reform, vocational qualifications settle down under employer–teacher panels. The number of young people of college age is increasing and there are many more local green jobs to train for, in turbine factories, insulation and construction, as well as design, planning, project management and regeneration. Universities have got the message, and higher education is now bifurcating: a research sector with an emphasis on postgraduate education, and the other focused on teaching, employability and twenty-first-century life skills. No one has yet had the courage to rename one of these latter as polytechnics, but that is what they are in essence, better keyed into local and regional economies. Young people are being weaned off the idea of spending three years at 'uni' a long way from home, facing high fees and living costs, and more are continuing to live at home and attend college locally. Colleges are training up a new cadre of older people, many returning to work after looking after children or relatives, for the National Care Service's new professionalized career structure, aligned with NHS bands and pay.

Working life is improving. Joining a union is easier as all employers now must allow them in to recruit. Unions have been regaining the confidence of employees with a professional, pragmatic approach to representing their interests, preventing exploitation and ensuring enforcement of new protections on dismissal, redundancy and working conditions. Ballots among union members have high turnouts now unions can use electronic voting, previously barred. Unionized workplaces have started to show productivity gains, with higher take-up of training and better customer service. 'Good work agreements' within individual firms and across whole sectors are becoming more common. Once adopted, the Resolution Foundation's proposal for a Single Enforcement Body brought together the regulators of wages and hours. This has had the strongest effect in social care and cleaning, where a predominantly female and low-paid work-force is more justly treated. The 'dignity premium' effect on prices, though real, was small and mostly accepted. The UK's great wasted resource – people aged 50 to 64 who have left the labour force, especially women – are being tempted back. A great push on occupational therapy is helping, adjusting hours and conditions to suit their health status. New sympa-thetic training schemes are giving them back confidence as they master IT and modern workplace skills. Improvements in nursery and childcare lift a burden from families, along with the new Homecheck care system in conjunction with Royal Mail in some areas, boosting the self-reliance of older people, freeing carers to re-enter the workforce.

The UK has become a much more pensions-aware country, in a dual sense. The success of Labour's auto-enrolment is being rolled out further to include the lowest-paid employees, many of them women and those on zero hours and short-term contracts. Policymakers had been rereading an old classic by the management guru Peter Drucker, in which he conjured the mobilization of the money owned by citizens inside pension schemes to use for promoting economic growth, in a virtuous circle. The total value of public service pensions alone was more than UK GDP: the £50 billion paid in each year was being invested in productive assets. The Local Government Pension scheme, already overfunded, was actively lending to both municipal and private projects – within the UK.

Resurrected after its near-death experience, the Confederation of British Industry has merged with the British Chambers of Commerce to become robust but cooperative with the government and unions, its members more prepared to take an interest in training, productivity and investment planning. They are central to national conversations about AI and R&D, low wages and regional imbalance. Employers and business leaders have not suddenly discovered a conscience or converted to full environmental, social and governance expectations, but most are more alert. Boardrooms are not exempt from flooding and overheating and companies are profiting from their involvement in the government-stimulated green economy.

Governing better

Creating this new impetus for growth was beyond the capacity of HM Treasury. It took a new national economic development council to do the heavy lifting. Former prime minister Gordon Brown had talked of putting government into battle mode to boost growth and productivity, with the new council as its general staff. The retreat of the Treasury had been as much intellectual as administrative. Why had it ignored report after report from the NAO suggesting improvements in efficiency? Why had it always conflated revenue and capital spending? International definitions of what counted as capital investment were at last being recast, the UK among those pressing for the change, so that human capital was valued alongside bricks and mortar. That allowed borrowing to invest in education, skills and research, adding to growth. The UK joined international moves to capture the capital value of nature, people and social fabric.

A new career structure for the senior civil service based on expertise and training sent them on secondments into local government and the NHS to get on-the-ground practical experience in how to pursue the national missions for productivity, transport, greening and investment. Civil service training has been reinvented in the new National College for Government, offering specialist courses to public managers of all kinds around the country, building up scarce skills like cybersecurity, data science and project management. Honing sharp management skills would soon pay for itself in saved management consultancy fees.

Gross inequality is now seen as a block on growth. Kristalina Georgieva, head of the International Monetary Fund, had made the point: 'We have an obligation to correct what has been most seriously wrong over the last 100 years – the persistence of high economic inequality. IMF research shows that lower income inequality can be associated with higher and more durable growth.' On that cue, growth plans were now harnessed to reduce inequalities of income and wealth.

Inequality questions were set out early to assess progress. Are fewer people poor, fewer children hungry? Is destiny any less fixed at birth? A raft of social supports, starting with Sure Start, are being measured. Every year benefits rise above inflation until they reach the 'essentials standard' drawn up by the Joseph Rowntree Foundation and the Trussell Trust. Until now no government was willing to spell out an official level that no one should fall below: it will be fixed into law.

In the public finances, borrowing builds human and physical potential. Taxation pays for policing, courts, day-to-day NHS services and the armed forces. But rescuing young NEETs, not in education, employment or training, counts as investment in a future where they contribute to growth instead of dragging on it, spending justly based on borrowing. Youth services are revived, incorporating careers advice amid help with the confusions and miseries of adolescence, catching young people before they fall through the cracks. Youth centres are coming back, sometimes allied to leisure and sports facilities, places to hang out with youth workers, an almost defunct profession reinstated. Through tagging and AI, more prisoners are released early: less crowded, prisons now have some hope of offering education, training and therapy.

Reformed council tax now raises sensible sums from larger properties and council finances are stabilizing. Municipal bankruptcy notices are being withdrawn as a new audit regime gives councils greater freedom to spend and invest within prudential guidelines. Already local services look and feel better: parks are less unkempt, streets swept, potholes filled, playground swings unchained and paddling pools filled.

A National Care Service is taking shape, staff better trained and paid. Rising dementia rates helped convince families that everyone gains when none face catastrophic costs for care. On retirement everyone now makes a capital contribution depending on their assets, usually taking the form of a lien on the value of a property, to be claimed on death. No one loses their home even if care costs are high. Councils are recalibrating the mix between public and private provision. Strict rules stop them sending vulnerable people miles away from their communities, but freer to borrow to invest, more are opening their own care homes.

Meanwhile in Hastings, the Isabel Blackman Centre has reopened! We had been sad witnesses to its closure in 2019, along with more than seven other Hastings day centres for the old and frail. Alas, this has come too late for Rose, Mary and Sal: closures accelerated old people's demise. Today the health secretary is in Hull, opening another polyclinic, a halfway house between community and hospital. GPs retain their autonomy but increasingly they are employed by community trusts to treat patients as close to home as possible. The polyclinics have diagnostic capacity and do minor surgery, which extends GP skills and maintains enthusiasm. Consultants come for clinics; others review patients remotely now that the clinics are equipped with monitoring and imaging equipment; both ways frail patients are spared a journey. This bright, light, airy primary care centre, paid for by a municipal bond, has a community café. It is attracting newly qualified GPs to come to stretch their skills and its crèche is a boon to female doctors.

GPs are more relaxed about assistant physicians in their teams, acknowledging their skill set and trusting their judgement, as they do experienced nurses. Social prescribing is commonplace, the polyclinic booking swimming sessions at the local pool and organizing walks and outdoor gyms. Quantifiable health benefits take years to verify, but already there are signs that demand for treatment is more manageable. Digital remote monitoring of frail people in their own homes and in care homes has cut ambulance call-outs, A&E visits and bed blocking.

Public health has ceased to be a Cinderella thanks to joint appointments of medical officers of health between the NHS and local government. Shifting resources towards prevention is under way: improvements in housing, jobs and the environment will do more for health in the long run. The new green consciousness has helped shift diets, with stricter regulation on junk food, salt and sugar. Public services are emphasizing freshness and local purchasing in catering contracts. Harder to deal with are widespread loneliness and family distress, but there is a welcome for the new regulations curbing the emotional harms and bullying done by social media.

Paying up

Fantasy falls on the hard rock of finance. Aside from the quantity of money available to the state, the political challenge is who pays, shifting the incidence of both direct and indirect taxation towards the better-off. Redistribution has sat at the heart of politics since the dawn of democratic politics, though so often, to the chagrin of progressives, the less well-off have failed to mobilize, or often even to vote. Does it always have to be the case that the small number of losers in any tax reform shout louder and more effectively than the winners, who are usually greater in number? Fiscal ignorance can be challenged. A concerted effort is starting to spread knowledge and understanding of where everyone sits on the income scale and who pays what – revealing how grotesque tax injustice has become.

Reform of property tax comes first. Buildings can't be offshored or hidden in vaults. Buckingham Palace sat in council tax band H and was charged just £1,828 by Westminster City Council for its use as a residence – less than the amount paid for an average three-bedroom semi in Blackpool. Re-banding relieved pressure on poorer households and helped nudge others to move out of over-large homes, freeing up living space.

Next is the great barnacle-encrusted tax code and its array of exemptions for industries and interests. Over many years chancellors added dubious incentives: the patent box, R&D tax relief, inheritance tax rollover for farmers and family businesses. Where there was no evidence they had a beneficial effect, out they went: reformers had a long list of exemptions and gifts overdue for abolition. Closer coordination with other countries makes fair taxation of wealth more practicable. An expert commission had calculated that a 1 per cent per year charge on estates worth more than £2 million would yield a massive £80 billion over five years. Devote that to schools, research, energy infrastructure and upskilling the workforce and that investment creates new endeavours that bring in more tax, in a virtuous circle.

Equalize the tax rate on capital gains and earned income. Low capital gains did nothing to encourage investment, said the IFS. The Office of Tax Simplification had urged the government to tax work at the same rate as unearned income from, for example, rents, shares, or property inherited from well-off parents. Sunak had shelved that report, then Truss abolished the agency that wrote it. Another anomaly was that when someone died, the obligation to pay tax on capital gains made during their lifetime was extinguished with them. The proceeds of abolition could be vast.

Everyone paying National Insurance on all income, regardless of its source, brings in a tidy sum. Apply it first to the earned income of people still in work over the official pension age – a growing (and welcome) army. Stop the self-employed avoiding it, high-earning City law partners and medical consultants among them. Equalize pension tax relief so that higher earners get no more proportionately than others. Green the tax code to end the long freeze on fuel duty: level up prices across road, rail and air. You might annoy Ryanair's Michael O'Leary, but growing public awareness of the true environmental costs of jets would start to cut flying, unless airlines speed up ordering the new generation of electric and non-carbon-powered aircraft.

The end and the new beginning

In this book we have laid out an alarming legacy. Responsibility is laid at the door of ideological and incompetent politicians, for whom Johnson and Truss stand not as outliers but as all-too-typical Tories. First-past-the-post elections to the House of Commons gave them artificial majorities when fairer electoral arrangements would have brought progressive governments at Westminster on the same votes. Nonetheless, many people chose to sustain the Tories in power to both their own and the UK's disadvantage and so delayed efforts to mitigate climate change and stem economic decline.

After the 2024 election, with the passage of the years, two terms of a new government maybe, the UK could look and feel so much better, productive, fairer, cleaner, greener, healthier and more contented. How much optimism does that demand? We don't need the heart-melting rhetoric of an Obama; we've had enough of Johnson's word-spinning. It's time for no-frills determination to push along the pathway we've tried to map here. Of course it's a steep gradient, but the only way is up.

Endnotes

Introduction: Their Legacy

p.3 **Office for Budget Responsibility** https://www.tuc.org.uk/news/tuc-uk-families-suffering-worst-decline-living-standards-g7#:~:text=UK%20workers%20are%20on%20course,financial%20crisis%20real%20wage%20trends

p.3 **A quarter of adults no safety net** https://www.money.co.uk/savings-accounts/savings-statistics#:~:text=According%20to%20a%20survey%20by,having%20no%20savings%20at%20all

p.3 **Citizens Advice estimated five million people** https://www.citizensadvice.org.uk/policy/publications/the-national-red-index-how-to-turn-the-tide-on-falling-living-standards/

p.5 **Book groups** https://www.theguardian.com/books/2024/feb/29/uk-in-the-midst-of-a-boom-in-book-clubs-as-gen-zs-hobbies-change

p.6 **John Burn-Murdoch** https://twitter.com/jburnmurdoch/status/1570832839318605824?lang=en

p.7 **Our European neighbours** https://economy2030.resolutionfoundation.org/wp-content/uploads/2022/07/Chapter-one-interim-report.pdf

p.8 **His autobiography** David Cameron, *For the Record*, William Collins, 2019

p.8 **Increased national indebtedness** https://www.independent.co.uk/news/uk/politics/the-uk-national-debt-has-risen-by-ps555-billion-since-2010-under-george-osborne-a6947661.html

p.11 **Oliver Letwin** *Hearts and Minds. The Battle for the Conservative Party from Thatcher to the Present*, Biteback, 2017

p.11 **The barmy army** Kwasi Kwarteng et al., *Britannia Unchained: Global Lessons for Growth and Prosperity*, Palgrave Macmillan, 2012

p.12 **Another loss of UK credibility** *Guardian*, 16 June 2020

p.12 **Grant Shapps claimed woke culture** https://www.express.co.uk/comment/expresscomment/1865551/Defence-Secretary-Grant-Shapps-Woke-policies-are-divisive

p.13 **May and just about managing** https://www.tuc.org.uk/blogs/mrs-mays-legacy-just-about-managing-are-worse-today-when-she-took-office

p.15 **Tooth decay so extreme** https://www.bda.org/news-and-opinion/news/child-hospital-admissions-caused-by-decay-going-unchallenged/

p.16 **Will Hutton** *This Time No Mistakes*, Apollo, 2024

p.16 **Built before the First World War** https://www.ons.gov.uk/people

populationandcommunity/housing/articles/ageofthepropertyis
thebiggestsinglefactorinenergyefficiencyofhomes/2021-11-01

p.16 **Properties at risk of being flooded** https://publications.parliament.uk/
pa/cm5804/cmselect/cmpubacc/71/report.html#:~:text=In%202022–
23%2C%20there%20were,table%20level%20rises%20about%20
ground

p.17 **'Young Britons had realistic expectations'** John Burn-Murdoch,
Financial Times, 10/11 February 2024

p.17 **Average number of children born to a woman** https://www.ons.
gov.uk/peoplepopulationandcommunity/birthsdeathsandmarriages/
livebirths/bulletins/birthsummarytablesenglandandwales/2022refr
eshedpopulations#:~:text=The%20total%20fertility%20rate%20
(TFR,has%20been%20decreasing%20since%202010

p.18 **Young are turning Tory** https://www.statista.com/statistics/1379439/
uk-election-polls-by-age/

p.19 **GDP growth in London** *Financial Times*, 24 January 2024

1 Children: A Case of Neglect

p.23 **Least physically active generation** https://assets.childrens
commissioner.gov.uk/wpuploads/2018/08/Play-final-report.pdf

p.24 **Children below the poverty line** https://cpag.org.uk/news-blogs/news-
listings/official-child-poverty-statistics-350000-more-children-poverty-
and-numbers

p.24 **School absence crisis** https://www.sec-ed.co.uk/content/news/school-
attendance-crisis-one-in-four-secondary-students-persistently-absent/
#:~:text=Official%20figures%20for%20the%20autumn,sessions
%20during%20the%20autumn%20term

p.24 **Football pitches** https://www.theguardian.com/society/2019/jun/
02/tory-cuts-force-sale-710-local-football-pitches

p.24 **Playing fields** https://www.thelondoneconomic.com/news/all-work-
and-no-play-as-215-school-playing-fields-sold-off-since-2010-
127649/#

p.24 **Swimming pools** https://www.theguardian.com/commentisfree/
2023/mar/14/the-guardian-view-on-swimming-pools-a-public-good-
for-everyone

p.24 **Libraries** https://www.theguardian.com/books/2019/dec/06/britain-
has-closed-almost-800-libraries-since-2010-figures-show#:~:text=
Since%202010%2C%20773%20have%20closed,on%20the%20
2017%2F2018%20spend

p.25 **Youth centres** *Financial Times*, 30/31 December 2023

p.25 **Government's commitment to the sporting legacy** https://www.
nao.org.uk/wp-content/uploads/2024/02/delivering-value-from-
government-investment.pdf

p.25 **Al Aynsley-Green** *The British Betrayal of Childhood*, Routledge,
2019

p.25 **Not toilet-trained** https://www.theguardian.com/education/2024/feb/

28/one-in-four-school-starters-in-england-and-wales-not-toilet-trained-say-teachers

p.25 **Child deaths** https://www.ncmd.info/publications/child-death-data-2023/

p.26 **Royal College of Paediatrics and Child Health** https://www.independent.co.uk/news/health/child-deaths-england-rise-covid-b2445204.html?utm_campaign=1525638_THN%20-%2013%20November%202023&utm_medium=email&utm_source=NHS%20Providers%20%28Main%20account%29&dm_i=514F,WP6U,13CBES,3S46A,1

p.26 **Expectant mothers** *Financial Times*, 2/3 December 2023

p.26 **Psychiatric referrals of under-18s** https://www.thelancet.com/journals/lanpsy/article/PIIS2215-0366(24)00038-5/fulltext?dgcid=hubspot_update_feature_updatealerts_lanpsy&utm_campaign=update-lanpsy&utm_medium=email&_hsmi=300104067&_hsenc=p2Anqtz-92Nk-mHrgfF48LTDTZaGdNd4Y13OBJx27oiUxF-g8ZjFKKhxq5DpUGxhq6DVuuREQ1ZZ1V_msvx6ucJ5YdFy-kSx5fv77FPOQRLSpXGA2as-RkWrc&utm_content=300031254&utm_source=hs_email

p.26 **A 2021 review of children's care** https://assets.publishing.service.gov.uk/media/640a17f28fa8f5560820da4b/Independent_review_of_children_s_social_care_-_Final_report.pdf

p.27 **The NAO concluded** https://www.nao.org.uk/press-releases/support-for-vulnerable-adolescents/

p.27 **Births 2012–19** https://www.ons.gov.uk/peoplepopulationandcommunity/birthsdeathsandmarriages/livebirths/bulletins/birthsummarytablesenglandandwales/2019

p.28 **Births lowest in two decades** https://www.ons.gov.uk/peoplepopulationandcommunity/birthsdeathsandmarriages/livebirths/bulletins/birthsummarytablesenglandandwales/2022

p.28 **Child-rearing had become unaffordable** https://www.resolutionfoundation.org/advanced/a-new-generational-contract/

p.28 **A third of their income on nursery fees** https://www.theguardian.com/money/2023/mar/08/some-parents-england-spending-80-per-cent-pay-childcare-study

p.28 **Women dying in pregnancy and childbirth** https://www.theguardian.com/society/2024/jan/11/why-are-so-many-women-dying-during-pregnancy-and-what-can-be-done

p.28 **Unsafe maternity units** https://www.bbc.co.uk/news/health-67238868

p.28 **Almost one in four English children** https://www.theguardian.com/society/2024/jan/24/child-obesity-in-england-still-above-pre-pandemic-levels-study-finds#:~:text=2%20months%20old-,Almost%20a%20quarter%20of%20English%20children%20are,the%20end%20of%20primary%20school&text=Almost%20one%20in%20four%20children,impact%20of%20the%20coronavirus%20pandemic

p.29 **Heightened risk of diabetes** https://imperialbrc.nihr.ac.uk/2024/01/25/rising-childhood-obesity-from-pandemic-could-cost-uk-billions/

p.29 **Children's Society on unhappiness** https://www.childrenssociety.org.uk/good-childhood

p.29 **The 2014 changes around SEND** https://www.theguardian.com/uk-news/2024/jan/28/from-social-care-to-homelessness-what-are-the-cost-pressures-facing-english-councils

p.29 **Hampshire financial meltdown** https://www.theguardian.com/uk-news/2023/oct/04/tory-run-hampshire-council-says-it-faces-financial-meltdown

p.30 **According to the NSPCC** https://www.nspcc.org.uk/about-us/news-opinion/2023/2023-12-07-106-increase-in-child-cruelty-and-neglect-offences-in-england-in-the-past-5-years/

p.30 **On vulnerable young people** https://www.nao.org.uk/reports/support-for-vulnerable-adolescents/

p.30 **Children in care** https://www.gov.uk/government/statistics/children-looked-after-by-local-authorities-in-england-year-ending-31-march-2010#:~:text=Main%20findings%3A,year%20ending%2031%20March%202010

p.30 **County councils said children's services** https://www.localgov.co.uk/Childrens-services-absolute-carnage/58269

p.30 **Dumped far away** https://www.theguardian.com/society/2023/jul/09/revealed-childrens-care-homes-flood-into-cheapest-areas-of-england-not-where-most-needed

p.30 **John Pearce** https://www.themj.co.uk/NCASC-Government-must-make-some-difficult-decisions-on-childrens-services/233353?__hstc=194848306.d11473d61f3410da17cb4a8c99c0cfe0.1699788986943.1700053342339.1701635693133.3&__hssc=194848306.1.1701635693133&__hsfp=4208101522

p.30 **Placements in private homes** https://www.room151.co.uk/funding/rise-childrens-social-care-placements/#:~:text=The%20number%20of%20such%20placements,91%25%20over%20the%20same%20period

p.32 **Joeli Brearley** https://pregnantthenscrewed.com/code-chaos-for-parents-as-just-1-in-10-secure-a-code-to-access-new-government-childcare-scheme/

p.32 **Fall in infant care providers** *Financial Times*, 4 January 2024

p.32 **IFS research** https://ifs.org.uk/news/sure-start-greatly-improved-disadvantaged-childrens-gcse-results

p.33 **Gap in per pupil funding** https://ifs.org.uk/publications/tax-private-school-fees-and-state-school-spending#:~:text=This%20is%20£7%2C200%20or,about%2040%25%20or%20£3%2C500

p.33 **Spending per primary school pupil** https://ifs.org.uk/news/school-spending-pupil-2024-remain-3-below-2010-levels-real-terms-once-you-account-actual-costs

p.34 **Institute for Government addressing the attainment gap** https://www.instituteforgovernment.org.uk/publication/performance-tracker-2023/schools; see also https://epi.org.uk/executive-summary/

p.34 **Persistent inequalities in outcomes** https://epi.org.uk/comments/gcse-results-day-2023/

p.34 **Every Child a Reader** https://ifs.org.uk/publications/evaluation-every-child-reader-ecar

p.34 **No social class narrowing** https://www.ucl.ac.uk/news/2018/jul/chaotic-government-reforms-are-failing-tackle-education-inequality

p.35 **John Goldthorpe** *Understanding – and misunderstanding – social mobility in Britain*, Barnett Papers in Social Research, Oxford, 2012

p.35 **Top in maths at primary school not proceeding** *Tes Magazine*, 16 January 2024

p.36 **Education Policy Institute** https://epi.org.uk/publications-and-research/free-schools-2019-report/

p.36 **Powers to direct academy schools to reduce places** https://www.theguardian.com/society/2024/feb/19/the-devestating-impact-of-covid-and-austerity-on-children-in-england

p.36 **Ofsted found they did not** https://lordslibrary.parliament.uk/improving-schools-performance-are-multi-academy-trusts-the-answer/#:~:text=The%20government%20highlighted%20that%20%E2%80%9Cmore,in%20the%20same%20government%20paper

p.37 **Highest-performing pupils do better** https://www.instituteforgovernment.org.uk/report/devolved-public-services

p.37 **Centre for Social Justice worried about** https://www.centreforsocialjustice.org.uk/library/suspending-reality

p.38 **Not reaching key measures of progress** *Guardian*, 6 January 2024

p.38 **Sir Kevan Collins** https://www.theguardian.com/politics/2021/jun/02/education-recovery-chief-kevan-collins-quit-english-schools-catch-up-row

p.38 **Government 'well behind' on its own target** https://epi.org.uk/publications-and-research/education-the-fundamentals-eleven-facts-about-the-education-system-in-england/

p.38 **OECD runs periodical assessments** https://www.oecd.org/publication/resultats-du-pisa-2022?utm_campaign=OECD%20Education%20%26%20Skills%20Newsletter%3A%20New%20PISA%20Results&utm_content=Lire%20le%20rapport%20numérique%20et%20les%20notes%20de%20pays&utm_term=edu&utm_medium=email&utm_source=Adestra

p.39 **Half of UK pupils were in schools whose head reported** https://publications.parliament.uk/pa/cm5803/cmselect/cmpubacc/998/report.html

p.40 **'Disgruntlement over workloads'** https://www.instituteforgovernment.org.uk/publication/performance-tracker-2023/schools

p.40 **IFS on school funds** https://ifs.org.uk/news/school-spending-pupil-2024-remain-3-below-2010-levels-real-terms-once-you-account-actual-costs

p.40 **Fall in GCSE arts** https://www.culturallearningalliance.org.uk/arts-gcse-and-a-level-entries-2022/

p.41 **Perry suicide verdict** https://schoolsweek.co.uk/ofsted-inspection-contributed-to-head-ruth-perrys-death-coroner/

p.41 **Gillian Keegan** https://www.theguardian.com/politics/2024/mar/09/labour-shadow-education-secretary-calls-gillian-keegan-ofsted-comments-pathetic p.42 **NAO on school buildings** https://www.nao.org.uk/reports/condition-of-school-buildings/

p.43 **FE budget cuts** https://ifs.org.uk/education-spending/further-education-and-sixth-forms

p.43 **FE staff pay** https://ifs.org.uk/publications/what-has-happened-college-teacher-pay-england

p.44 **IFS said these reforms** https://ifs.org.uk/education-spending/further-education-and-sixth-forms

p.44 **Ofsted on T levels** https://www.gov.uk/government/publications/t-level-thematic-review-final-report/t-level-thematic-review-final-report

p.44 **NAO on digital skills** https://www.nao.org.uk/reports/the-digital-strategy-for-defence-a-review-of-early-implementation/

2 The Economy: Going Nowhere

p.46 **'Stagnation' and various figures** Resolution Foundation & Centre for Economic Performance, LSE, *Stagnation nation: Navigating a route to a fairer and more prosperous Britain*, July 2022; *Ending Stagnation: A New Economic Strategy For Britain*, December 2023

p.46 **Jeremy Hunt 'We had Brexit'** https://www.theguardian.com/politics/2023/dec/04/jeremy-hunt-blames-brexit-instability

p.48 **'If you think you could do a better job'** *The Times*, 20 March 2024

p.48 **Legal & General** https://www.theguardian.com/business/2023/dec/17/l-and-g-investment-manangement-us-style-bonuses-london-listed-firms-pay-policy#:~:text=Legal%20%26%20General%20Investment%20Management%20has,to%20US%2Dstyle%20pay

p.49 **More opaque ownership** *Financial Times*, 9 February 2024

p.49 **John Plender** *Financial Times*, 11/12 November 2023

p.49 **Martin Wolf** *Financial Times*, 16 October 2023

p.49 **Chartered accountants' professional body** https://www.icaew.com/insights/viewpoints-on-the-news/2022/may-2022/audit-reform-plans-announced-a-lopsided-package

p.50 **Attitudes towards austerity** Ipsos Mori Almanac 2018, www.ipsos-mori.com

p.51 **Keynes quote** https://www.economicsnetwork.ac.uk/archive/keynes_persuasion/The_Great_Slump_of_1930.htm

p.51 **Raab quote** https://www.independent.co.uk/news/uk/politics/brexit-latest-dominic-raab-trade-eu-france-calais-dover-economy-finance-deal-a8624036.html

p.51 **OBR on Brexit** https://obr.uk/forecasts-in-depth/the-economy-forecast/brexit-analysis/#assumptions

p.54 **Harrington quote** *Financial Times*, 23 November 2023

p.54 **May's industrial strategy** https://www.gov.uk/government/publications/industrial-strategy-building-a-britain-fit-for-the-future?utm_source=substack&utm_medium=email

p.54 **Maier quote** https://www.ippr.org/media-office/business-groups-back-new-ippr-blueprint-to-end-flip-flopping-and-to-get-serious-about-green-industrial-growth

p.54 **Phipson quote** https://lordslibrary.parliament.uk/calls-for-a-uk-industrial-strategy/

p.54 **David Edgerton** *The Rise and Fall of the British Nation*, Allen Lane, 2018

p.54 **Will Hutton** https://www.theguardian.com/books/2024/mar/31/will-hutton-this-time-no-mistakes-extract

p.55 **Hitachi** https://www.business-live.co.uk/manufacturing/hitachi-slashes-value-durham-factory-28266691

p.55 **Alstom** https://www.theguardian.com/business/2023/nov/15/train-maker-alstom-jobs-derby

p.55 **Train leasing companies** https://www.theguardian.com/business/2024/feb/18/profits-of-uks-private-train-leasing-firms-treble-in-a-year

p.55 **Switch to electric cars** *Financial Times*, 25 January 2024

p.56 **Deals rose to £8.6 billion** https://www.ons.gov.uk/business industryandtrade/changestobusiness/mergersandacquisitions/bulletins/mergersandacquisitionsinvolvingukcompanies/octobertodecembe r2023#:~:text=The%20provisional%20estimated%20value%20 of,2022%20(£5.8%20billion)

p.57 **Bank tax bailout** http://blogs.lse.ac.uk/politicsandpolicy/the-curious-case-of-bank-tax-since-the-bailout/#Author

p.57 **Professor Nicholas Crafts** https://voxeu.org/article/brexit-blame-it-banking-crisis#.XD4X6rmboi0.twitter

p.58 **Make UK said two thirds of manufacturers** *Financial Times*, 22 October 2023

p.58 **Download speeds** https://www.synergy-mobile.co.uk/2024/01/03/in-2023-the-uk-had-slowest-5g-mobile-download-speeds-in-the-g7/#:~:text=The%20research%20from%20Opensignal%20 found,average%20speeds%20in%20the%20UK

p.58 **Openreach** https://www.openreach.com/news-and-opinion/2023/12-5-million-build-milestone

p.58 **'Altnets'** https://www.ispreview.co.uk/index.php/2023/05/alternative-full-fibre-isps-cover-8-2-million-uk-premises-as-build-slows.html

p.59 **Public charging points** https://www.fleetnews.co.uk/news/latest-fleet-news/electric-fleet-news/2023/07/06/charge-point-installation-rate-increases-by-more-than-80

p.59 **Southend councillor** https://www.echo-news.co.uk/news/24100027.southend-seafront-see-car-charging-points-created/

p.59 **Asphalt Industry Alliance** https://www.asphaltuk.org/wp-content/uploads/ALARM-survey-2023-FINAL-with-links.pdf

p.59 **AA patrols called to 52,541 incidents** https://www.localgov.co.uk/Worst-October-in-history-for-pothole-breakdowns/58409

p.60 **Andy Haldane** *Financial Times*, 10 November 2023

p.60 **Edwin Heathcote** *Financial Times*, 7/8 May 2022

p.61 **Keith Williams** https://www.newcivilengineer.com/latest/rail-review-chair-calls-for-guiding-mind-to-oversee-sector-30-10-2019/

p.61 **Mark Harper** *Financial Times*, 4 April 2024

p.61 **Avanti West Coast** https://inews.co.uk/news/avanti-cancel-trains-rail-contract-government-2967888?ico=above_article_ticker

p.61 **Executives chortled** https://www.theguardian.com/business/2024/jan/16/free-money-avanti-west-coast-bosses-caught-joking-about-uk-government-handouts

p.62 **Thameslink** *Financial Times*, 9 February 2024

p.62 **NAO on major capital projects** https://www.nao.org.uk/insights/delivering-value-from-government-investment-in-major-projects/

p.63 **Duchess of Westminster** https://fullfact.org/news/margaret-thatcher-bus/

p.63 **Bus passengers** https://www.gov.uk/government/statistics/annual-bus-statistics-year-ending-march-2022/annual-bus-statistics-year-ending-march-2022#:~:text=Passenger%20journeys-,England,the%20financial%20year%20ending%202021

p.63 **Centre for Cities** https://www.centreforcities.org/wp-content/uploads/2019/11/Improving-urban-bus-services.pdf

p.63 **Birmingham buses** *Financial Times*, 8 November 2023

p.64 **CIPD on the gig economy** https://www.cipd.org/uk/views-and-insights/thought-leadership/cipd-voice/uk-gig-economy/

p.64 **TUC on the gig economy** https://www.tuc.org.uk/news/gig-economy-workforce-england-and-wales-has-almost-tripled-last-five-years-new-tuc-research

p.65 **Self-employment** https://cep.lse.ac.uk/pubs/download/cepcovid-19-028.pdf

p.65 **OBR on PIP** https://obr.uk/efo/economic-and-fiscal-outlook-march-2024/

p.65 **NEETs** https://www.ons.gov.uk/employmentandlabourmarket/people notinwork/unemployment/bulletins/youngpeoplenotineducation employmentortrainingneet/august2023

p.66 **OECD on skills** https://www.oecd-ilibrary.org/sites/1f029d8f-en/index.html?itemId=/content/publication/1f029d8f-en

p.67 **NAO on skills** https://www.nao.org.uk/press-releases/developing-workforce-skills-for-a-strong-economy/

p.67 **Firms' spending on workforce training** https://assets.publishing.service.gov.uk/media/65855506fc07f3000d8d46bd/Employer_skills_survey_2022_research_report.pdf

p.67 **UK companies spent** *Financial Times*, 10/11 February 2024

p.68 **Apprenticeship starts** https://commonslibrary.parliament.uk/research-briefings/sn06113/#:~:text=48%25%20of%20the%20apprenticeships%20started,25%20and%20over%20age%20groups

p.68 **New Economics Foundation** https://neweconomics.org/2024/03/solving-the-uks-skills-shortage

p.68 **Spending on the youngest** https://data.oecd.org/eduresource/education-spending.htm

p.69 **University ranking** https://www.topuniversities.com/university-rankings-articles/world-university-rankings/top-universities-uk#:~:text=The%20UK%20is%20home%20to,in%20the%20global%20top%2050 p.69 **Student rent** https://www.theguardian.com/money/2023/oct/26/university-students-england-50p-a-week-after-rent

p.69 **Student sex** https://www.hepi.ac.uk/wp-content/uploads/2021/04/Sex-and-Relationships-Among-Students-Summary-Report.pdf

p.70 **Loan repayments** *Financial Times*, 5 February 2024

p.70 **Migration Observatory** https://migrationobservatory.ox.ac.uk/resources/briefings/long-term-international-migration-flows-to-and-from-the-uk/

p.70 **Educated in the UK** https://commonslibrary.parliament.uk/research-briefings/cbp-7976/#:~:text=The%20analysis%20said%20the%20economic,%C2%A3560%20per%20UK%20resident

p.70 **University towns** https://www.theguardian.com/education/2024/feb/29/student-immigration-restrictions-will-damage-uk-economy-universities-say

p.71 **Sir John Bell** *Financial Times*, 21 February 2024

p.71 **Johnson-era report** https://assets.publishing.service.gov.uk/media/60f04432e90e0764ccfbd7bc/CST_Global_Britain.pdf

p.71 **Kate Bingham** *Guardian*, 27 August 2022

p.72 **Scientists' visas** *Financial Times*, 12 February 2024

3 Climate: High Water Everywhere

p.74 **Flood defences** *Guardian*, 6 January 2024

p.74 **Spending on flood risk** https://www.gov.uk/government/news/increasing-flood-resilience-in-the-great-river-ouse#:~:text=Throughout%20history%20the%20River%20Great,more%20recent%20memory%20in%201998

p.74 **NAO on flood protection** https://www.nao.org.uk/reports/resilience-to-flooding/

p.74 **MPs asked that same month** https://publications.parliament.uk/pa/cm5804/cmselect/cmpubacc/71/report.html

p.75 **Cavity or solid wall insulation** https://www.gov.uk/government/statistics/chapters-for-english-housing-survey-2022-to-2023-headline-report/chapter-5-energy-efficiency

p.75 **Owen Paterson** https://www.theguardian.com/politics/2012/oct/11/owen-paterson-environment-guardian-profile

p.76 **'We're going all out for shale'** https://www.theguardian.com/environment/2014/jan/13/shale-gas-fracking-cameron-all-out

p.76 **Cummings trolley quote** https://www.bbc.co.uk/news/uk-politics-67276394

p.76 **Trees target** https://committees.parliament.uk/committee/62/environmental-auditcommittee/news/196527/government-tree-planting-meets-less-than-half-its-annual-targets-despite-the-growing-demands-on-uk-woodland-for-net-zero/#:~:text=Increasing%20productive%20forestry%20is%20welcome,challenges%20and%20demands%20on%20woodland p.77 **Rates of planting** https://www.nao.org.uk/wp-content/uploads/2022/03/Tree-planting-in-England.pdf

p.77 **Mark Spencer quote** https://www.fwi.co.uk/news/land-use-framework-wont-be-communist-says-defra-minister

p.77 **Environmental Audit Committee** https://committees.parliament.uk/publications/40938/documents/199465/default/

p.78 **Climate Change Committee annual report** https://www.theccc.org.uk/publication/2022-progress-report-to-parliament/

p.78 **'Not appropriate' to stop supporting** https://www.edie.net/transport-secretary-rejects-calls-to-oppose-heathrow-airport-expansion-on-climate-grounds/

p.79 **Two thirds did not know they lived inside one** https://www.transport-network.co.uk/LTNs-popular-and-effective-leaked-report-says/19225

p.79 **Alok Sharma** *Financial Times*, 11 January 2024

p.79 **Chris Skidmore** *Daily Telegraph*, 25 November 2023

p.79 **NAO, 'it still had more work to do'** https://www.nao.org.uk/press-releases/decarbonising-the-power-sector/

p.80 **Low-carbon sector failed to grow** https://www.theguardian.com/environment/2022/feb/17/uk-green-economy-has-failed-to-grow-since-2014-official-figures-show

p.80 **Carbon Brief** https://www.theguardian.com/environment/2023/jan/23/low-carbon-jobs-fell-after-david-cameron-kibosh-on-green-crap-policies-study

p.80 **C&AG** https://www.nao.org.uk/press-releases/the-governments-support-for-biomass/

p.80 **Office for Environmental Protection** https://www.theoep.org.uk/report/government-remains-largely-track-meet-its-environmental-ambitions-finds-oep-annual-progress

p.81 **Resolution Foundation** *Ending Stagnation, a new economic strategy for Britain* December 2023 https://economy2030.resolutionfoundation.org/reports/ending-stagnation/

p.81 **Survey of charging points** https://www.localgov.co.uk/Nearly-70-of-EV-owners-unhappy-with-public-chargers/58782?actId=ebwp0YMB8s3Mv0I20l85odUcvuQDVN7aZHxMk8Rn99QlVf5ROUCALcXRBRDbz-zr&actCampaignType=CAMPAIGN_MAIL&actSource=510521Productions%20/%20Shutterstock.com

p.81 **Expert Lords committee** https://committees.parliament.uk/committee/515/environment-and-climate-change-committee/news/199773/the-uks-electric-vehicle-strategy-needs-a-rapid-recharge-says-lords-committee/

p.81 **Official ambition to power every home** https://www.theguardian.com/politics/2020/oct/05/boris-johnson-to-unveil-plan-to-power-all-uk-homes-with-wind-by-2030

p.82 **'Clear measures of overall progress'** https://www.nao.org.uk/wp-content/uploads/2023/03/decarbonising-the-power-sector.pdf

p.83 **Sunak swimming pool** https://www.theguardian.com/politics/2023/mar/12/rishi-sunak-has-electricity-grid-upgraded-to-heat-his-private-pool p.83 **Winser review** https://assets.publishing.service.gov.uk/media/64c8e96e19f5622360f3c0f0/electricity-networks-commissioner-letter-to-desnz-secretary.pdf

p.83 **Clark MacFarlane** https://www.siemensgamesa.com/newsroom/2021/08/210809-siemens-gamesa-double-blade-facility-offshore-hull-uk

p.84 **'aggressively' cyberattacking MPs** https://www.theguardian.com/uk-news/2024/mar/23/china-targets-group-of-mps-and-peers-with-string-of-cyber-attacks

p.85 **Hinkley Point electricity** *Financial Times*, 24 January 2024

p.85 **Sellafield cyberattack** https://www.theguardian.com/business/2023/dec/04/sellafield-nuclear-site-hacked-groups-russia-china

p.85 **Building Back Britain commission** https://www.nhbc.co.uk/media-centre/industry-news/2021/11/05/building-back-britain-commission-publishes-its-first-report-levelling-up-and-the-housing-challenge

p.86 **Properties valued at less than £162,000; Resolution Foundation did the sums** https://economy2030.resolutionfoundation.org/reports/ending-stagnation/

p.86 **National Infrastructure Commission** https://nic.org.uk/studies-reports/recommendations/government-should-not-support-the-rollout-of-hydrogen-heating/

p.87 **Clare Moriarty** *Financial Times*, 22 January 2024

p.87 **NAO on smart meters** https://www.nao.org.uk/reports/update-on-the-rollout-of-smart-meters/

p.88 **To ensnare customers without sufficient cover** https://www.nao.org.uk/reports/the-energy-supplier-market/

p.88 **UK Biobank** *Guardian*, 12 January 2024

p.89 **Pollution levels are a fifth lower** https://www.london.gov.uk/new-report-reveals-transformational-impact-expanded-ultra-low-emission-zone-so-far#:~:text=%E2%80%9Cthe%20evidence%20from%20this%20landmark,air%20for%20four%20million%20Londoners

p.89 **'Government does not clearly and consistently communicate'** https://www.nao.org.uk/wp-content/uploads/2022/01/Tackling-local-breaches-of-air-quality.pdf

p.89 **District Councils Network** https://www.localgov.co.uk/Concern-over-waste-reform-costs/58704

p.90 **Delayed blueprint for land use** https://www.theguardian.com/environment/2023/jan/05/ministers-run-scared-of-targeting-meat-consumption-in-land-use-strategy

p.90 **'Moved the goal posts'** https://www.bbc.co.uk/news/uk-england-24459424

p.90 **Climate Change Commission 2023 report to Parliament** https://www.theccc.org.uk/publication/2023-progress-report-to-parliament/

p.90 **National Infrastructure Commission** https://nic.org.uk/studies-reports/infrastructure-progress-review-2023/

p.91 **Alastair Chisholm** *Guardian*, 10 January 2024

p.91 **State of the rivers** https://www.theguardian.com/environment/2024/feb/26/british-irish-rivers-desperate-state-pollution-report-trust

p.92 **Oldest cast-iron pipes** *Financial Times*, 9 January 2024
p.92 **'Sufficient preliminary treatment'** *Financial Times*, 13 February 2024
p.93 **Thames Tideway** *Financial Times*, 20 August 2018
p.93 **Michael Benke** *Camden New Journal*, 25 January 2024
p.93 **Thames Water raising charges** *Financial Times*, 28 February 2024
p.94 **South West Water** https://www.theguardian.com/business/2024/jan/15/south-west-water-drought-preparations-devon-cornwall

4 Housing: A Property-Owning Plutocracy

p.95 **Steve McQueen** https://grenfell.film
p.96 **Competition and Markets Authority** https://www.gov.uk/government/news/cma-finds-fundamental-concerns-in-housebuilding-market
p.97 **Families with children** https://www.gov.uk/government/statistics/english-private-landlord-survey-2021-main-report/english-private-landlord-survey-2021-main-report—2
p.98 **Decency standard** https://www.gov.uk/government/statistics/english-housing-survey-2021-to-2022-private-rented-sector/english-housing-survey-2021-to-2022-private-rented-sector
p.99 **Transparency International** https://www.transparency.org.uk/mps-three-times-more-likely-own-second-home-public-research-reveals
p.100 **Gap between renters and owner-occupiers** https://www.gov.uk/government/statistics/english-housing-survey-2021-to-2022-headline-report/english-housing-survey-2021-to-2022-headline-report
p.100 **Renting in Andover** https://www.onthemarket.com/details/11214002/
p.100 **Affordability of rentals** https://www.scottishhousingnews.com/articles/only-85-of-private-rental-homes-affordable-to-uc-claimants-research-finds
p.100 **Rent rises** https://www.theguardian.com/money/2024/mar/20/average-monthly-uk-rent-up-9-the-highest-annual-increase-recorded
p.100 *Inside Housing* 17 December 2010
p.101 **Units completed** https://www.gov.uk/government/statistical-data-sets/live-tables-on-affordable-housing-supply#full-publication-update-history
p.101 **NAO on new homes** https://www.nao.org.uk/wp-content/uploads/2019/02/Planning-for-new-homes.pdf
p.102 **Councils' building record** https://www.local.gov.uk/topics/housing-and-planning/council-housing-100/why-council-housing-important
p.102 **National Housing Federation** https://commonslibrary.parliament.uk/research-briefings/cbp-8963/#:~:text=Research%20conducted%20by%20Heriot%2Dwatt,should%20be%20for%20social%20rent
p.103 **Housing ombudsman** https://www.theguardian.com/society/2024/jan/22/richard-blakeway-ombudsman-england-social-housing-health
p.103 **Council homes owned by landlords** https://www.insidehousing.co.uk/news/exclusive-7-rise-in-former-right-to-buy-homes-now-rented-privately-53507

p.105 **Private rents in the countryside** https://propertyindustryeye.com/rural-tenants-face-brunt-of-rent-hikes-new-data-shows/

p.105 **Migration driving growth** *Financial Times*, 21 February 2024

p.105 **English Housing Survey** https://www.gov.uk/government/statistics/english-housing-survey-2021-to-2022-headline-report

p.105 **Royal College of Paediatrics** https://www.theguardian.com/global/2023/nov/12/thousands-of-babies-and-toddlers-falling-sick-from-damp-homes-in-britain-nhs-doctor-warns

p.106 **Freedom to build** https://cps.org.uk/research/the-language-of-freedom/

p.106 **Martin Wolf** *Financial Times*, 6 February 2023

p.106 **National Planning Framework** https://assets.publishing.service.gov.uk/media/65a11af7e8f5ec000f1f8c46/NPPF_December_2023.pdf

p.107 **Public Accounts Committee** https://committees.parliament.uk/committee/127/public-accounts-committee/news/199357/flood-resilience-eroded-by-poorly-maintained-defences-with-government-in-the-dark-on-progress/

p.107 **Grid connections** https://www.theguardian.com/money/2024/mar/20/average-monthly-uk-rent-up-9-the-highest-annual-increase-recorded

p.107 **Ownership trends** https://www.insidehousing.co.uk/news/news/morning-briefing-homeownership-rate-halves-among-young-adults-62983

p.107 **Saving for a deposit** Bobby Duffy, *Generations*, Atlantic Books, 2021

p.108 **Help to Buy** https://blogs.lse.ac.uk/politicsandpolicy/who-is-helped-by-help-to-buy/#:~:text=Who%20benefits%3F,have%20recently%20attracted%20media%20attentionhave

p.108 **Aspirations towards owning** https://yougov.co.uk/economy/articles/36686-global-who-does-and-I-want-own-home

p.109 **New housing was available** https://www.gov.uk/government/statistics/housing-supply-net-additional-dwellings-england-2022-to-2023/housing-supply-net-additional-dwellings-england-2022-to-2023

p.110 **Housing Infrastructure Fund** https://www.housingtoday.co.uk/news/two-thirds-of-42bn-housing-infrastructure-fund-remains-unspent/5127043.article

p.110 **Some flats lacked windows** *Financial Times*, 14 February 2024

p.110 **'Work tirelessly'** *Guardian*, 6 November 2023

p.111 **Liverpool** https://www.insidehousing.co.uk/news/city-councils-spend-on-temporary-accommodation-up-7660-83922

p.111 **Rough sleeping** *Financial Times*, 13 November 2023

p.111 **Braverman** https://www.theguardian.com/society/2023/nov/04/suella-braverman-says-rough-sleeping-is-lifestyle-choice

p.112 **Nicholas Boys Smith** https://www.theguardian.com/politics/2024/jan/02/green-belt-building-design-tsar-nicholas-boys-smith

p.113 **Chief planner for the Corporation of London** *Guardian*, 15 January 2024

p.114 **Cambridge sustainability** *Financial Times*, 27/28 January 2024

5 Health: Waiting and Waiting

p.117 **Budget deficit** https://fullfact.org/economy/factcheck-has-budget-deficit-been-halved/

p.118 **NHS spending** https://www.kingsfund.org.uk/insight-and-analysis/data-and-charts/nhs-budget-nutshell#:~:text=Public%20funding%20for%20health%20services,as%20staff%20salaries%20and%20medicines

p.118 **Per capita spending** https://data.oecd.org/healthres/health-spending.htm

p.118 **Health Foundation** https://www.health.org.uk/news-and-comment/charts-and-infographics/how-does-uk-health-spending-compare-across-europe-over-the-past-decade

p.119 **Royal College of Nursing** https://www.theguardian.com/society/2023/aug/25/numbers-accepted-on-to-nursing-courses-in-england-falls-13-per-cent-future-of-nhs

p.120 **Cameron and Lansley** David Cameron, *For the Record*, William Collins, 2019

p.120 **David Nicholson** https://www.bmj.com/content/bmj/364/bmj.l422.full.pdf

p.121 **'Some sort of private solution'** *Daily Telegraph*, 20 March 2024

p.121 **Hinchingbrooke** https://www.theguardian.com/society/2015/jan/09/circle-hospital-private-firms-nhs-report-poor-care-hinchingbrooke

p.121 **NHS spending on private suppliers** https://www.gov.uk/government/publications/dhsc-annual-report-and-accounts-2022-to-2023

p.123 **NAO new hospitals** https://www.nao.org.uk/reports/progress-with-the-new-hospital-programme/

p.124 **Satisfaction with the NHS** https://www.kingsfund.org.uk/insight-and-analysis/press-releases/british-social-attitudes-satisfaction-nhs-falls-lowest-level#:~:text=Overall%20satisfaction%20with%20the%20NHS,BSA%20survey%20began%20in%201983

p.124 **GP popularity** https://www.england.nhs.uk/statistics/2023/07/13/gp-patient-survey-2023/

p.127 **Dementia** https://www.nice.org.uk/about/what-we-do/into-practice/measuring-the-use-of-nice-guidance/impact-of-our-guidance/niceimpact-dementia/ch3-hospital-care

p.127 **Mental health bed occupancy** *Financial Times*, 7 January 2024

p.127 **NAO** https://www.nao.org.uk/wp-content/uploads/2023/02/Progress-in-improving-mental-health-services-CS.pdf

p.129 **Smoking and health** https://www.bbc.co.uk/news/health-17264442

p.129 **Russell Jones** *The Decade in Tory: an inventory of idiocy from the Coalition to Covid*, Unbound, 2023

p.130 **Fast-food billboards** https://www.theguardian.com/media/2024/mar/04/four-in-five-billboard-ads-in-england-and-wales-in-poorer-areas

p.130 **Health status** https://www.smf.co.uk/wp-content/uploads/2023/07/Carrots-and-sticks-July-2023.pdf

p.130 **Getting fatter** https://data.oecd.org/healthrisk/overweight-or-obese-population.htm

p.130 Health Survey of England https://digital.nhs.uk/data-and-information/areas-of-interest/public-health/health-survey-for-england---health-social-care-and-lifestyles

p.130 **Obesity Health Alliance** https://obesityhealthalliance.org.uk/wp-content/uploads/2023/02/OHA-Health-Inequalities-Position-Statement-Final.pdf

p.131 **Sugar levy** https://www.kingsfund.org.uk/sites/default/files/2020-03/tax-regulation-briefing-2020.pdf

p.131 **IfG on diets** https://www.instituteforgovernment.org.uk/publication/tackling-obesity

p.132 **Nuffield Trust on dentists** https://www.nuffieldtrust.org.uk/news-item/nuffield-trust-response-to-imminent-nhs-dental-recovery-plan#:~:text="Last%20year%20we%20said%20that,state%20of%20near%2Dterminal%20decline

p.133 **Physical activity** https://digital.nhs.uk/data-and-information/publications/statistical/health-survey-for-england/2021-part-2/physical-activity

p.133 **Chief Medical Officers' guidance** https://assets.publishing.service.gov.uk/media/5d839543ed915d52428dc134/uk-chief-medical-officers-physical-activity-guidelines.pdf

p.133 **Health visitors** https://committees.parliament.uk/writtenevidence/120201/pdf/

p.134 **MMR vaccine** https://www.gov.uk/government/news/london-at-risk-of-measles-outbreaks-with-modelling-estimating-tens-of-thousands-of-cases#:~:text=Between%201%20January%20and%2030,the%20UK%20is%20considered%20low

p.134 **Sexual health budgets** https://www.local.gov.uk/publications/breaking-point-securing-future-sexual-health-services

p.135 **Health Survey England** https://digital.nhs.uk/data-and-information/publications/statistical/health-survey-for-england/2021/part-3-drinking-alcohol#:~:text=In%202021%2C%20a%20minority%20of,than%2014%20units%20per%20week

p.135 **Children's Commissioner** https://www.childrenscommissioner.gov.uk/chldrn/

p.135 **Portman Group** https://www.theguardian.com/society/2023/nov/18/firms-earn-53bn-a-year-from-uk-smoking-excess-drinking-and-junk-food-study

p.136 **Truss quote** https://twitter.com/trussliz/status/1751878969278796209?lang=en

p.136 **Johnson quote** https://www.bbc.co.uk/news/uk-politics-68787914

p.136 **Sales of harmful products** https://www.theguardian.com/society/2023/nov/18/firms-earn-53bn-a-year-from-uk-smoking-excess-drinking-and-junk-food-study#:~:text=People%20who%20smoke%20or%20drink,UK%20£31bn%20a%20year

p.136 **Spending on drug and alcohol treatment** https://committees.parliament.uk/committee/127/public-accounts-committee/news/199803/illegal-drugs-progress-mixed-on-government-harm-reduction-efforts-pac-report-finds/#:~:text=The%20PAC's%20report%20

highlights%20that,Government%20has%20not%20yet%20
addressed

p.137 **Public Accounts Committee on test and trace** https://committees.
parliament.uk/committee/127/public-accounts-committee/
news/150988/unimaginable-cost-of-test-trace-failed-to-deliver-central-
promise-of-averting-another-lockdown/

p.137 **Leicester report on lessons learned** https://www.leicester.gov.uk/
content/beyond-the-lockdowns-lessons-learned-from-leicester-s-covid-
story/lessons-for-the-future/

p.138 **Social care shortfall** https://researchbriefings.files.parliament.uk/
documents/CBP-7903/CBP-7903.pdf

p.138 **Social care spending** https://www.kingsfund.org.uk/insight-and-
analysis/data-and-charts/key-facts-figures-adult-social-care

p.138 **Unpaid care** https://www.nao.org.uk/wp-content/uploads/2023/11/
Report-reforming-adult-social-care-in-England.pdf

p.138 **NAO on social care** https://www.nao.org.uk/reports/reforming-
adult-social-care-in-england/

6 Misgovernment

p.141 **Steve Barclay** *Daily Telegraph*, 12 February 2022

p.141 **UK public sector** https://www.statista.com/statistics/623259/public-
sector-workforce-uk/

p.142 **Public spending and tax figures** https://www.resolutionfoundation.
org/publications/four-of-a-kind/; https://economy2030.resolution
foundation.org/wp-content/uploads/2023/06/Tax-planning.pdf;
https://ifs.org.uk/taxlab/taxlab-key-questions/what-does-government-
spend-money?tab=tab-545

p.144 **C&AG said it was crucial** https://www.nao.org.uk/insights/
efficiency-savings-require-learning-past-lessons/

p.144 **OECD had complacently observed** https://www.oecd.org/gov/ethics/
ethicscodesandcodesofconductinoecdcountries.htm#:~:text=
Citizens%20expect%20public%20servants%20to,their%20tasks%20
in%20daily%20operations

p.145 **Chair of Ofcom lauding GB News** *Financial Times*, 13 November
2023

p.145 **'Naked obsession'** *Financial Times*, 9/10 April 2022

p.146 **David Neal** https://www.theguardian.com/uk-news/2024/mar/27/
home-office-tried-cover-up-critical-reports-sacked-uk-border-chief-
david-neal

p.147 **'Generalist leaders who lacked expertise'** https://www.nao.org.uk/press-
releases/digital-transformation-in-government-addressing-the-barriers/

p.148 **'Ideological purge'** https://www.bbc.co.uk/news/uk-politics-62869880

p.149 **In the form of temporary staff** https://publications.parliament.uk/
pa/cm5804/cmselect/cmpubacc/452/report.html

p.150 **A study across the European Economic Area** *Lancet Public Health*
2024, 9: e166–77

p.151 **Centre for Cities** *Financial Times*, 22 January 2024
p.151 **Gains made on property sales** https://www.theguardian.com/money/2024/feb/20/notting-hill-residents-capital-gains-exceed-people-of-three-cities-combined
p.151 **An average property in Westminster** https://www.themj.co.uk/Reform-council-tax-to-level-up/233805
p.152 **Sunak on funding formulas** https://www.theguardian.com/politics/2022/aug/05/video-emerges-of-rishi-sunak-admitting-to-taking-money-from-deprived-areas
p.152 **Sir Steve Houghton** https://www.sigoma.gov.uk/news/2024/sigoma-warns-local-government-finance-settlement-undermining-levelling-up
p.152 **IFS on funding systems** https://ifs.org.uk/news/public-service-cuts-and-disjointed-funding-systems-local-services-put-levelling-danger#:~:text=Geography-,A%20new%20report%20out%20today%20finds%20that%20the%20current%20funding,the%20'Levelling%20Up'%20agenda
p.153 **Caught short in Woking** https://www.bbc.co.uk/news/articles/cv2yzver5vpo#:~:text=All%20council%2Drun%20toilets%20in,declaring%20effective%20bankruptcy%20in%20June
p.153 **Joseph Chamberlain** https://chamberlainhighburytrust.co.uk/2021/04/28/joseph-chamberlains-time-in-birmingham/Thurrock *Public Finance* Nov-Dec 2023
p.154 **Chartered Trading Standards Institute spot check** https://www.theguardian.com/commentisfree/2023/jun/20/trading-standards-uk-consumer-goods-britain-europe
p.155 **Thurrock** https://www.theguardian.com/society/2023/jun/15/thurrock-council-hid-losses-gambled-millions-risky-investments
p.155 **David Hodge** https://www.theguardian.com/commentisfree/2017/feb/09/surrey-council-tax-referendum-david-hodge-cuts
p.156 **NewFrontiersreport**https://businesscornwall.co.uk/news-by-industry/public-sector-news-categories/2018/05/cornwall-exploring-new-frontiers/
p.157 **Lord Amyas Morse** https://www.themj.co.uk/Lord-Morse-I-do-not-blame-all-council-failure-on-bad-management/233527
p.157 **NAO on Towns Fund** https://www.nao.org.uk/reports/review-of-the-town-deals-selection-process/
p.158 **Teesside** *Financial Times*, 2 February 2024
p.158 **Matt Griffith** *Financial Times*, 17 November 2023
p.158 **County Councils Network** https://www.localgov.co.uk/Culture-spend-down-by-500m/58783?actId=ebwp0YMB8s3Mv0I2Ol85odUcvuQDVN7aZHxMk8Rn99QlVf5ROUCALcXRBRDbz-zr&actCampaignType=CAMPAIGN_MAIL&actSource=510517
p.158 **Arts funding** https://musiciansunion.org.uk/news/the-damage-caused-by-a-decade-of-arts-funding-cuts; https://www.campaignforthearts.org/news/arts-index-2019/
p.159 **Ipswich theatre** *Observer*, 7 January 2024
p.161 **NAO on Unboxed festival** https://www.nao.org.uk/reports/investigation-into-the-unboxed-festival/

p.163 **Four out of every ten pounds** https://www.deliveringforscotland. gov.uk/scotland-in-the-uk/public-spending/

p.164 **Big gaps between better-off and disadvantaged** http s://ifs.org. uk/sites/default/files/2023-08/Employment-earnings-and-incomes-in-Scotland-IFS-Report.pdf

p.164 **World Health Organization** https://www.who.int/europe/news/ item/26-07-2023-no-place-for-cheap-alcohol--scotland-s-minimum-unit-pricing-policy-is-protecting-lives

p.164 **End of emergency rent caps** https://www.theguardian.com/uk-news/2024/feb/11/tenants-scotland-face-big-rent-rises-mass-evictions-from-april-emergency-protections-expire

p.165 **Child poverty** https://www.gov.scot/publications/cash-first-towards-ending-need-food-banks-scotland-child-rights-wellbeing-impact-assessment-crwia/

p.165 **In 2015, academics had concluded** https://social-policy.org.uk/ wordpress/wp-content/uploads/2015/04/Rummery.pdf

p.165 **IfG did stout-hearted work** https://www.instituteforgovernment. org.uk/report/devolved-public-services

p.166 **OECD 2022 student assessment survey** https://www.oecd.org/ publication/pisa-2022-results/

p.166 **Welsh spending per person** https://commonslibrary.parliament.uk/ research-briefings/sn04033/

p.166 **'Challenging and radical'** https://www.theguardian.com/ commentisfree/2024/jan/30/wales-council-tax-england-real-levelling-up

p.167 **Welsh social care** https://www.instituteforgovernment.org.uk/ report/devolved-public-services

7 Security: Criminal Neglect

p.170 **Gavin Williamson** https://ukdefencejournal.org.uk/defence-secretary-suggests-firing-paintballs-at-spanish-ships-off-gibraltar/

p.170 **General Sanders** https://www.independent.co.uk/news/uk/home-news/uk-going-to-war-russia-nato-conscription-age-b2484473.html

p.171 **Grant Shapps** https://www.bbc.co.uk/news/uk-68097048

p.171 **Truss and Trump** https://www.telegraph.co.uk/world-news/2024/ 02/23/liz-truss-donald-trump-joe-biden-us-election/

p.171 **Mhairi Fraser** *Guardian*, 10 February 2024

p.171 **Forces mental health** https://publications.parliament.uk/pa/ cm201719/cmselect/cmdfence/813/81306.htm#:~:text=There%20 have%20been%20significant%20increases,nearly%20 doubled%2C%20to%203.1%25

p.172 **Tanks** https://www.army-technology.com/news/british-army-has-just-157-challenger-2-tanks-available-for-operations/?cf-view

p.173 **Sir Richard Barrons** *Financial Times*, 16 September 2016

p.174 **NAO on equipment budget** https://www.nao.org.uk/reports/ equipment-plan-2023-to-2033/

p.174 **Malcolm Chalmers** *Financial Times*, 4 December 2023

p.174 **Francis Tusa** *Financial Times*, 5 February 2024

p.175 **Naval recruitment** https://ukdefencejournal.org.uk/figures-show-royal-navy-not-meeting-recruitment-targets/

p.175 **'Muddling through'** *Financial Times*, 3/4 February 2024

p.175 **'Not fit for purpose'** https://www.theguardian.com/uk-news/2018/sep/21/uks-nuclear-deterrent-infrastructure-not-fit-for-purpose-say-mps

p.175 **'Very close allies'** https://questions-statements.parliament.uk/written-questions/detail/2018-01-22/123985/

p.176 **Blackham** https://publications.parliament.uk/pa/cm201719/cmselect/cmdfence/818/818.pdf

p.177 **Bobbies on the beat** https://www.instituteforgovernment.org.uk/publication/performance-tracker-2023/police#footnoteref207_jdptqgd

p.177 **Perceptions of crime** https://www.ons.gov.uk/peoplepopulationandcommunity/crimeandjustice/articles/publicperceptionsofcrimeinenglandandwales/yearendingmarch2016

p.178 **Hospital reports on stabbings** https://researchbriefings.files.parliament.uk/documents/SN04304/SN04304.pdf

p.178 **Young people in trouble with the law** https://youthendowmentfund.org.uk/wp-content/uploads/2022/02/YEF-Statistics-update-February-2022-FINAL.pdf

p.178 **Crime Survey** https://www.ons.gov.uk/peoplepopulationandcommunity/crimeandjustice/bulletins/crimeinenglandandwales/yearendingseptember2023

p.178 **Centre for Social Justice** https://www.centreforsocialjustice.org.uk/wp-content/uploads/2023/12/CSJ-Two_Nations.pdf

p.179 **Social Justice Commission** https://www.centreforsocialjustice.org.uk/the-social-justice-commission

p.179 **Courts and offenders** https://www.theguardian.com/uk-news/2022/jul/21/recorded-in-england-and-wales-at-20-year-high-as-charge-rate-hits-new-low

p.179 **Falling crime figures** https://ec.europa.eu/eurostat/statistics-explained/index.php?title=Crime_statistics#:~:text=Between%202020%20and%202021%2C%20police,%2C%20Spain%2C%20Italy%20and%20Luxembourg

p.179 **Sex offences** https://www.ons.gov.uk/peoplepopulationandcommunity/crimeandjustice/articles/sexualoffencesprevalenceandtrendsenglandandwales/yearendingmarch2022

p.180 **Walking alone after dark** https://www.endviolenceagainstwomen.org.uk/new-data-women-feel-unsafe-at-night/

p.180 **Roadside breath tests** https://www.ukroed.org.uk/roadside-breath-test-figures-lowest-on-record/

p.180 **Drink-driving deaths** https://www.rac.co.uk/drive/news/motoring-news/the-battle-against-drink-driving-is-far-from-over/

p.180 **Fall in charging** https://www.instituteforgovernment.org.uk/publication/performance-tracker-2023/police#footnoteref165_lhbmq6m p.180 **Police understanding of sexual violence** https://www.bbc.co.uk/news/uk-england-london-63984813

p.181 **Casey review of Met** https://www.met.police.uk/cyGB/SysSiteAssets/media/downloads/met/about-us/baroness-casey-review/update-march-2023/baroness-casey-review-march-2023a.pdf

p.181 **Tom Harper** *The Fall of the Metropolitan Police*, Biteback, 2022

p.181 **Cuts in Tory areas** https://www.localgov.co.uk/Crime-prevention-budgets-slashed-under-Tories/46727

p.181 **Police and crime commissioners** https://www.nao.org.uk/reports/police-accountability-landscape-review-2/

p.182 **Appointing new officers** https://www.instituteforgovernment.org.uk/sites/default/files/2024-01/performance-tracker-2023.pdf

p.182 **Adrian Mardell** *Financial Times*, 2 February 2024

p.183 **Rise of antisocial behaviour** *Financial Times*, 10 April 2023 https://www.ft.com/content/6d765d94-5c5a-4313-a473-525d7814721e

p.183 **Police and psychiatric cases** https://www.bbc.co.uk/news/uk-66304472

p.184 **BDO** *Guardian*, 19 February 2024

p.184 **Police Foundation** https://www.police-foundation.org.uk/category/cyber-crime/

p.184 **Untaxed vehicles** https://www.gov.uk/government/statistics/vehicle-excise-duty-evasion-statistics-2023/vehicle-excise-duty-evasion-statistics-2023#:~:text=The%20rate%20for%202023%20corresponds,rate%20seen%20in%20active%20stock

p.184 **NAO on stealing during COVID** https://www.nao.org.uk/reports/tackling-fraud-and-corruption-against-government/

p.186 **Legal aid funding and C&AG on cuts** *Financial Times*, 9 February 2024

p.187 **Sam Townend KC** *Financial Times*, 6 February 2024

p.188 **Court closures** https://commonslibrary.parliament.uk/constituency-data-magistrates-court-closures/

p.189 **Blackpool magistrates** https://www.theguardian.com/law/2023/nov/30/stripped-bone-lancashire-courts-chaos-raac-adds-crisis-blackpool-blackburn-preston

p.189 **Prison numbers** https://commonslibrary.parliament.uk/research-briefings/sn04334/

p.191 **Prison spending** https://www.instituteforgovernment.org.uk/publication/performance-tracker-2023/prisons#:~:text=Spending%20increased%20to%20£4.06,4.34%20billion%20in%202024%2F25.&text=Following%20deep%20cuts%20in%20the,spending%20increased%20from%202015%2F16

p.191 **HMP Woodhill** https://www.miltonkeynes.co.uk/news/crime/milton-keynes-prison-is-calling-on-new-recruits-to-make-a-difference-4073507

p.192 **NAO on prisons** https://www.nao.org.uk/reports/improving-resettlement-support-for-prison-leavers-to-reduce-reoffending/

p.192 **Grayling on experts** https://publications.parliament.uk/pa/cm201213/cmhansrd/cm130109/debtext/130109-0001.htm p.193 **Private probation** https://www.theguardian.com/society/2017/dec/14/private-probation-firms-criticised-supervising-offenders-phone

p.193 **Ian Dunt** *How Westminster Works ... and Why It Doesn't*, Weidenfeld, 2023

p.193 **Michaela Hall inquest** https://www.theguardian.com/society/2024/mar/24/father-michaela-hall-murder-victim-probation-service

p.193 **Community sentences** *Guardian*, 25 December 2023

8 Equalities: Unjust Rewards

p.195 **Rich were richer** https://equalitytrust.org.uk/how-has-inequality-changed#:~:text=Inequality%20in%20Recent%20Years&text=After%20falling%20slightly%20over%20the,has%20stayed%20relatively%20level%20since

p.196 **Wealth of the top 1 per cent** Liam Byrne, *The Inequality of Wealth: Why it Matters and How to Fix it*, Apollo, 2024

p.196 **Minister for loneliness** https://www.gov.uk/government/news/pm-launches-governments-first-loneliness-strategy

p.196 **Casey review** https://www.ein.org.uk/news/government-publishes-casey-review-social-integration-great-britain

p.198 **Andy Haldane** https://www.civilsociety.co.uk/voices/andy-haldane-covid-19-has-reinforced-the-values-of-community-purpose-and-social-solidarity.html

p.198 **Peter Hennessy** *A Duty of Care: Britain Before and After COVID*, Allen Lane, 2022

p.198 **Sebastian Payne** *Broken Heartlands: A Journey Through Labour's Lost England*, Pan, 2021

p.198 **National Council for Voluntary Organizations** https://www.ncvo.org.uk/news-and-insights/news-index/key-findings-from-time-well-spent-2023/

p.198 **Charitable giving** https://www.centreforcities.org/press/north-east-of-england-more-generous-with-earnings-than-the-south-centre-for-cities-finds/#:~:text=Centre%20for%20Cities'%20analysis%20shows,in%20the%20most%20affluent%20places

p.200 **Trussell Trust** https://www.trusselltrust.org/?gad_source=1&gclid=CjwKCAjw9IayBhBJEiwAVuc3frMLqLE3OyOZeriIkk0cRaMkHs-DDsrFqo-IkoCHtT6hmgMrdXqQDxoC_94QAvD_BwE&gclsrc=aw.ds

p.200 **Lord Freud** https://www.independent.co.uk/news/uk/politics/demand-for-food-banks-has-nothing-to-do-with-benefits-squeeze-says-work-minister-lord-freud-8684005.html

p.200 **Johnny Mercer** https://www.standard.co.uk/news/politics/johnny-mercer-food-banks-poverty-uk-b1091987.html

p.200 **DWP referrals to food banks** https://www.theguardian.com/society/2024/feb/16/jobcentres-told-to-stop-referring-benefit-claimants-to-food-banks

p.202 **Low pay** https://www.resolutionfoundation.org/publications/a-pre-election-statement/#:~:text=Although%20nominal%20wages%20 are%20growing,unprecedented%2020%2Dyear%20pay%20 stagnation

p.203 **Beecroft report on employment law** https://www.gov.uk/government/ news/beecroft-report-on-employment-law

p.203 **Sarah O'Connor** *Financial Times*, 18 May 2018

p.205 **Refugee numbers** https://kantar.turtl.co/story/public-attitudes-to-immigration/page/3/14; https://researchbriefings.files.parliament.uk/ documents/SN01403/SN01403.pdf

p.205 **Welfare and asylum** https://migrationobservatory.ox.ac.uk/resources/ commentaries/uk-policies-to-deter-people-from-claiming-asylum/

p.205 **Rwanda costs** https://www.theguardian.com/uk-news/2024/mar/01/ rwanda-plan-uk-asylum-seeker-cost-figures

p.206 **Reasons for migrating** https://commonslibrary.parliament.uk/ research-briefings/sn06077/

p.206 **Christina McAnea** *Financial Times*, 28 November 2023

p.206 **Brian Bell** *Financial Times*, 26 January 2024

p.206 **May on entering Number 10** https://www.gov.uk/government/ speeches/statement-from-the-new-prime-minister-theresa-may

p.207 **Income gap** Anthony Heath, *Social Progress in Britain*, OUP, 2018

p.207 **Michael Marmot** https://www.instituteofhealthequity.org/resources-reports/marmot-review-10-years-on

p.207 **Damian Hinds** https://www.gov.uk/government/speeches/education-secretary-sets-vision-for-boosting-social-mobility

p.208 **Centre for Social Justice** *Two Nations*, December 2023

p.208 **Army housing** *Daily Telegraph*, 26 February 2024

p.209 **Suella Braverman** https://www.telegraph.co.uk/politics/2024/02/22/ islamism-suella-braverman-gaza-ceasefire-lindsay-hoyle/

p.209 **Survey of black Britons** https://www.cam.ac.uk/stories/black-british-voices-report

p.209 **Ethnic and religious minorities** https://bristoluniversitypress.co.uk/ ethnic-inequalities-in-a-time-of-crisis

p.209 **Ethnic minority earnings** https://www.ucl.ac.uk/news/2023/ jul/lessons-must-be-learnt-covid-19s-unequal-impact-minority-groups#:~:text=Black%20and%20Asian%20communities%20 had,access%20to%20it%20at%20all

p.210 **Casey review** https://www.gov.uk/government/publications/the-casey-review-a-review-into-opportunity-and-integration

p.210 **At ease with racial difference** https://www.kcl.ac.uk/policy-institute/ assets/love-thy-neighbour.pdf

p.210 **Johnson race inquiry** https://www.gov.uk/government/publications/ the-report-of-the-commission-on-race-and-ethnic-disparities/foreword-introduction-and-full-recommendations

p.211 **Opinium survey** https://www.opinium.com/racism-rising-since-brexit-vote/

p.212 **Absolute poverty** https://www.gov.uk/government/statistics/ households-below-average-income-for-financial-years-ending-1995-to-2023/households-below-average-income-an-analysis-of-the-uk-income-distribution-fye-1995-to-fye-2023?mc_cid=94b8cfb210&mc_

eid=a7b8777863#long-term-trends-data-prior-to-fye-1995-are-not-accredited-official-statistics

p.212 **Digital living standards** https://www.theguardian.com/technology/2024/mar/17/half-uk-families-excluded-modern-digital-society-study

p.212 **Minimum Income Standard** https://dmscdn.vuelio.co.uk/publicitem/5bb4b0e5-9959-4a6f-9e7e-cffb64618d2e

p.213 **Poverty threshold** https://cpag.org.uk/child-poverty/poverty-facts-and-figures#:~:text=From%20the%20latest%20figures%20(2019,14%20(seek%20UK%20wide%20reference)

p.213 **Cameron on births** https://www.gov.uk/government/speeches/welfare-speech

p.213 **Children becoming shorter** https://www.theguardian.com/business/2023/jun/21/children-raised-under-uk-austerity-shorter-than-european-peers-study

p.213 **Blair poverty target** https://www.resolutionfoundation.org/publications/the-living-standards-audit-2018/

p.213 **Poverty rates** https://publications.parliament.uk/pa/cm200304/cmselect/cmworpen/85/85.pdf

p.213 **Children in poverty** https://www.jrf.org.uk/uk-poverty-2024-the-essential-guide-to-understanding-poverty-in-the-uk#:~:text=Poverty%20has%20increased%2C%20close%20to%20pre%2Dpandemic%20levels,-More%20than%201&text=This%20included%3A,nearly%203%20in%202010)%20children

p.214 **Unemployment benefits** https://www.resolutionfoundation.org/comment/policy-lessons-on-how-to-have-children-and-how-to-bribe-them/

p.214 **Children in families out of work** https://www.theguardian.com/commentisfree/2023/sep/29/poverty-tory-britain-essential-bills-social-tariff-covid-universal-credit

p.214 **Universal Credit in the pandemic** https://www.theguardian.com/business/2023/jul/09/end-to-universal-credits-covid-top-up-is-fuelling-rise-in-poverty-warns-ifs

p.214 **Single people** Donald Hirsch, *The UK's inadequate and unfair safety net*, abrdn Financial Fairness Trust, 2024

p.214 **UN rapporteurs** *Guardian*, 5 November 2023

p.214 **Torsten Bell** https://www.resolutionfoundation.org/comment/fraying-safety-nets/#:~:text=Second%2C%20we%20treat%20different%20groups,to%20that%20minimum%20income%20standard

p.215 **British Social Attitudes** https://natcen.ac.uk/sites/default/files/2023-09/BSA%2040%20Poverty.pdf

p.215 **Universal Credit claim costs** https://www.nao.org.uk/wp-content/uploads/2018/06/Rolling-out-Universal-Credit-Summary.pdf

p.215 **NAO on transfer to Universal Credit** https://www.nao.org.uk/press-releases/one-in-five-legacy-benefit-claimants-not-switching-to-universal-credit/

p.216 **Bedroom tax** https://assets.publishing.service.gov.uk/government/uploads/system/uploads/attachment_data/file/329949/rr882-evaluation-of-removal-of-the-spare-room-subsidy-summary.pdf p.217 **Marriage** https://www.ons.gov.uk/peoplepopulationandcommunity/ birthsdeathsandmarriages/marriagecohabitationandcivilpartnerships/ bulletins/marriagesinenglandandwalesprovisional/2020

p.218 **The old less likely to be poor** https://www.ons.gov.uk/economy/ investmentspensionsandtrusts/compendium/pensiontrends/2014-11-28/ chapter13inequalitiesandpovertyinretirement2012edition

p.218 **David Willetts** *The Pinch: How the Baby Boomers Took Their Children's Future*, Atlantic, 2011

p.218 **Voting preferences of the old and young** https://yougov.co.uk/ politics/articles/48476-how-is-britain-voting-as-we-enter-the-2024-election-year

p.219 **Gap between rich and poor old** https://ageing-better.org.uk/sites/ default/files/2023-12/The-State-of-Ageing-interactive-summary-2023-4.pdf

p.220 **Equality as a value** https://cps.org.uk/research/the-language-of-freedom/

p.220 **Martin Wolf** *Financial Times*, 6 December 2023

p.220 **Proportion of income paid in tax** https://docs.google.com/ spreadsheets/d/1CPIm9U5KYZiEPAZ64IHZVdVMm1rds8yY/ edit?pli=1#gid=966296506

p.221 **Millionaire bankers** https://www.theguardian.com/business/2022/feb/ 16/weve-had-a-run-on-champagne-biggest-uk-banker-bonuses-since-financial-crash

p.221 **Bankers' bonuses** https://www.theguardian.com/business/2023/ oct/24/uk-financial-regulators-scrap-cap-on-bankers-bonuses

p.221 **Sunak tax return** *Financial Times*, 9 February 2024; https://www. theguardian.com/politics/2024/feb/09/rishi-sunak-paid-effective-tax-rate-of-23-on-22m-income-last-year#:~:text=Rishi%20Sunak-, Rishi%20Sunak%20paid%20effective%20tax%20rate%20of%20 23%25%20on,2.2m%20income%20last%20year&text=Rishi%20 Sunak%20paid%20more%20than,of%20his%20tax%20affairs%20 shows

p.221 **Sunak wife loophole** https://taxpolicy.org.uk/2023/09/28/obscure_ loophole/

p.222 **Richest 50 families** https://equalitytrust.org.uk/scale-economic-inequality-uk#:~:text=GB%20Wealth%20Inequality&text=In%20 2020%2C%20the%20ONS%20calculated,and%202013%2C%20 reaching%209%25

p.222 **ONS on wealth** https://www.ons.gov.uk/peoplepopulationand community/personalandhouseholdfinances/incomeandwealth/bulletins/ totalwealthingreatbritain/april2018tomarch2020

p.223 **Sue Hawley** https://www.spotlightcorruption.org/hold-senior-executives-to-account/

p.224 **Resolution Foundation** https://www.resolutionfoundation.org/ publications/happy-new-tax-year-2024/

Conclusion: Up, Up and Away

p.229 **Exeter University** https://www.theguardian.com/environment/2024/apr/09/england-could-produce-13-times-more-renewable-energy-using-less-than-3-of-land-analysis

p.233 **Lack of water planning** https://www.nao.org.uk/reports/water-supply-and-demand-management/

p.233 **John Muellbauer and David Soskice** *The Thatcher Legacy: Lessons for the Future of the UK Economy*, Resolution Foundation, November 2022

p.233 **Martin Weale** *Financial Times*, 1 January 2024

p.234 **Within a two-kilometre radius of railway stations** https://www.citymetric.com/fabric/within-2km-station-south-east-england-has-golf-courses-room-500000-homes-373

p.234 **Brett Christophers** *The New Enclosure: Appropriation of Public Land in Neoliberal Britain*, Verso, 2018

p.234 **National Housing Federation** *Financial Times*, 27 February 2024

p.237 **Ashton-under-Lyne leisure centre** https://www.placenorthwest.co.uk/tameside-calls-in-wrecking-ball-at-ashton-swimming-pool/

p.238 **IFS on Sure Start** https://www.theguardian.com/education/2024/apr/09/senior-labour-figures-call-for-life-transforming-sure-start-policy

p.240 **Resolution Foundation Single Enforcement Body** https://www.resolutionfoundation.org/publications/enforce-for-good/

p.240 **Peter Drucker** *The Unseen Revolution: How Pension Fund Socialism Came to America*, Harper Collins, 1976

p.242 **Kristalina Georgieva** https://www.theguardian.com/business/2024/mar/14/imf-kristalina-georgieva-inequality-growth-living-standards-john-maynard-keynes#:~:text="We%20have%20an%20obligation%20to,durable%20growth%2C%20she%20said

p.245 **Buckingham Palace council tax** https://fullfact.org/news/buckingham-palace-pay-council-tax/

p.245 **An expert commission** https://www.lse.ac.uk/News/Latest-news-from-LSE/2020/L-December/Wealth-Commission-report

Index

Abbott, Diane, 210
Advanced Research and Invention Agency, 71
Afghanistan, 171, 173
ageing, 17–18
Albania, 205
alcohol consumption, 135–6, 164
Almond, Kirsty, 98
ALMOs (arm's-length management organizations), 101
Alstom, 55
Anderson, Lee, 11, 201
Andover, Hampshire, 100
Anglia Water, 114
apprenticeships, 68, 153, 226
Arm (tech company), 56
armed forces, 173–5, 208
arts and leisure, 225–6
funding, 158–60
Arts Council England, 158–60
Asphalt Industry Alliance, 59
Association of Directors of Children's Services, 30
Association of Prison Lawyers, 188
AstraZeneca, 71
Audit Commission, 156
austerity, 8–10, 26, 31, 50, 100, 119, 126, 173, 183, 196–9, 207
autism, 15–16, 23, 27
'Awaab's law', 125
Aynsley-Green, Al, 25

Badenoch, Kemi, 144, 210
badgers, 90
Bank of England, 57, 197
bankers' bonuses, 220, 221
Barclay, Stephen, 75, 141, 210
Barnett formula, 163, 166
Barratt Homes, 106
Barrons, Richard, 172
BBC (British Broadcasting Corporation), 11, 120, 145, 167–8
beavers, 90
Bedfordshire, 183–4
'bedroom tax', 104, 216–17
Beecroft, Adrian, 203
Bell, Brian, 206
Bell, John, 71
Bell, Torsten, 104, 214
benefit system, 7, 14, 65–6, 104, 178, 185–6, 200–202, 205, 211–17
'bedroom tax', 104, 216–17
disability benefits, 66, 98, 214–16
housing benefit, 99–100
Personal Independence Payments (PIP), 65, 214
sickness benefits, 65, 128
unemployment benefits, 214
Universal Credit, 7, 202, 214, 215–17
Benke, Michael, 93
BHS, 49
Biden, Joe, 54
Big Help Project, 200
'Big Society', 198
Bingham, Kate, 71
biodiversity, 89–90
Birkinshaw, Steve, 113
Birmingham, 153
birth rate, 17, 28, 213
Black Lives Matter, 209–10
Blackham, Jeremy, 176
Blair, Tony, 122, 178, 213
Boohoo, 203
Boots, 48
Boyle, Danny, 120
Boys Smith, Nicholas, 112
Braverman, Suella, 111, 182, 205, 209
Brearley, Joeli, 32
Brexit, 7–9, 19, 42, 67, 84, 92, 129, 141, 143, 158, 206, 211
economy and, 46–7

immigration and, 119, 139
NHS and, 119, 122
referendum, 13, 162
science and, 71
sovereignty, 176
trade and, 51–3, 55–7, 175–6
Unboxed festival, 161
devolution and, 161–2, 164, 197
Bristol council, 160
Britannia Unchained, 11
British Dental Association 132
British Museum, 11, 161, 195
British Steel, 53
'Britishness', 197, 201
broadband, 58
'Broken Britain', 179
Brooks, Rebekah, 168
Brown, Gordon, 50, 162, 211–12, 241
Browne, Ivan, 134–5, 137
BT, 58
Bucknall, Rosie, 208
Buffett, Warren, 82
Building Back Britain Commission, 85
Building Better, Building Beautiful Commission, 110
Bulb Energy, 88
Burke, Edmund, 11
Burn-Murdoch, John, 6
Burnham, Andy, 63
Burnley, 151
bus services, 63–4
Business and Technology Council, 43
Business, Energy and Industrial Strategy (BEIS), 79

Cadent, 86
Cambridge, 114–15
Cambridge University, 69, 71, 159

Cameron, David, 7–8, 11–13, 34, 53, 62, 143, 145–6, 162, 168, 201, 207
Big Society, 198
Brexit, 13
'Broken Britain', 179
defence and, 172–3
employment and, 203
green issues, 75–6, 81
Greensill Capital and, 145, 195
housing and, 101–2
NHS and, 7, 117–20
police and, 176, 181
poverty and, 213
prisons and, 189, 192
CAMHS (Child and Adolescent Mental Health Services), 45
Canada, 144
cancer, 118–19, 125
capitalism, 47–9, 54
car industry, 55, 56, 88
electric vehicles (EVs), 55, 56, 58–9, 78, 81, 232
Carbon Brief, 80
Care Quality Commission (CQC), 41, 117, 127
care workers, 206
Carillion, 49
Carney, Mark, 197
Casey, Louise, 181, 196, 210
Centre for Cities, 63
Centre for Social Justice, 32, 37, 178–9, 208
CGN (China General Nuclear Power Group), 84
Chalk, Alex, 191
Chalmers, Malcolm, 174
Chamberlain, Joseph, 112, 153
Chambers, Mike, 1
Channel Four, 168
charities, 167, 198–200
Charles III, King of the

United Kingdom, 168
Chartered Institute of Personnel and Development (CIPD), 64
Chartered Trading Standards Institute, 154
Child Trust Fund, 24
children, 18, 20, 23–45, 135, 237–8
careers advice, 25
child abuse/neglect, 30, 33, 45, 153
child poverty, 24, 26, 44, 165, 213–14
childbirth, 28
childcare, 28, 31–2, 66
COVID and, 38–40
health, 28–9, 131–2, 133
infant mortality, 25–6
mental health, 2, 26–7, 45, 127–8
obesity and, 28–9, 130–31
private children's homes, 183–4
social care, 30–31
special needs, 29, 30–32
see also education
Children's Commissioner, 135
Children's Society, 29
China, 53, 56, 84–5, 143
Chisholm, Alastair, 91
Chote, Robert, 9
Christophers, Brett, 234
Circle Health, 121
Citizens Advice, 3, 98, 198, 217
civil service, 9, 146–9
Civitas, 17
Clapham Park estate, Lambeth, 101–2
Clark, David, 128
Clarke, Kenneth, 188, 191
class, 206–8

clean air strategy, 88–9
Clegg, Nick, 27
climate change, 15, 20, 73–94, 228–30
  air quality, 88–9
  carbon emissions, 80–82, 88
  flooding, 16, 73–4, 90–91
  net zero target, 2, 10, 20, 75, 77–9, 83, 85
  tree planting, 76–7
  see also energy
Climate Change Act (2008), 75
Climate Change Commission
Climate Change Committee, 78, 90
Co-op Food, 183
Coffey, Therese, 75
Collins, Kevan, 38
Colston, Edward, 209
Competition and Markets Authority, 96, 106, 120
Comptroller and Auditor General (C&AG), 80, 144, 157, 186
Confederation of British Industry, 48
Conformité Européenne (CE), 52
Connolly, Frances and Patrick, 199
constitutional spoliation, 142–5
COP26, 77, 79
Coram, 187–8
Cornwall, 156
Corruption Watch, 223
councils see local government
County Councils Network, 158
COVID, 14, 21, 26, 28–9, 50, 61, 104–5, 108, 126, 137, 139, 142–4, 180, 197–8, 224
  benefits and, 216

children and, 38–40
contracts, 8, 144, 195
crime and, 184–5
education and, 38–9, 43, 137–8
Crafts, Nicholas, 57
crime, 5, 164, 176–91
  antisocial behaviour, 183
  car theft, 182–3
  COVID and, 184–5
  justice system, 185–91
  knife crime, 177–8
  online fraud, 184
  sex offences, 179–81
  shoplifting, 183
Crime Survey of England and Wales, 177, 178
culture wars, 12, 201
Cummings, Dominic, 33, 76, 147–8
Currys, 56
cyberattacks, 172

Dacre, Paul, 145
Daily Express, 12
Daily Mail, 6, 12, 70, 134, 143, 145, 153, 163, 188, 191, 199, 209, 211, 212, 224
Daily Mirror, 36
Daily Telegraph, 12, 14, 56, 77, 121, 141, 191
Dean-Curtis, Kyle, 116
Deben, Lord, see Gummer, John Selwyn, Baron Deben
defence, 170–76
Defence Analysis, 174
Defra (Department for Environment, Food & Rural Affairs), 89, 91
dementia, 128
dentistry, 131–3
Department for Business, Energy & Industrial Strategy, 55

Department for Culture, Media and Sport, 158
Department for Education, 25, 42
Department for Work and Pension, 128
Department of Economic Affairs, 54
Department of Health and Social Care, 123, 138
Department of Levelling Up, Housing and Communities, 101
Department of Transport, 62
Deregulation Act (2015), 110
devolution, 161–6
Diamond, HMS, 175
digital services legislation, 27
Direct Line, 56
disability, 66, 98, 214–16
District Councils Network, 89
Dorling, Danny, 108
Dorries, Nadine, 160
Douglas-Home, Alec, 11
Drake, Francis, 6
Drakeford, Mark, 166
drink-driving, 180
Driver and Vehicle Standards Agency (DVSA), 148–9
driving examiners, 148–9
Drucker, Peter, 240
drug abuse, 135–6, 164
DS Smith, 56
Duncan Smith, Iain, 178–9, 201, 214–15, 217
Dunt, Ian, 193
Dyson, James, 36, 48

'Eat Out to Help Out' scheme, 14

economy, 46–72
  GDP, 46–7, 50, 64, 142
  productivity, 47–8, 51, 58, 60, 64
  public spending, 142
  stagnation, 46–7, 50
  state borrowing, 50
EDF, 84–5
Edgerton, David, 54
Edinburgh, 165
education, 20–21, 23–4, 27, 32, 33–45, 67–72, 165–7, 209, 211, 230, 237–9
  A levels, 40, 43, 44
  absenteeism, 68
  academies, 37
  Advanced British Standard, 44
  arts, 40
  BTECs, 43–4
  COVID and, 38–9, 43, 137–8
  curriculum, 35
  EBacc, 35
  free schools, 35–6
  further education, 43–4, 45, 67, 239
  GCSEs, 34, 35, 39, 40, 43
  nurseries, 28, 31–2, 44–5
  Ofsted inspections, 41
  overseas students, 70
  school buildings, 42
  sports, 40
  student loans, 69–70
  T levels, 44, 68
  teachers, 39–40
  tuition fees, 70
  universities, 68–72, 239
Education Policy Institute, 36, 38
employment, 5, 64–8, 141, 150, 202–3, 214, 239–41
  apprenticeships, 68
  income, 64–6, 195–6, 202–3, 220
  minimum wage, 202–3

National Living Wage, 153
  NEETs (young people not in education or employment), 65–6
  self-employment, 65
  skills shortages, 66–7
  unemployment, 64, 135–6, 201–2
  unemployment benefits, 214
  unions, 202–3
  workforce training, 67–8
  zero-hours contracts, 64–5
Employment Support Allowance, 216
energy, 229–30
  coal mining, 78
  domestic energy, 85–8
  electricity distribution, 82–3
  energy companies, 80, 82–3, 88
  hydrogen, 86
  natural gas, 82
  nuclear power, 84–5
  smart meters, 87
  solar power, 82
  wind power, 76, 78, 81–3
Enfield, north London, 154
English National Opera, 160–61
environment, 73–94
  flooding, 16, 73–4, 90–91
  insulation, 75, 78, 86, 230–31
  see also climate change; energy; water
Environment Agency, 73–4, 79, 94, 114
Environmental Audit Committee, 77
Equality Act (2010), 6, 208
Equality and Human

Rights Commission, 209
Equality Hub, 210
European Convention on Human Rights, 205
European Union, 7, 51–2, 64, 92, 200, 205–6
  Erasmus scheme, 71–2
  grants, 156
  Horizon programme, 72
Evening Standard, 195
Everard, Sarah, 180
Every Child a Reader programme, 34, 45
Every Child Matters programme, 23
executive pay, 48
exercise, 133
exports, 51–2

Facebook, 27
Fairburn, Jeff, 221
Farage, Nigel, 143
Financial Conduct Authority, 219
Financial Ombudsman Service, 218
Financial Times, 49, 203, 221
flooding, 16, 73–4, 90–91
food banks, 21, 200–201
Food Standards Agency, 129
football, 146
Forensic Science Service, 193
Forestry and Land Scotland, 77
Forestry Commission, 76–7
fracking, 75–6, 79
France, 7, 47, 58, 64, 68, 76, 105, 189, 201–2, 205
Fraser, Mhairi, 171
Frazer, Lucy, 168

free ports, 157
Freud, David Anthony, Baron Freud, 200
Friedman, Milton, 49
Frost, David, 52, 78

GB News, 6, 12, 145, 168
generation wars, 97
Georgieva, Kristalina, 242
Germany, 7, 47, 68, 76, 97, 108, 205, 221
Gibraltar, 170
'gig economy', 64, 202
Glasgow, 165
global financial crisis (2007–8), 8, 57, 142, 220
Global Warming Policy Foundation, 78
Glyndebourne, 160
Goddard, Vic, 40–41, 43
Goldsmith Street, Norwich, 103
Goldthorpe, John, 35
Goodwin, Fred, 51
Gove, Michae, 23–4, 33–7, 40, 42, 66l, 107, 109–10, 112, 114, 147, 149, 152, 155, 211
Grade, Michael, Baron Grade of Yarmouth, 145
Gramsci, Antonio, 247
Grayling, Chris, 8, 90, 155, 171, 189, 192–3, 215
Great British Railways (GBR), 61
Great Ouse river, 73–4
green belts, 112
Green Investment Bank, 75
green policies, 75–80
Greenpeace, 74
Greensill Capital, 145, 195
Grenfell Tower fire, 7, 95–6, 101

Griffith, Matt, 158
growth, 18–19
Guardian, 61, 74, 85, 132
Guardiola, Pep, 197
Gummer, John Selwyn, Baron Deben, 78

Haldane, Andy, 60, 198
Hall, Michaela, 193
Hamas, 197
Hammond, Philip, 155
Hancock, Matt, 130
Harmsworth, Alfred, 1st Viscount Northcliffe, 12
Harper, Mark, 61
Harper, Tom, 181
Harrington, Richard, 54
Hartlepool, County Durham, 151, 199
hate crimes, 211
Hawley, Sue, 223
Hayek, Friedrich, 10, 49
health, 65–6, 129–30, 150
    cancer, 118–19, 125
    HIV, 134
    mental health, 66, 127–8
    obesity, 130–31, 136
    prevention, 128–9
    public health, 122, 129, 133, 243–4
    sexual health, 134–5
    sickness benefits, 65, 128
    vaccinations, 133–4
    see also NHS
Health Foundation, 118
heat pumps, 86, 107
Heath, Edward, 54
Heathcote, Edwin, 60
Heathrow Airport, 2, 78
Help to Buy scheme, 8, 108
Henderson, Kate, 110
Hennessy, Peter, 198
Henry, Donna Charmaine, 101

Heseltine, Michael, 112
high streets, 4, 196, 235
Hillier, Meg, 10
Hinds, Damian, 207
Hinkley Point, Somerset, 84–5
Hitachi, 55
HIV, 134
HM Inspectorate of Constabulary, 180
HM Revenue & Customs (HMRC), 203
Hodge, David, 155–6
Hodge, Margaret, 10
homelessness, 96, 99, 103, 110–12, 134–5, 149–50
Honda, 158
Houchen, Ben, 158
Houghton, Steve, 152
House of Commons, 143–4
House of Lords, 143
household waste, 89
housing, 16–17, 85–6, 95–115–10, 150–51, 186, 233–4, 236–7
    building standards, 110
    developers, 4, 96, 105–7, 109, 112–14
    energy efficiency, 85–6
    evictions, 98–9
    home ownership, 96, 107–9
    house prices, 96–7, 107–8
    housebuilding, 104–7, 109–10, 236
    housing benefit, 99–100
    housing crisis, 10, 105
    insulation, 75, 78, 86, 230–31
    leaseholders, 110
    planning, 111–14, 234–5
    private rentals,

97–100, 105, 125,
236–7
renewal, 233–4
retirement homes,
104
social housing, 99,
100–103
underoccupied
housing, 103–4
Housing Infrastructure
Fund, 110
Howard League for
Penal Reform, 190
Howard, Michael, 190
HS2, 62–3
HSBC, 57
Huawei, 58
Hulme, Nick, 121–2
Hunt, Jeremy, 46–7,
155
Hutton, Will, 16, 54

I, Daniel Blake (film),
216
IKEA, 110
immigration, 15, 70,
197, 203–6, 228
imports, 53
income *see* employment
inequality, 15, 19, 34–5,
66–7, 129–30, 150–
52, 195–224, 242
infrastructure, 58–60
Inside Housing, 100
Institute for Fiscal
Studies (IFS), 9, 32,
34, 44
Institute for
Government (IfG),
34, 131, 165, 167,
176–7
insulation *see* housing
International Labour
Organization, 203
International Monetary
Fund (IMF), 242
Iraq, 171–2
Isabel Blackman Centre,
Hastings, 139–40
Israel, 197
Italy, 205
ITV, 14, 1685

Jaguar Land Rover, 55
Japan, 56, 64
Javid, Sajid, 132
Jayawardena, Ranil, 75
Jenrick, Robert, 114
Jingye, 53
Johnson, Boris, 3,
13–14, 61, 139,
141, 143–5, 147,
152, 160, 172, 182,
195, 246
Brexit and, 52
business and, 47
climate and, 76, 77,
84
COVID and, 131,
136–7, 143, 165
health and, 123, 131
housing and, 105, 110
levelling-up, 150, 166
police and, 182
racism and, 210
Jones, Russell, 129
Joseph Rowntree
Foundation, 212,
242
junk food, 130–31
Just Eat, 64
justice system, 185–91

Kabul, Afghanistan, 8
Keegan, Gillian, 41
Kensington and
Chelsea, Royal
Borough of, 95
Keynes, John Maynard,
51
Khan, Sadiq, 89
King's Fund health
think tank, 138
Kingdon, Camilla, 26
Kirkcaldy, Scotland, 4

Labour Party, 51, 179
birth rate, 17
child poverty and,
23–4, 213
climate change, 75
economy, 142
education, 25, 31,
33–4, 36–7, 41–3,
69

equality, 6, 208
housing, 100–101,
107, 112
local government and,
149, 152–3, 155,
156–8
NHS and, 120–21,
123, 128
pensions and, 218,
240
Lansley, Andrew, 120–
22, 133, 167
Latimer, David, 55
Lawson, Nigel, 116, 120
Layard, Richard, 128
Leadsom, Andrea, 75
Lebedev, Evgeny, 143
legal aid, 185–8
Legal & General, 48
Legal Aid, Sentencing
and Punishment
of Offenders Act
(2012), 186
Letwin, Oliver, 11
'levelling up', 13–14,
150–52, 157–60,
166
Leveson inquiry, 182
Li Ka-shing, 82
Liberal Democrats, 24,
69, 75, 121–2, 155
coalition government,
13, 69, 143, 216,
219
libraries, 24–5, 153,
160
Libya, 172
life expectancy, 130,
150, 164
Lifelong Loan
Entitlement, 68
Lifetime Skills
Guarantee, 68
Liverpool city council,
111
Loach, Ken, 216
loan companies,
217–18
local government, 149–
50, 152–8
arts and leisure
funding, 158–9

bankruptcy, 153–5, 157
council tax, 103–4, 151
funding, 29, 152–3
Local Government Association, 156\
London, 19, 34, 36, 57, 60
ultra-low emission zone, 78, 89
London Stock Exchange, 19, 57

MacFarlane, Clark, 83
Macmillan, Harold, 11, 105, 112
Macquarie Group, 86–7
Macron, Emmanuel, 201
Magnomatics, 55
Maier, Jürgen, 54
Major, John, 145
Manchester, 63, 160
Mardell, Adrian, 182
Marfleet, Nikki, 191
Marmot, Michael, 207
marriage rate, 217
Match of the Day, 205
May, Theresa, 3, 13, 54, 143, 159, 170, 196, 198, 211, 220, 223
climate change and, 77
health and, 122, 128
housing and, 99, 102, 112
immigration and, 204
inequality, 206–7
levelling-up, 150
police and, 181–2
probation service and, 193
social care, 107, 139
transport and, 63
McAnea, Christina, 206
McQueen, Steve, 95
mental health see health
Mercer, Johnny, 200
#Metoo movement, 180
Metropolitan Housing Trust, 102

Metropolitan Police, 145, 181
Milton Keynes, 151, 177, 191–2
miners' strike, 181
Minford, Patrick, 53
Minimum Income Standard (MIS), 212–13
minimum wage, 202
ministerial honesty, 144–5
Ministry of Defence, 55, 208
Missguided, 203
Mitchell, Andrew, 181
Mitchell, Peter, 200
mobile phones, 58, 212
Moriarty, Clare, 87
Morrisons, 56
Morse, Amyas, Baron Morse, 157
Mossack Fonseca, 223
Muellbauer, John, 233
multi-academy trusts (MATs), 37
Murdoch, Rupert, 12, 92, 168
National Audit Office (NAO), 9–10, 27, 30, 42, 44, 62, 67, 74, 79, 82, 87–9, 101, 128, 144, 157, 161, 174, 181
National Council for Voluntary Organizations, 198
national debt, 50
National Grid, 82–3
National Housing Federation, 102, 110, 234
National Infrastructure Commission, 86, 90
National Lottery, 159
Heritage Fund, 153
National Planning Framework, 106
National Portrait Gallery, London, 6, 161
National Security and

Investment Act (2021), 56, 175
national skill set, 42–4
National Trust, 11, 76, 209
NATO, 172, 175
Natural England, 91
Natural Resources Wales, 73, 77
Neal, David, 146
Netherlands, 150
New Deal for Communities project, 101–2
New Economics Foundation, 68
New Wolsey Theatre, Ipswich, 159
Newcastle United FC, 2
NHS (National Health Service), 1–2, 5, 7–8, 11, 21, 66, 71, 116–40, 167, 172, 185, 210–11, 243–4
charging, 132–3
COVID and, 136–8
dentistry, 1–2, 15, 131–3
GPs, 121, 123–5, 130, 244
maternity, 28
mental health services, 2, 5, 127–8
Office for Health Disparities, 210
privatization, 120–22
reorganization, 119–23, 133
spending, 117–18
staffing, 119, 126
strikes, 117
Talking Therapies, 128
waiting lists, 121
Nicholson, David, 120
North Sea oil and gas, 79, 163
Northamptonshire, 154
Northcliffe, Lord, see Alfred Harmsworth, 1st Viscount Northcliffe

Northern Ireland, 64, 162, 197
Notting Hill, London, 151
NSPCC, 30
Nuclear Decommissioning Authority, 84
nuclear power, 84–5
Nuffield Trust, 132

O'Connor, Sarah, 203
obesity, 130–31, 136
Obesity Health Alliance, 130
Ofcom, 145
Office for Budget Responsibility (OBR), 3, 9, 51, 65
Office for Environmental Protection, 80
Office for Local Government (Oflog), 157
Office for National Statistics (ONS), 9, 184, 222
Office for Place, 112
Office for Students, 69
Office of Government Property, 42
Office of Road and Rail Regulation, 145
Office of Tax Simplification, 246
Ofgem, 83, 88, 145
Ofsted, 167
Ofwat, 93, 145
Olympics Games, London (2012), 25, 120
online communications, 145
Openreach, 58
Opera North, 160
opera, 160–61
Operation Deter, 177–8
Organisation for Economic Co-operation and Development

(OECD), 38–40, 66, 68, 144, 167
Osborne, George, 8, 16–17, 50, 53–4, 57, 100, 142, 150, 161, 195, 201
Oxford University, 70, 71, 114–15, 195
    Migration Observatory, 70

Paris Agreement, 75
Parker Morris Committee, 110
Passmores Academy, Harlow, 40
Patel, Priti, 42, 82–4, 148
Patterson, Owen, 75, 90
Payne, Sebastian, 198
PayPlan, 217
Pearce, John, 30
pensions/pensioners, 18, 104, 142, 153, 218–19, 240
Percy, Emma and Rob, 108–9
Perry, Ruth, 41
Persimmon, 221
Personal Independence Payment (PIP), 65, 214
Phipson, Stephen, 54
Pickles, Eric, 91
Pinch, The (Willetts), 218
Plender, John, 49
police, 145, 176–84
    maladministration, 180
    Metropolitan Police, 145, 181
    police and crime commissioners, 181
    Thames Valley Police, 177
    traffic police, 180
Police, Crime, Sentencing and Courts Act (2022), 182

Police Foundation, 184
pollution, 88–9, 91–2, 232–3
Portman Group, 135
Post Office, 167
    prosecutions scandal, 7
potholes, 59, 149
poverty, 24, 26, 66, 126, 130, 165, 178, 202, 211–15
'Pregnant Then Screwed' campaign, 32
Prison and Probation Service, 192
prison service, 189–93
privatization, 10, 145, 167
probation service, 192–3
    privatization, 8
productivity, 47–8, 51, 58, 60, 64
Public Accounts Committee, 137
public finances, 242–3
public health see health
public procurement, 55
Public Sector Fraud Authority, 185
public spending, 142
Putin, Vladimir, 171–2

Queen Elizabeth, HMS, 175
QuickQuid, 217

Raab, Dominic, 51, 155, 173
RAAC (reinforced autoclaved aerated concrete), 7, 42
race/racism, 11, 204, 208–11
railways, 10, 55, 60–63, 231
    Avanti West Coast, 61
    Crossrail, 60
    Elizabeth Line, 60
    Great British Railways (GBR), 61

HS2, 55, 62
Thameslink, 62
Transpennine line, 60
Reagan, Ronald, 10, 14
recycling, 89
Red Arrows, 175–6
Rees-Mogg, Jacob, 148
regulators, 145–6
Republic of Ireland, 150
Research & Development (R&D), 71
Resilience Framework, 90
Resolution Foundation, 9, 46, 81, 86, 104, 186, 202, 214, 224, 240
retirement, 17–18
Richmond, Enid, 116
Right to Buy scheme, 10, 99, 101–3, 162, 166
Road to Serfdom (Hayek), 10
Robinson, Liam, 111
Rochdale, 153
rough sleeping, 111
Royal College of Nursing, 117
Royal College of Paediatrics and Child Health, 105
Royal Mail, 167
Royal National Lifeboat Institution (RNLI), 11, 167, 199
Royal Society, 72
Royal Society for the Protection of Birds (RSPB), 167
Royal Society for the Prevention of Cruelty to Animals (RSPCA), 199
Royal Society of Arts, 198
Russia, 85, 170–73
Rwanda, 205

Sainsbury Foundation 190
same-sex marriage, 12
Sanders, Patrick, 170–71, 208
Savills estate agency, 100
Scholar, Tom, 148
Scholz, Olaf, 205
science, 71–2
Scilly Isles, 156
Scotland, 4, 81, 92–3, 161–6, 197
Scottish independence, 162
Scotland Act (2012), 163
Scottish Environment Protection Agency, 73
Scottish Forestry, 77
Scottish National Party (SNP), 163, 165–6
Scottish Power, 82
Scottish Water, 92–3, 164
Seetru, 52
Sellafield, Cumbria, 85
SEND (special educational needs and disabilities), 29
Shankland, Ben, 124–5
Shapps, Grant, 12, 171, 175
Shared Prosperity Fund, 157
shareholders, 19, 48–9
Sharkey, Feargal, 91
Sharma, Alok, 79
shipbuilding, 55
sickness benefits, 65, 128
Siemens UK, 54
Gamesa plant, Hull, 83
Sizewell, Suffolk, 84–5
Skidmore, Chris, 79
Skripal, Sergei and Yulia, 170
slavery, 6, 209
Slough council, 157
Smith, Adam, 4–5

smoking, 135–6
social care, 30–31, 107, 128, 138–40, 153, 240, 243
social media, 12, 45
social mobility, 207
Social Mobility Commission, 207
Society of Motor Manufacturers and Trades, 55
SoftBank, 56
solar power, 82
Soskice, David, 233
South East Water, 92, 94
South West Water, 94
Southern Water, 92
Spectator, 14, 56
Spencer, Mark, 77
SSE, 82
St Ives, Cambridgeshire, 73–4
St Mungo's homelessness charity, 111
St Pauls, Bristol, 1–2
stamp duty, 108
Star Blizzard group, 172
steel industry, 53–5, 78
StepChange, 217
Stephenson, Norman, 1
Stevens, Simon, 122, 124
Sturgeon, Nicola, 165
Sunak, Rishi, 11, 83, 141, 203, 221, 246
badgers and, 90
climate change and, 78–9
COVID and, 14
defence, 173
education and, 33, 44
health and, 116, 131, 135, 165
immigration and, 205–6
levelling-up, 152, 163
racism and, 210
transport and, 62–3
Sure Start programme,

23, 32–3, 44, 191, 238, 242

Surrey county council, 155–6

Swindon, 158

Syria, 172

Tata Group, 54, 55, 78

taxation, 19, 51, 142, 163, 220–24, 242–6
  corporation tax, 48, 57–8, 222–3
  council tax, 103–4, 151
  income tax, 220–21
  marriage allowance, 217
  tax avoidance, 185, 221
  tax evasion, 185
  tax havens, 222–3
  vehicle tax, 184

Thales, 174

Thames Valley Police, 177

Thames Water, 10, 48, 87, 92–3

Thatcher, Margaret, 10, 48, 63, 82, 104, 110, 111, 145, 181, 203–4

Thatcherism, 10, 13–14, 91, 96, 99

Thomas, David, 106

Times, The, 92

Tower Hamlets, London, 114, 124

Townend, Sam, 187

Towns Fund, 157

trading standards officers (TSOs), 154

transgender issues, 12, 201

Transparency International UK, 99

transport, 60–64, 81, 231–2, 236
  car industry, 55, 56, 88
  electric charging points, 58–9, 81

electric vehicles (EVs), 55, 56, 78, 81, 232
  see also railways

Transport Focus, 63

Trenitalia, 61

Trump, Donald, 53, 171, 173, 175–6

Truss, Liz, 3, 6, 9, 11, 14, 50–51, 70, 75, 87, 126, 148, 171, 173, 195, 219–20, 246
  health and, 131, 136

Trussell Trust, 20, 2420

TUC, 64

Tunbridge Wells, 152, 163

Turing Scheme, 72

Tusa, Francis, 174–5

Uber, 64

UK Biobank, 88

UK Conformity Assessed (UKCA), 52

UK Power Networks, 82

UKIP (UK Independence Party), 204

Ukraine war, 53, 87, 172–3

United Arab Emirates, 56, 174–5

United States, 47–8, 64, 175, 207, 220

Universal Credit, 7, 202, 214, 215–17

Unjust Rewards (Toynbee & Walker), 34, 199

Uxbridge by-election (2023), 78

Vallance, Patrick, 77

Vanguard, HMS, 175

vaping, 135–6

Varga, Andrew, 52

Vattenfall, 83

Vestas plant, Isle of Wight, 83

Villiers, Theresa, 75

Virgin, 120–21

Vodafone, 175

volunteering, 198

Wales, 54, 161–3, 166–7, 197

water, 91–4
  flooding, 16, 73–4, 90–91
  sewage, 2, 91–4
  water companies, 2, 10, 92–4, 232–3

Weale, Martin, 233

wealth, 220–23, 227, 227

Webb, Steve, 219

Welby, Justin, 168

Welsh Opera, 160

Wessely, Simon, 128

Westminster, London, 151–2

Westminster council, 149

Wiegman, Sarina, 197

Willetts, David, 218

Williams, Keith, 61

Williamson, Gavin, 90, 170, 215

Wincanton, 56

wind power, 76, 78, 81–3

Windrush scandal, 7, 204

Winser, Nick, 83

Witney, Oxfordshire, 200

'wokeism', 12–13, 69, 201

Woking, 153

Wolf, Martin, 49, 106, 220

Wonga, 218

Woodhill Prison, Milton Keynes, 191–2

World Health Organization, 119, 164

Xi Jinping, 53, 58